WITHDRAWN

Israel Through the
Jewish-American Imagination

SUNY Series in
Modern Jewish Literature and Culture

Sarah Blacher Cohen, Editor

Israel Through the Jewish-American Imagination

A Survey of Jewish-American Literature on Israel, 1928–1995

Andrew Furman

STATE UNIVERSITY OF NEW YORK PRESS

Production by Ruth Fisher
Marketing by Dana E. Yanulavich

Published by
State University of New York Press, Albany

©1997 State University of New York

For information, address the State University of New York Press,
State University Plaza, Albany, NY 12246

Library of Congress Cataloging-in-Publication Data

Furman, Andrew, 1968–
    Israel through the Jewish-American imagination : a survey of
Jewish-American literature on Israel, 1928–1995 / Andrew Furman.
        p.   cm. — (SUNY series in modern Jewish literature and
culture)
    Includes bibliographical references and index.
    ISBN 0–7914–3251–3 (hc : alk. paper). — ISBN 0–7914–3252–1 (pb :
alk. paper)
    1. American fiction—Jewish authors—History and criticism.
2. Israel—In literature. 3. Jewish fiction—United States—History
and criticism.   I. Title.   II. Series.
PS153. J4F87   1997
813'.509325694'089924–dc20   96–18577
                                                                                       CIP

10 9 8 7 6 5 4 3 2 1

To my grandparents,
Ruth and Herbert Dickstein, and Dorothy and Ralph Furman
and
To my parents,
Nancy and Stephen Furman, who still correct my English

CONTENTS

ACKNOWLEDGMENTS

I would like to express my warmest appreciation to Robert Burkholder, Gloria Cronin, James L. W. West III, Erella Brown, and Sarah Blacher Cohen. They have each contributed greatly to the strength of this project through their enthusiastic support and their careful criticism of the manuscript.

I would also like to express my special indebtedness to Daniel Walden and Sanford Pinsker.

Earlier versions of some of these chapters or significant excerpts from them have appeared in various publications. For permission to reprint the material here I am grateful to *Contemporary Literature* ("A New 'Other' Emerges in American-Jewish Literature: Philip Roth's Israel Fiction," Winter 1995 [The University of Wisconsin Press]), *Studies in American Jewish Literature, Saul Bellow Journal, MELUS, Response,* and *Midstream.*

Chapter 1

INTRODUCTION
Israel, the Foremost Preoccupation
of the American Jew

In 1955, just seven short years after the founding of the Jewish state, Harold Ribalow recognized a revelatory characteristic of Jewish-American literature on Israel:

> [T]he American Jew today represents the largest Jewish community in the world: his reaction to Israel, creatively as well as philanthropically, may well measure the intimacy between the Israeli and the American Jew, as well as the chasm between them. The establishment of Israel already has led to a handful of novels on Israel and, inferentially, on the relationship between the Israeli and the Diaspora Jew. The wealth of the future literature on Israel, its depth, its sensitivity and its authenticity, is bound to be a true gauge of the impact of Zion reborn on a Jewish people which has survived to enjoy the miracle of Israel. ("Zion" 591)

As we near Israel's fiftieth birthday, the time seems ripe to explore the Jewish-American fiction on Israel that Ribalow anxiously anticipated. How have Jewish-American writers imagined Israel? What does this imaginative writing reveal about the relationship between the Israeli and the Diaspora Jew over the years? How has the literature gauged the impact of the Jewish state on the American Jewish community?

It would be difficult to overstate this "impact" of the Jewish state in forging the ethos of Jewish-Americans. Arthur Hertzberg and Leonard Fein only slightly overstate matters when they suggest that Israel *became* the religion of the American Jews after the Six-Day War of 1967 (Solotaroff, "The Open Community" xv). In an insightful article published in *The New York Times Book Review*, Ted Solotaroff observes that "since the Six-Day War the survival of Israel has been the paramount concern of organized Jewish life and probably the paramount source of Jewish identity" ("American Jewish Writers" 33). However, while Jewish-American writers have written prolifically since the 1960s about the Holocaust (the other central Jewish event of the twentieth century), it would be disingenuous to suggest that Israel has carved out an equally substantial niche for itself in the Jewish-American writer's imagination. Ribalow, writing in 1955, surely expected that "the future literature on Israel" would demand more space today in the library stacks than it presently does.

Several critics have bemoaned the relatively minor role Israel has played in Jewish-American fiction. Looking back recently upon the 1960s, Robert Alter recalls his bewilderment that Jewish-American writers "could so regularly imagine a world in which Israel was scarcely even a presence on a distant horizon" ("Defenders" 55). Naomi Sokoloff also notes the relative dearth of Jewish-American fiction on Israel given the enormous impact of the state upon Jewish existence: "Given the importance of Israel for American Jewish identity and communal self-expression, considering the quantities of ink spilled on polemics about relations between the two cultures, and taking into account the increasing familiarity of each with the other, not much imaginative writing has addressed this topic in a substantive way" (65).

Despite Alter's and Sokoloff's puzzlement concerning the shortage of Jewish-American imaginings of Israel, one can readily enough understand the reluctance on the part of these writers to engage Israel seriously in their work. After all, one must remember that Israel is not their country; most Jewish-American writers thus lack the palpable and intimate knowledge of Israel that could stimulate good fiction. Leslie Fiedler, a forceful critical voice in literary matters Jewish, expressed how "strange" Israel appears to, perhaps, most American Jews when he remarked poignantly, ". . . I feel myself more hopelessly a foreigner in Jerusalem and Tel Aviv and the Holy City of Safad than I do in Rome or Bologna or Florence. . . . Israel remains for me, even when I walk its streets, somehow an abstraction, a metaphor from a dull, half-forgotten sermon" (8). It is this very strangeness of Israel that prompted Bernard Malamud to announce that he would write about Israel if he knew about it, but since he didn't, he would leave it to the Israeli writers (Field 50). Sanford Pinsker suggests some other reasons why Jewish-American writers tend to "shy away from writing about the Middle East"—most notably, their wariness of the possible sentimentality of such fiction and, conversely, their recognition of the *chutzpah* implicit in any attempt to offer a critical glance at Israel's political landscape from "the smug safety of American soil" ("William Faulkner" 412, 400). Small wonder, indeed, that the protagonist's feet in Jewish-American fiction have, for the most part, been planted squarely on American terrain (see Chapter 7 for a more elaborate discussion concerning the Jewish-American writers' reluctance to engage Israel in their work).

Given such a gloomy description of Jewish-American literature about Israel, one might reasonably question whether the fiction warrants a book-length study in the first place. Despite my own skepticism, I discovered that two principal characteristics of the literature demanded the undertaking of such a study. First, as Harold Ribalow predicted, the literature that does exist serves as an incisive gauge of the impact of Israel upon the Jewish-American ethos. Secondly, the zeitgeist in the American Jewish intellectual community has shifted dramatically to precipitate a recent surge of Jewish-American fiction on Israel. To place this paradigm shift in historical perspective, one must remember that the renowned (predominantly Jewish) New York intellectuals earlier in this century—Philip Rahv, Irving Howe, Alfred Kazin, Lionel Trilling, and Daniel Bell, to sound off a few—haggled over the hot topics of alienation, marginality, and anti-Stalinism in the pages of such magazines as *Partisan Review, Dissent, Commentary,* and *Midstream.* Concomitantly, the fiction of Jewish-American writers like Abraham Cahan, Anzia Yezierska, Saul Bellow, Isaac Rosenfeld, Delmore Schwartz, Bernard Malamud, and others revolved largely around these same themes. Today, the Middle East, rather than anti-Stalinism, is the pressing issue. In the very periodicals listed above (and in additional ones like *Tikkun* and *The New Republic*), intellectuals like Ruth Wisse, Michael Walzer, Norman Podhoretz, Robert Alter, Edward Alexander, Cynthia Ozick, Michael Lerner, and Martin Peretz prove that their Hawk and Dove disputes in regard to Israeli foreign policy have replaced the battles, waged earlier in this century, between warring socialist factions of the Jewish-American intelligentsia.

Likewise, Jewish-American writers ("post-alienated," as Lillian Kremer contends) are increasingly abandoning the nearly tapped-out muses of marginality and alienation to engage Israel seriously as a theme (Kremer, "Post-alienation" 571). The ever-growing list of these works includes such novels as Mark Helprin's *Refiner's Fire* (1977), E. M.

Broner's *A Weave of Women* (1978), Jay Neugeboren's *The Stolen Jew* (1981), Nessa Rapoport's *Preparing for Sabbath* (1981), Anne Roiphe's *Lovingkindness* (1987), Deena Metzger's *What Dinah Thought* (1989), Philip Roth's *The Counterlife* (1986) and *Operation Shylock: A Confession* (1993), Carol Magun's *Circling Eden: A Novel of Israel* (1995), and Tova Reich's *Master of the Return* (1988) and *The Jewish War* (1995). That Ted Solotaroff and Nessa Rapoport's recent anthology of Jewish-American fiction, *Writing Our Way Home: Contemporary Stories by American Jewish Writers* (1992), contains three stories set in Israel also illustrates the increasing attention the Jewish state presently demands from Jewish-American writers. Solotaroff notes that, "given the welter of new social and cultural influences that are redefining America as a multi-ingredient soup rather than a melting pot, it is not surprising that the subject of Jewish identity is increasingly being set against an Israeli background" ("The Open Community" xxii). Moreover, in a recent article in the *Philadelphia Jewish Exponent*, Sanford Pinsker puts forward his own prediction concerning Jewish-American fiction on Israel: "if my reading of the Zeitgeist is correct, one can look forward to a new renaissance of Jewish-American fiction about Israel in the next decade" ("They Dream" 8-x).

I would like to suggest that the Jewish-American writers' relatively new exploration of the fictional possibilities of Israel contributes greatly to the renaissance today in Jewish-American fiction as a whole. For Irving Howe's cynical suggestion in 1977 that "American Jewish fiction has probably moved past its high point" was rooted in his view that American Jewish life after the immigrant experience of marginality and alienation would prove too sterile and unrecognizably Jewish to inspire a new wave of Jewish-American literature ("Introduction" 16). "[T]here just isn't enough left of that [immigrant] experience," Howe lamented (16); and at least one other prominent critic, Leslie Fiedler, agreed (see Fiedler xii, 117). Thankfully, Howe (while correct about a good many things) was wrong in assuming that the immigrant experience alone embodied the Jewish-American identity. What the present surge of Jewish-American literature on Israel tells us, in the most general sense, is that American Jews define themselves today by looking not only toward Eastern Europe and the Lower East side of New York—toward the dimming "world of our fathers," to borrow Howe's phrase—but toward the West Bank, Jerusalem, Tel Aviv, and the Golan Heights as well.

What specifically, though, does Jewish-American fiction on Israel tell us about American Jews, Israel, and the relationship between the two communities? These are the questions I endeavor to answer in the chapters to follow. I will resist the temptation here merely to summarize the main arguments of these chapters. Instead, it might prove helpful to flesh out the historical context surrounding the authors whom I discuss by adumbrating three essential relational phases between American Jews and Israel during this century: pre-Zionism, Zionism, and post-Zionism. For the eight authors included in this study have all necessarily challenged or espoused the prevailing temper of their day.

Since I consider works spanning from 1928 to 1995, it should come as no surprise that the American Jewish relationship toward Israel throughout these sixty-seven years has fluctuated every bit as much as the generic conventions of fiction during this time. Indeed, the relationship has proven both dynamic and tumultuous, and these qualities manifest themselves prevalently as Jewish-American writers choose to imagine Israel in their work. To impose a somewhat reductive framework upon this relationship, one might use the term pre-Zionist (or anti-Zionist) to define the American Jewish perspective toward the idea of a Jewish state from the time of Theodor Herzl's first Zionist Congress in 1897 in Basel, Switzerland, until roughly 1947 (when the atrocities of the Holocaust gained clarity in the United States). As Martin Peretz, the Editor-in-Chief of *The New Republic,* notes in a recent speech, "the Zionists before the war were surely a minority among Jews, in some countries a very small minority. Their authority came with the war and after, when their admixture of analysis and prophecy that European soil was doomed territory for the Jews had already been proven true in the blood of millions" (7–8). Before the war, to elaborate upon Peretz's comment, practically every kind of Jew one can imagine excoriated Zionism. As Irving Howe writes in his landmark study, *World of Our Fathers:*

> A good number of Orthodox Jews regarded [Zionism] as "Torahless," a heretical effort to transpose messianic expectation from the transcendent to the mundane sphere. . . . the Reform rabbis had passed a resolution declaring themselves "unalterably opposed to political Zionism" and, in a startling sentence, had added, "America is our Zion." The Jewish socialists regarded Zionism as a troublesome competitor, a bourgeois delusion that could only distract the masses from struggling for their liberation. The Yiddishists were enraged by the Zionist depreciation of the whole Diaspora experience. (207)

Indeed, for religious, assimilationist, socialist, or downright traditionalist reasons, Zionism was a staggeringly unpopular movement among American Jews until the Holocaust convinced a majority of the dissenters that Jews needed their own state if they were to survive as a people.

The term pre-Zionist, then, accurately describes the zeitgeist of the American Jewish community before the Holocaust. The terms Zionist and post-Zionist—which I use to describe the latter two phases of the American Jewish relationship with Israel—are more nebulous and demand careful scrutiny. For Zionism, at its philosophical core, is a critical orientation of inquiry, not the complacent, uncritical "pro-Israel" orientation as most people believe. A leading Jewish magazine, *Midstream,* aptly defines Zionism as "a questioning of the Jewish *status quo,* and a steady confrontation of the problems of Jewish existence." So, essentially, a true Zionist should engage Israel from the very same critical perspective as those who today carry the "post-Zionist" banner. Now, before one even hazards to define the term, post-Zionist, it demands immediate qualification, because it implies something that the vast majority of those calling themselves post-Zionists do not mean to imply—namely, that they do not believe in the legitimacy of Israel's existence. As Michael Lerner, perhaps the most vociferous post-Zionist, argues, "Post-Zionists are Jews who fervently support the State of Israel, believe that its welfare and military security must be ensured, but who wish to see an Israel based on tolerance; an honoring of the multicultural realities of the people living within its borders . . ." ("Post-Zionism" 261).

A true understanding of Zionism, then, should render the term "post-Zionism" obsolete. Sadly, perhaps, anyone who has flipped through a Jewish or political magazine lately knows that the "post" prefix, like its cousin "neo," is here to stay. So, the "Zionist" phase in America, for better or for worse, refers to the period of the greatest, most uncritical, American Jewish support of Israel, the period when most (though not all) American Jews accepted Israel's moral righteousness almost without question. The founding of Israel in 1948 precipitated this period, and it reached its zenith just after Israel's stunning defeat of the combined Arab forces in the 1967 Six-Day War. Midge Decter captures this euphoric Jewish-American vision of Israel during the Zionist phase in some recent reminiscences: "Created out of an act of long overdue international justice, the country was, at once and at last, to be a safe haven for Jews, a model of social existence, and a rich ground for the efflorescence of a new and lovely Jewish culture" ("American Jews" 31).

Given the spiritual stock that American Jews placed in Israel, one can easily grasp why Hebrew schools (like the one I attended) taught young Jews not to question Israel's policies and encouraged unflinching loyalty toward the state.

Indeed, American Jews only reluctantly began to speak out against Israel; irrespective of Hebrew school indoctrination, most American Jews who criticize Israeli policy do so with the sobering recognition that their Israeli counterparts are the ones who must live with these policies, that the *Israelis* are the ones who cannot take their lives for granted. Henry Feingold describes this practically untenable position of American Jews when it comes to anything that they might have to say about the Middle East: "I have heard American Zionism called 'air conditioned Zionism' . . . Just as American Jews have developed Judaism without the yoke of Torah, so they also have Zionism without the yoke of aliya" (22). But despite the precarious position of those who would criticize Israel, there can be little doubt that American Jewry's heady Zionist phase of overwhelming uncritical support of Israel has come to an end. It was only a matter of time, perhaps, before Jews would begin to redefine how one might express one's "loyalty" toward the Jewish state; and recently, a growing number of American Jews express their commitment to the state, they believe, through their careful scrutiny—rather than unreflective support—of Israeli policy. Michael Lerner marks the beginning of this "post-Zionist" period in the 1990s as Israel implicitly acknowledged the credibility of the post-Zionist critiques of the Israeli Occupation:

> In the 1990s, Israel received a second birth, this time in joy and in peace. After decades of building itself into one of the world's strongest military powers, Israel chose a new direction. In 1993 it signed an accord with the Palestine Liberation Organization. Mutual recognition and peace were the central goals of that accord. In so doing, Israel had started on the path of post-Zionism, in which Jewish values could eventually triumph over the worship of power, and Jewish compassion could replace Jewish rage. ("Post-Zionism" 221)

True, some American Jews do not share Michael Lerner's optimistic account of the 1993 accord between Israel and the PLO. Ruth Wisse, for one, wonders in her article, "Peace Not," "If Arabs went to war against Israel in 1967 when all the disputed territories were in their hands, what's to keep them from repeating the process?" ("Peace Not" 16). Still, no one who has kept an ear to the ground regarding the American Jewish relationship with Israel would deny that American Jews have increasingly spoken out both for Palestinian rights and against perceived Israeli wrongs. In regard to Lerner's use of the term, post-Zionism, I would only mark an earlier date at which this phase ensued in America. For Israel's military incursions into Lebanon from June to September of 1982—and, more precisely, Israel's well-publicized role while there in facilitating the Phalangist militiamen's massacre of hundreds of Palestinians in the Sabra and Shatila refugee camps—initiated the post-Zionist phase. As Elaine M. Kauvar suggests, "[t]he Israeli incursion into Lebanon elicited an outbreak of criticism from members of the American Jewish community," as large numbers of American Jews began finally to question their previously intransigent presumption of Israel's moral purity (343).

Two events later in the 1980s exacerbated these initial tensions between American Jews and Israel and set the post-Zionist phase in full swing. First, in November 1985, a Jewish-American Navy intelligence analyst, Jonathan J. Pollard, was arrested in the United States for providing top-secret military data to the Israelis. Several American Jews were shocked that Israel would sink so low as to spy on their long-time benefactor, the United States, and rushed to express their American patriotism by vociferously repudiating both Pollard and the Israelis (one might rightly view in analogous terms the Jewish-American community's repudiation of the Rosenbergs earlier in this century). Then, in December 1987, the Palestinian uprising, or *intifada,* began. The nightly news film of heavily armed Israeli soldiers chasing down and occasionally shooting or beating rock-wielding Palestinian teenagers went a long way toward shattering the heroic image of the Israeli soldier to which most American Jews had clung up until that point. A January 28, 1988, Op-Ed piece in *The New York Times* by one notorious American Jew, Woody Allen, betrays the post-Zionist shift in the tide of the American Jewish relationship with Israel subsequent to the *intifada.* The barrage of media coverage illustrating apparent excessive force by the Israeli military toward the Palestinians in the Occupied Territories provoked Allen to write, "I am appalled beyond measure by the treatment of the rioting Palestinians by Jews. I mean, fellas, are you kidding? . . . Breaking the hands of men and women so they can't throw stones? Dragging civilians out of their houses at random to smash them with sticks in an effort to terrorize a population into quiet? . . . Am I reading the newspapers correctly?" (A27). Enough is enough, Allen seems to say, and he does not stand alone. An unprecedented number of American Jews today apparently believe that ". . . for all of us who are rooting for Israel to continue to exist and prosper the obligation is to speak out" when Israel violates its democratic principles by committing human rights abuses (Allen A27).

Let me emphasize that large segments of the American Jewish population were, and continue to be, outraged by public American Jewish denunciations of Israeli policy, a la Woody Allen. As recently as 1993, several prominent American Jewish intellectuals like Edward Alexander, Cynthia Ozick, Marie Syrkin, and Jacob Neusner contributed to a collection of essays entitled, *With Friends Like These: The Jewish Critics of Israel*, in which they challenge the validity of such Allen-like American Jewish critiques of Israel. A year earlier, Ruth Wisse also took Israel's critics to task in her book-length study, *If I Am Not For Myself . . . : The Liberal Betrayal of the Jews*. However, though several intelligent and sensitive American Jews refuse to subscribe to the post-Zionist temper, one would be hard pressed to argue that their ardent pro-Israel message resonates through the American Jewish community with the same force as it did, say, fifteen years ago. The aforementioned events of the 1980s forced most American Jews to take a more critical look at Israel. Moreover, while the 1991 Israeli Information Center for Human Rights report on the torture of Palestinian prisoners probably eluded most American Jews, Amnesty International's July 1993 report that Palestinians under interrogation by the Israelis are "systematically tortured or ill-treated" was widely publicized and certainly took its toll on the PR between Israel and American Jews (Qtd. in Greenberg 3). In the pages of *The New York Times*, American Jews read detailed reports of Israel's alleged abuses of Palestinian prisoners in the Occupied Territories. One such article highlighted Amnesty International's conclusion that Palestinian prisoners were deprived of sleep for days on end while "typically held on small chairs, their heads covered with dirty, foul-smelling sacks and their hands tied behind them to the chair or to a wall" (Greenberg 3). Alas, as Thomas Friedman notes, "the Lebanon invasion, the Pollard espionage affair, and the Palestinian *intifada* really forced American Jews to look at some of the more unpleasant, but very real, rhythms of political life in today's Israel—instead of just the episodic moments of celebration" (478). Israel's most recent 1996 incursions into Lebanon, during which scores of Lebanese civilians lost their lives, threaten to strain relations further between American and Israeli Jews.

Lest one infer that Israeli agression alone precipitated America's post-Zionist milieu, let me emphasize that other, more welcome, factors than the regrettable events of the 1980s have worked to define our present, skeptical mood in regard to the Middle East. Most significantly, perhaps, the normalization of Israel as a nation provides for an atmosphere in which Jews on the left are much less reluctant to speak out against Israeli policy. That is, as Israel becomes more established as a nation and its existence becomes less and less tenuous, American Jews on the left feel (prematurely, some argue) that they can publicly scrutinize Israeli human rights abuses just as they publicly denounce, say, China's or South Africa's human rights violations. Interestingly, American Jews on the political right (most of whom carry the Zionist banner free of its current "post" prefix) also scarcely hesitate these days to criticize Israeli policies. However, what prompts their criticism is the fear that Shimon Peres's Labor government, as evidenced in its dovish policies toward the Palestinians, has placed too much stock in Israel's normalcy. Just after the late Yitzhak Rabin initiated a peace accord with the PLO, the neoconservative Norman Podhoretz retracted his former position that "American Jews had no moral right to criticize Israel's security policies" (19). The advent of the Labor government's more progressive agenda toward its Arab neighbors presented an "entirely new situation," according to Podhoretz, in which "the real danger . . . is that Israel will be too 'flexible' in its desperate eagerness to conclude agreements both with the Syrians and with the Palestinians" (20). Podhoretz thus roundly criticizes Israel's peace accord with the PLO in three separate articles (see *Commentary*, April and June 1993 and December 1994). American Jewish criticism of Israeli policy, then, bristles currently in both the progressive pages of *Tikkun* and the conservative pages of *Commentary*.

Before one laments this surge of American Jewish criticism of Israel as if it were an indication of the American Jews' flagging commitment to the state, one should at least note that Israelis themselves are immersed every bit as much in the contentious spirit of the day. A wave of Israeli "new historians" have just begun in the last seven or eight years to offer unprecedented, critical analyses of the Zionist movement and, specifically, of Israel's culpability for the present Palestinian crisis in the Middle East (Avi Shlaim's *Collusion Across the Jordan* and Benny Morris's *The Birth of the Palestinian Refugee Problem, 1947–1949* and *Israel's Border Wars, 1949–1956* immediately come to mind). As Clyde Haberman notes, "Even legendary Zionist heroes are being re-evaluated.... Israelis have long been told that [Joseph Trumpeldor's] last words were, 'It is good to die for our land.' Now, new accounts say he actually died with curses in his native Russian on his lips" ("Meet a New" A1, A7). Certainly, a good many Israelis closer to the political right bemoan this post-Zionist hoopla in Israel. Hillel Halkin, for one, is more than a bit perturbed that "the central myths of Zionism, which for four or five generations successfully linked Jewish settlement in Palestine, and the existence of the state of Israel, to 3,000 years of Jewish history, no longer speak to much of Israeli society and its current political leadership" ("Israel Against Itself" 35). Furthermore, in a leading Israeli newspaper, *Ha'aretz,* the Israeli novelist Aharon Megged recently admonished Israeli post-Zionist scholars like Benny Morris. He goes so far as to accuse them of doing Satan's work. Other Israelis, however, like Gershom Gorenberg, welcome the advent of Israeli post-Zionist scholarship as it "allows for writing a more nuanced, balanced drama, in which both Arabs and Jews are flawed figures in history's tragedy" (22). At any rate, my hunch is that both Israeli and American Jews, from both the traditional Zionist and post-Zionist perspectives, will continue to wrangle over whose version of history merits transmission to the next generation. Since Israel has now miraculously survived to create almost a half-century of history for itself, it strikes me as only prudent that scholars and lay people should begin to examine this history and clash over it in essential ways.

Which is simply to suggest that our current post-Zionist milieu does not so much mark the end of the American Jewish relationship with Israel as it does mark the beginning, perhaps, of a more honest relationship between the two communities. For, whatever positive things one might say about American Jewry's most fervently Zionist phase, one must also acknowledge that the American Jewish affinity for Israeli Jews during this period was based largely (though not wholly) upon a sentimental vision of the heroic Israeli *kibbutznik* or soldier. After the Holocaust, Jews were eager to embrace the image of the strong and courageous Israeli soldier—no matter how accurate that image was—to replace the image of the *nebbisheh* (weak) Diaspora Jew, the victim of Hitler's Holocaust. One Israeli, Haim Chertok, recognizes this superficial element of the American Jewish relationship with Israel when he notes, "American support for Israel is like anti-Semitism. Both are not much affected by what Jews do or do not do" (189). As one might infer from the tenor of Chertok's comment, he and other Israelis grow increasingly weary of such American Jewish "support," characteristic of America's "Zionist" phase. Fortunately, most Israelis have not given up on American Jews and, instead, encourage American Jews to eschew their romantic notions of Israelis and to embrace them for whom they really are. In a recent *Wall Street Journal* article, Amy Dockser Marcus reports that the United Israel office, in its effort "to create a future with Americans . . . is attempting to immerse visiting American Jewish donors in Israeli life as it really is, rather than indulge them in the old stereotypes of settlers and soldiers" (A4). To their credit, American post-Zionists, in defiance of those who still "want to see the heroic Israel, Israel facing the odds," do endeavor to see Israeli life as it really is (Marcus A4). Likewise, those Jewish-American intellectuals today who tout a more hard-line Zionism (like Ruth Wisse, Norman Podhoretz, Cynthia Ozick, and Edward Alexander) argue from a critical and historically astute, rather than nostalgic, perspective. Thus, if my reading of the zeitgeist is correct, post-Zionism just might mark the birth of a genuine relationship between American and Israeli Jews, in which American Jews will finally know Israeli Jews (and vice-versa) by what they do rather than by what they symbolize.

I hope that my cursory description of the three phases thus far of the American Jewish relationship with Israel provides a contextual lens through which the reader might read not only the following chapters but also Jewish-American literature on Israel in general. In the eight chapters that follow, I will, of course, have more specific things to say about these relationship phases; as I have already implied, each of the eight writers I consider sheds light (and sometimes heat) upon these phases, because they necessarily generate their fiction amid the tumult of one phase or the other. While I make no claims at comprehensiveness, I have endeavored to offer a fairly representative analysis of Jewish-American literature on Israel by selecting at least one author from each of the three phases and by selecting a group of writers whose works, taken as a whole, encompass the wide range of Middle East concerns that Jewish-Americans (both writers and lay people) have expressed during this century.

I have, thus far, argued that (a) the American Jewish relationship with Israel has evolved in concrete ways, and that (b) a thorough understanding of how this relationship has evolved yields a richer interpretation of Jewish-American literature on Israel. I would like now to focus more specifically upon this literature, to explore how it has evolved as well. Tempting though it may be, I will resist the urge to name three evolutionary phases of the literature to complement the three relational phases named above. While the terms pre-Zionist, Zionist, and post-Zionist aptly characterize the evolution of the Jewish-American relationship with Israel, the evolution of Jewish-American fiction on Israel—though inextricably connected to the relational phases—has evolved in ways too various and complex to be reducible to three discrete categories. This is not to say that there exists no general principle governing the evolution of the literature. For the eight authors I chose to explore (in relatively chronological order) betray major shifts in the political orientation and, hence, imaginative power of the Jewish-American author in regard to the Middle East.

How, one might ask, does a writer's political orientation inform his or her imaginative powers? Irving Howe's description of the "political novel," in *Politics and the Novel* (1957), proves helpful in illustrating this relationship between ideology and imagination. In the study, he describes the political novel as one in which "political ideas play a dominant role or in which the political milieu is the dominant setting. . . . Perhaps it would be better to say: a novel in which *we take to be dominant* political ideas or the political milieu . . ." (*Politics* 17). Reading these lines from Irving Howe's 1957 study today, one recognizes readily—in spite of Howe's italicized proviso—how out of favor his essential premise has become. Indeed, any graduate student in English worth his or her salt these days would hasten to note the absurdity of singling out, as Howe does, certain overtly political novels. Howe's introduction would, no doubt, be welcomed by today's graduate students with a resounding chorus of "*All* novels are political," or perhaps "ideology permeates *all* modes of discourse." There is no dearth of scholars today, for example, who find it fascinating to stoke out the insidious political agenda interwoven into the fabric of, say, Jane Austen's novels (a writer who was fortunate enough, Howe contends, not to have to worry about politics in her novels).

Still, what strikes me in re-reading Howe's study is how relevant, how eminently usable, some of his precepts remain as we consider how Jewish-American fiction on Israel has evolved during this century. Consider, for example, Howe's elaboration upon the "ideal" political novel:

> The political novel—I have in mind its "ideal" form—is peculiarly a
> work of internal tensions. To be a novel at all, it must contain the

usual representation of human behavior and feeling; yet it must also absorb into its stream of movement the hard and perhaps insoluble pellets of modern ideology. . . . The conflict is inescapable: the novel tries to confront experience in its immediacy and closeness, while ideology is by its nature general and inclusive. Yet it is precisely from this conflict that the political novel gains its interest and takes on the aura of high drama. (*Politics* 20)

Political novelists, then, must somehow assert their broad, inclusive ideology through (rather than in spite of) the personal, felt life of their protagonists.

We might ponder here how well the Jewish-American novelists, from Meyer Levin to Tova Reich, have balanced this "internal tension" in their work. Every novel in this study, after all, qualifies as a "political" one, certainly by our current paradigm of literary study, and even under Howe's more exclusive model. To be sure, a writer who engages Israel or other Middle East matters necessarily adopts a "political milieu" as a setting and grapples with "political ideas," either overtly or tacitly. In regard to Jewish-American fiction on Israel, it is my contention that we can trace a definite progression, or evolution, insofar as the recent authors have balanced the internal tension with greater skill and have engaged Israel with far greater intellectual rigor than their predecessors, Meyer Levin and Leon Uris. This development would not prove so significant if it were not for the intriguing historical circumstances which, at least in part, precipitated the evolution.

The novels of Meyer Levin and Leon Uris, for example, were informed by and have much to tell us about the American pre-Zionist and Zionist phases. In writing their Israel fiction, both Meyer Levin and Leon Uris were driven primarily by their strong ideological convictions concerning both the Middle East and what, in their day, passed for Jewish-American literature in general. Levin self-consciously wrote a Zionist novel in *Yehuda* (1931) both to challenge the pre-Zionist milieu within the Jewish-American community and to assert what he considered to be a sorely needed *Jewish* artistic vision. He thereby challenged, preemptively, what he called the "hidden assimilationist quality" in the work of his most notable literary peers: Saul Bellow, Philip Roth, and Bernard Malamud (Levin, "A Conversation" 40). The lackluster public and critical reception of his early Zionist work and the harsh treatment afforded to him by the Jewish-American intelligentsia at the time reveals—at least in part—the American Jews' fierce opposition to the idea of a Jewish state prior to the Holocaust.

Uris, in contrast to Levin, faced a decidedly Zionist milieu when he wrote *Exodus* (1958), but, like Levin, he was driven by his ideological convictions concerning the Middle East and Jewish-American fiction. He wrote *Exodus* to tout the heroism of the Israeli *sabra*, to confirm the maliciousness of the Arab, and to challenge what had emerged by the late 1950s as the archetypal Jewish protagonist in American literature. "*Exodus*," Uris claims in a prefatory note to the paperback edition, "is about a fighting people," not about "the cliché Jewish characters who have cluttered up our American fiction." Lamentably, Uris merely replaced one set of clichés with another. From his canned depiction of the heroic Israeli freedom fighter to his facile demonization of the Arabs, Uris affirmed everything that American Jews wanted so desperately to believe about the Middle East. The overwhelmingly enthusiastic public reception of *Exodus* reveals how eager American Jews were in the wake of the Holocaust to embrace Uris's image of the stoic, courageous Jew. Who cared that Uris's portrait was merely an inverse stereotype, one that even Israelis forthrightly disowned? Thirty-five years after the publication of Uris's novel, the commercial success of Herman Wouk's *The Hope* (1993)—in which he largely revives Uris's pulp formula for depicting the Israeli soldier—illustrates that some American Jews (and gentiles) still yearn for images of heroic Israeli soldiers and malicious Arabs.

One need only weigh Levin's and Uris's fiction against Howe's criteria above to isolate the weakness of their efforts. For while Uris and Levin make their own ideological convictions abundantly clear, these "hard pellets of ideology," as Howe puts it, are not satisfactorily absorbed into a credible depiction of human behavior and feeling. Their failure, like most novelistic failures, can be seen as a failure of expression. *Yehuda*, for example, fails as a novel because its protagonist's fatty sigh of unqualified Zionist fervor at the end of the novel strains credulity. Given what we know about Yehuda—his individualist aspirations to become a concert violinist and his spiritual longings, neither of which can be fulfilled on the *kibbutz*—it rings false. In the final analysis, Levin refuses to qualify his ideology to conclude the novel, though the experiences of his protagonist, Yehuda, refuse to sustain this broad, inclusive political statement.

In *Exodus,* Uris arguably fashions an even less plausible protagonist in his effort to bolster the comfortable Zionist pieties of his milieu and to fashion a new, decidedly un-neurotic Jewish character. As Ruth Wisse and others note, Uris's Ari Ben Canaan bears more in common with the stolid heroes of American films set in the Wild West than with Israeli *sabras.* The characters in *Exodus,* one reviewer comments, "stand in roughly the same relation to the reality of Israel as Scarlett O'Hara, Rhett Butler, and Ashley Wilkes do to the American Civil War and Reconstruction South" (Blocker 539). Like Levin, Uris, in deference to his political agenda, fails to filter his ideological convictions through three-dimensional, believable characters. Midge Decter aptly character-izes Uris's fiction as "genuine trash about Jews," insofar as "he has cre-ated the possibility of seeing Jews not as the troublesome and incom-prehensible heroes that decent social conscience has always demanded but as the kind of heroes that middle-class dream-life has conditioned us all to make our most immediate responses to" ("Popular Jews" 360). Indeed, Uris creates a fantasy through the stolid and tough Ari Ben Canaan—a fantasy that American readers anxiously embraced at the time, but one that earmarks *Exodus* as a novel in which the author can-not (or at least refuses to) express the political through the immediacy and closeness of credible experience.

The Israel fiction of Meyer Levin and Leon Uris, then, fails to achieve a level of "high drama" because the writers cannot reconcile their ideological agenda with the generic demands of the novel. Wouk's recent novel notwithstanding, Uris's *Exodus* distinguishes itself today as the trap that most Jewish-American writers seek to avoid (though the novel does contain significant and overlooked strengths, which I explore in Chapter 3). Fortunately, the succeeding Jewish-American writers on Israel—from Saul Bellow to Tova Reich—have demonstrated a far greater ability to engage the vexing ideological problems swirling about the Middle East through (rather than at the expense of) credible characters. To be sure, this development has a good deal to do with the variance in individual talent between, say, a Levin and a Bellow, a Uris and a Roth. However, as I have already implied, it also has a good bit to do with the historical circumstances surrounding the authors—circum-stances that bode well for the future Jewish-American fiction on Israel.

Perhaps the overarching point that I would like to make in this introduction is that the zeitgeist today encourages the surge of quality Jewish-American fiction that we are currently beginning to enjoy, just as the zeitgeist of Levin's and Uris's day discouraged Jewish-American writers from engaging Israel seriously in their work. The Jewish state, I would argue, needed to establish itself as a viable political reality before it could inspire quality fiction from Jewish-American authors. It needed to outgrow its role as the "transcendent object," to borrow a phrase from Ted Solotaroff, of the American Jews' political and spiritual dreams ("The Open Community" xv). Meyer Levin, one must remember, wrote his earlier Israel novels, *Yehuda* and *My Father's House* (1947), before the establishment of the Jewish state. Israel thus manifests itself in these novels as the dream, the transcendent object, yet to be realized. Leon Uris wrote *Exodus*, of course, after the dream became a reality. But just how long Israel would remain a reality was a matter for debate. Israel would not establish itself as a viable national entity in the Middle East until after its victory in the 1967 Six-Day War. The war, in a very real sense, represented Israel's moment of reckoning. Israel would either be wiped off the map or it would prevail. Israel, of course, prevailed. Now, given the historical circumstances that faced Levin and Uris, should it really surprise us that these Jewish-American authors refused to qualify their ardent Zionism? Should it surprise us that most other Jewish-American writers, no doubt recognizing the tenuousness of the historical circumstances, refused to even broach the topic of Israel in their fiction? The stakes, one might say, were simply too high for the Jewish-American author to approach the Middle East in all its complexity and moral ambiguousness.

Small wonder that it was only after Israel's overwhelming victory in the Six-Day War that Hugh Nissenson, in *In the Reign of Peace* (1972), and Saul Bellow, in *Mr. Sammler's Planet* (1970), were able to eschew Levin's and Uris's Zionist pieties to explore the psychological costs of Israeli militarism through less heroic, but ultimately, more human characters. Likewise, Potok was prescient enough in *The Chosen* (1967) to recognize the complications that would beset the American Jewish community after they eschewed messianic Judaism to embrace secular Zionism as a primary source of identity. The more recent works of Philip Roth, Anne Roiphe, and Tova Reich represent a further development of the Jewish-American novel on Israel. Roth takes on the Palestinian problem in both of his Middle East novels while Reich and Roiphe engage the problem of Israel's gender discrimination. These are novelists who, unlike Uris and Levin, seek out rather than obfuscate, the real, felt moral quandaries of Jewish identity as it plays itself out in Israel. Bellow, Nissenson, Potok, Roth, Roiphe, and Reich: they all write in the thoughtful, critical spirit of true Zionism, or "post-Zionism" (a notable accomplishment for Bellow, Nissenson, and Potok, who addressed Israel in their work during America's most deliriously "Zionist" phase) and explore the central issues that have linked and divided the two Jewish communities: the role of Israel as both safe haven and spiritual core for Jews everywhere pitted against its rampant secularism and spiritual sterility, its militarism, its deference (given Israel's parliamentary government) to the ultra-Orthodox, and its entrenched sexism.

A broad survey of the literature, then, illustrates the complex and varied ways in which American Jews have imagined Israel in their fiction, and the concomitantly dynamic relationship between American Jews and the Jewish state. Our post-Zionist milieu should inspire, I believe, the continued outcropping of sophisticated Jewish-American fictional approaches toward the Middle East. A comprehensive peace between Israel and its Arab neighbors seems more imminent today than impossible. So Jewish-American authors, I suspect, will follow the example of Roth, Roiphe, and Reich to grapple with the issue of Jewish identity against a more tangible Middle East landscape. As Israel evolves as a nation, so does Jewish-American fiction about Israel, and I anticipate that they will both continue to evolve at a rapid rate. But regardless of this changeable nature of the Jewish-American imagination, the very persistence of Israel in occupying that imagination tells us a great deal. Indeed, each of the eight writers illustrates, above all, how prominent a role Israel played and continues to play in forging the Jewish-American identity. Israel, after all, has emerged as the American Jew's favorite preoccupation. A single moment in Philip Roth's latest novel, *Sabbath's Theater* (1995), illustrates how ineluctable this preoccupation truly is for American Jews. The aging protagonist, Mickey Sabbath, does not travel to the Middle East, nor does he give any indication that Israel has ever entered his mind; but when he imagines his own eulogy, the final line reads curiously, "Mr. Sabbath did nothing for Israel" (*ST* 195). Israel, it seems, looms in the consciousness of even the most disaffected American Jews.

In regard to my own Middle East preoccupations, they do manifest themselves throughout the study—subtly in the first few chapters, and more explicitly in the later chapters on Chaim Potok, Philip Roth, and Anne Roiphe. Nonetheless, I would like now to articulate briefly my essential perspective of the Middle East to preclude the reader from rifling through the first chapters in a frustrating search for my political orientation. So, let me say up front that, as a Jew growing up in Los

Angeles in the 1970s (during the zenith of America's Zionist phase), I was brought up to be a Zionist. The Hebrew school I attended could just as well have been named "Israel school," for Holocaust remembrance and Zionism were seared into our consciousness more than aleph, bet, gimmel, and daleth. The suffering of fellow Jews during the Holocaust did not seem a thing of the distant past at all, as we witnessed it three afternoons a week (after "regular" school) at Temple Ramat Zion. The thick European accent of our *morah* [teacher], her occasional fits of sobbing, and her inability to participate in any of our principal's special assemblies dedicated to Holocaust remembrance made us painfully aware that she was a "survivor" and, probably, the only one so fortunate in her family. The message drilled home to us time and time again was that Holocaust remembrance was essential, not only to honor the Jewish victims, but because *it could happen again.*

Here, of course, is where Israel came in. What else did the recent 1973 attack against the Jewish state by its hostile Arab neighbors (launched on Yom Kippur, no less!) signify except that it could happen again? It was up to us to see that the Jews in Israel flourish rather than suffer a second annihilation. Thus, we set out around the neighborhood with our parents and our powder-blue collection cans with the detail of Israel set off in white like an ivory sliver. Our Zionist education was unclouded by the vexing Palestinian problem. The slaughter of six million Jews during the Holocaust made Israel a necessity while the Arabs—a monolithic group who already occupied 99 percent of the Middle East anyway—wished, not unlike Hitler, to wipe the Jews off the face of the earth (my Zionism was so unclouded, in fact, that I was dumbfounded as late as my freshman year in college when a fellow student whose intelligence I admired let on in the college newspaper that his hero was Yasir Arafat, a "freedom fighter who dedicated his life to getting back for the Palestinians what was rightfully theirs").

Today I still consider myself a Zionist. That is, I believe as strongly as ever in Israel's right to exist; and, moreover, I believe that the spiritual and physical condition of Jews everywhere in the Diaspora depends upon Israel's survival. I would only qualify my brand of Zionism in two ways. First, in embracing Zionism, I do not mean to imply that Zionism alone can carry the day as the religion of American Jews. As I hope I make clear in Chapter 6, on Chaim Potok, American Jews need Zionism *and* Judaism. The former, as the dizzying rate of assimilation illustrates (at least in part), has proven a weak substitute for the latter.

Second, like many progressive American Jews today, I have culti-
vated a healthy dose of skepticism in regard to Israeli policy toward the
Palestinians—hence my sensitivity to the way in which Jewish-American writers depict, or refuse to depict, Arab characters in their fiction
(see especially Chapter 7, on Philip Roth). Sheer demographics are
enough to convince me that Yitzhak Rabin's Labor party made the right
decision when they agreed on the "declaration of principles" with the
PLO in 1993, principles that honor the Palestinians' demand for self-
determination, and principles for which Rabin paid the ultimate price.
Indeed, the alternative—to continue ruling over an ever-growing
minority population with its own distinct history and culture—is an
altogether untenable one given the contemporary Middle East landscape. Despite the surge of fundamentalist violence in Israel since the
1993 Israel-PLO accord, I remain hopeful that the Israeli government
will persevere and continue on its present course with the Palestinians.
While I espouse a more gradual transition to full Palestinian national
self-determination than some progressive Jews (especially given the
reluctance of the Palestinians to strike the language in their National
Covenant that, until recently, called for Israel's destruction), I look forward to the establishment of a demilitarized Palestinian state in the
Middle East in the not too distant future.

Unlike an increasing number of academics, I am under no illusions
that this academic study will play a significant role in this political process. I only hope that the study serves as a touchstone through which the
reader might engage the past, present, and future Jewish-American fiction on Israel. If my own critical model helps guide readers toward a
richer, more historically informed, interpretation of Jewish-American
fiction—if it inspires, in the bargain, even a handful of readers to question their own assumptions about the Middle East—it will exceed my
wildest expectations.

Chapter 2

MEYER LEVIN
AGAINST THE GRAIN
A Zionist Writer Takes on
America's Pre-Zionist Zeitgeist

There can be little doubt that in the last ten years we have witnessed a shift in the tide of the American Jewish relationship with Israel. Some observers insist that we now live in a "post-Zionist" milieu, in large part because American Jews so readily come forward today to criticize the state of Israel. Indeed, those in the know would agree that Israel's incursions into Lebanon in the early 1980s, the Pollard affair, and the Palestinian *intifada* have all claimed a hefty toll on Israel's PR amid American (and American Jewish) circles. What fewer people realize, however, is that there was a time in America when the very idea of a Jewish state, in the first place, was not a popular one within the American Jewish community. After the Holocaust, of course, American Jews recognized the need for Israel, and the most prominent Jews were roundly admonished if they hesitated to express their new-found Zionism. "Even Ludwig Lewisohn," Daniel Walden notes, "was criticized by fellow Jews [shortly after the Holocaust], though he early became a Zionist and Judeophile" ("Introduction" 17). But prior to the Shoah, the zeitgeist was decidedly anti-Zionist as the idea of an autonomous Jewish state clashed with Marxist, plain old assimilationist, or religious precepts (see Chapter 6, on Chaim Potok, for a related discussion). As Michael Lerner reminds us, "to be a Zionist in the 1930s and 1940s was *not* to be a part of the American-Jewish establishment" ("The Editor" xxiv).

During this pre-Zionist period in America, Meyer Levin emerged as the most notable and courageous Zionist writer, a writer against the grain of popular American Jewish sentiment. Levin's own Zionism took hold, remarkably, in the 1920s ("pretty damn prematurely" as one Levin interviewer observes), after an editor of the *Menorah Journal*—which would shortly become *Commentary*—convinced Levin in 1925 to report for the magazine on the opening of Hebrew University in Jerusalem (Morton 32). While there, he met Golda Meir. Levin asserts that this first trip "made the whole Zionist experience real for me" (Morton 32). Although this first visit lasted only several weeks, the idea of making *aliyah* evidently occupied Levin's mind; he returned to Israel two years later and spent half a year at the *kibbutz* Yagur near Haifa (Levin, "The Writer" 527). From this experience, he wrote a short story in 1928, "Maurie Finds His Medium," which details the *aliyah* of an American Jewish artist, and published *Yehuda*, the first significant Zionist novel (in America) in 1931—a time, lest we forget, when "American Jews were generally opposed to the establishment of an independent Jewish homeland in Palestine" (Guttmann 108). Levin produced a Zionist film in 1947, *The Illegals,* about the underground exodus of Polish Holocaust survivors to Palestine. That same year, he published his second Zionist novel, *My Father's House,* and he would publish an intriguing short story, "After All I Did For Israel," in 1951.

Levin, of course, went on to publish a voluminous Zionist novel in 1972, *The Settlers,* and a sequel six years later, *The Harvest.* Owing largely to the scope of this chapter, I will not discuss these later novels (published during America's most fervently Zionist period). The scope of the chapter notwithstanding, however, other Jewish-American writers begin to "imagine" Israel in a more timely and critically astute manner than does the 1970s Levin even before the 1970s, and certainly during that decade (see the following chapters on Saul Bellow, Hugh Nissenson, and Chaim Potok). As Steven J. Rubin notes, "the fiction that Meyer Levin wrote after 1960 . . . does not seem well suited for the sophisticated tastes of the modern reader. . . . Too much of his later fiction appears to be a statement of the author's view of existence, rather than a rendering of experience" (Rubin 150). Readers interested in *The Settlers* and *The Harvest* might consult Rubin's adept treatment of these novels in his recent book. While Levin's later efforts largely fail as fiction, his early fiction on Israel—"Maurie Finds His Medium," *Yehuda, My Father's House,* and "After All I Did For Israel"—manifest themselves today not only as original and courageous, but also as works of extraordinary vision. For, in these works, Levin anticipates some of the problems that would beset Israel and, concomitantly, anticipates the concerns of Jewish-American writers who would eventually follow his lead to imagine Israel in their fiction.

One cannot fully appreciate the courage of Levin's early Zionist fiction without considering the scorn Levin thereby provoked from the ranks of the Jewish literary left. That Meyer Levin was ostracized from this epicenter of Jewish literary culture is no secret. Levin would bemoan the "anti-Levin conspiracy" and blast back throughout his career at the more popular writers who he believed were responsible for the "silent treatment." The holy triumvirate in Jewish-American literature—Bellow, Roth, and Malamud—were really "anti-Jewish" as far as Levin was concerned (Levin, "A Conversation" 39). In numerous interviews, Levin attacks the "hidden assimilationist quality in their work" and suggests that these most lauded Jewish writers, ironically, "don't know a thing about [the Jewish community]" ("A Conversation" 40). As recently as 1978, Levin insists that Bellow, Roth, and Malamud (and Irving Howe, as well) "are totally detached from the living Jewish community" (Morton 33). In the introduction to *The Rise of American Jewish Literature,* which Levin co-edited with Charles Angoff, Levin takes the opportunity to castigate Bellow, Roth, and Malamud once again. Discussing the "rise" of the three writers, Levin and Angoff comment, "Was this literary trend a valid interpretation of postwar Jewish psychology, or was it leading Jews to assimilation by—purposively or not—omitting the inner continuation as well as the creative and identifying activities in Jewish life?" (14).

Several critics, such as Benno Weiser Varon, Pearl Bell, and Harold Ribalow, explore the antipathies running both ways between Levin and the left-wing *Partisan Review* crowd, which included the eminent likes of Saul Bellow and Irving Howe (see also Lawrence Graver's recent study, *An Obsession with Anne Frank: Meyer Levin and the Diary,* for his detailed discussion of Levin's tumultuous relationship with the Jewish literary left). What demands emphasis today, however, is the extent to which Levin's unpopular Zionist vision, specifically, accounted for his ostracism from the Jewish literary left during the pre-Zionist period of the 1930s and 40s. For Levin's less valid complaints of the "literary mafia" during the 1970s—in the wake of his unsuccessful Zionist novels, *The Settlers* and *The Harvest*—tends to obscure the validity of his similar complaints in the 1930s and 40s. Pearl Bell, for example, can make a convincing case, in reviewing *The Harvest,* that "it is not just Levin's stubborn dedication 'to the Jewish life around me and to Jewish problems,' as he claims, that has kept him out of the pantheon of American Jewish writing" (68). Indeed, one must agree with Bell that anti-Levin "conspiracies" had little to do with the disappointing reception of Levin's 1970s Zionist novels; they were published, after all, during America's most Zionist period to date. Rather, owing largely to their overblown sentimentality (or perhaps their "sententious banality," as Bell puts it), these 1970s novels simply fail as art.

That said, one should not assume—as does Bell—that the Zionist Levin during the 1930s and 40s suffered merely the legitimate, artistic critiques of the 1970s Levin. Enough evidence exists today to conclude that the Jewish literary left judged Levin's early Zionist fiction largely on political, not artistic, grounds (and, yes, I count myself among those who insist that, although they are inextricably connected, certain distinctions can be drawn between art and politics). In Benno Weiser Varon's "The Haunting of Meyer Levin," he convincingly affirms that Levin was, indeed, "singled out for attack because of his consistent pro-Zionism sometimes by one Marxist clique, sometimes by another . . ." (13). Varon strays occasionally to offer unreliable, anecdotal evidence of the anti-Levin conspiracy, and performs overly generous, sentimental readings of Levin's work. However, Varon also effectively renders the anti-Zionist milieu of the 1930s and 40s. He quotes Norman Podhoretz's *Making It* to emphasize that "As good Marxists, they [the Jewish literary left of the *Partisan Review*] regarded Zionism as yet another form of bourgeois nationalism . . ." (16). What is more, Varon convincingly argues that the literary left did, predictably, "haunt" Levin, who courageously produced Zionist fiction during this period.

Case in point, Bellow's introduction to the first edition of *Great Jewish Short Stories* (1963). Bellow predictably excludes Levin from the anthology (not, in itself, proof of anything), but also blatantly misreads Levin's 1928 story, "Maurie Finds His Medium," to castigate Levin for his skewed artistic sensibilities. The story revolves around a foundering Jewish-American writer who decides, all too conveniently, that his alienation from his Jewish roots causes his artistic failure in America. He thus takes off for Palestine, where he discovers that painting offers him the artistic language through which to express his Jewish identity. Or so he thinks. Importantly, Levin concludes the story by making it clear that Maurie's art, in a word, stinks. He paints "hackneyed, common repetitions of landscapes and Arab heads, banal . . ." (Levin, "Maurie" 181). Varon aptly notes that "Levin obviously uses [Maurie] as a caricature for many a self-styled 'artist'" (14). Clearly, then, one should not confuse Maurie with Levin. But Bellow does precisely this as he assumes that Levin shares Maurie's artistic precepts:

> A curious surrender to xenophobia is concealed in this theorizing about art, and I am sure that Mr. Levin would not like to be identified with Oswald Spengler who is . . . an exponent of views of this sort. According to Spengler, the Jews are permanently identified with a period of culture he calls the Magian, and will never belong to modern order. . . . Theories like Mr. Levin's about the "perfect unit of time and place" seldom bring any art into the world. . . . ("Introduction" 15)

In subsequent editions of *Great Jewish Short Stories,* Bellow's editors persuaded him (after Levin's justifiable complaints) to revise the above passage to read, "Theories like those *expressed by Mr. Levin's character* . . . seldom bring any art into the world" [emphasis mine] (Bellow, "Introduction" 15). Now, Bellow is nothing if not an astute and canny reader, one eminently familiar with T. S. Eliot's dictum about narrative voice. So why does he insist upon reading Maurie's narrow artistic precepts as Levin's own? Most likely because Bellow viewed Levin's early Zionism (the one thing the author does share with his protagonist) as the pernicious influence responsible for Maurie's skewed vision of art. Put another way, because Levin is a Zionist, he must share his Zionist character's "xenophobic" artistic views. Steven Rubin also suggests that "Saul Bellow's harsh judgment of Levin as 'xenophobic' in his introduction to the first Dell edition of *Great Jewish Short Stories* (1963), serves to illustrate the general disregard for Levin's Zionist views" (149). Ironically, Bellow and most of his anti-Zionist (*ergo,* anti-Levin) cohorts would adopt Levin's Zionism shortly after the horrors in Europe gained full clarity, and Bellow would eventually insist upon the importance of Israel in his fiction and non-fiction (see Chapter 4). As Varon insists, "Levin's crime consisted in becoming a Zionist 'too soon'" (17).

Bellow's myopic reading of "Maurie Finds His Medium" serves as an instructive starting point at which to assess the courage and vision of Levin's early Zionist fiction. One can glean from Bellow's critique of the story both how Levin's early Zionist fiction has been received in the past and how it should be reinterpreted today. For Bellow's aversion toward Levin's early Zionism prevents him from recognizing Levin's foresight in "Maurie Finds His Medium." So intent is Bellow upon seeing Levin as Maurie that he refuses to see that Levin uses his protagonist to predict just what type of American Jew the future state of Israel will likely attract. Though Israel will desperately need able-bodied men and women to build up the Jewish state, Levin suggests (through his creation of Maurie) that the prospect of making *aliyah* will more likely appeal to the maladjusted, alienated American Jew.

To be sure, the past several years bear out Levin's 1928 prediction. As Thomas Friedman recently observed, the majority of Americans making *aliyah* today do not move to Israel to strengthen the state, but to salvage their own flagging spirituality; they join the yeshiva, not the *kibbutz*. At one such yeshiva, Friedman asks a group of these new Israelis, "What are you doing here? . . . You're not supposed to be in a yeshiva. That's not why Americans come here. . . . You're supposed to be on kibbutzim, draining swamps, dreaming about being an Israeli fighter pilot . . ." (303). Levin envisions the onslaught of these new Israelis in "Maurie Finds His Medium." Moreover, he anticipates the creations of later Jewish-American writers who imagine Israel. The characters who make *aliyah* in Philip Roth's *The Counterlife* (1986), Anne Roiphe's *Lovingkindness* (1987), and Tova Reich's *Master of the Return* (1988) (see Chapters 7–9) share Maurie's disillusionment with the shallowness of Jewish life in America. Like Maurie, they move to Israel to reclaim their religious roots, and the secular state of Israel just might be better off without any of them.

Levin would go on to publish the first significant Zionist novel in America, *Yehuda*, three years later, in 1931. The novel revolves principally around a *kibbutznik*, Yehuda, who struggles throughout the novel to reconcile his socialist ideals with his individualist aspirations to become a concert violinist. Not many people were buying books during the Depression, and the novel sold only about 3,000 copies. Regardless of the Depression, however, the subject matter and title of the book probably turned off some potential readers (Rubin 25). *Yehuda's* poor reception greatly disappointed Levin, who "expected to be launched as a Jewish writer of significance to my fellow Jews" (Levin, "The Writer" 527). Levin reflects that "when *Yehuda* appeared and touched off no response in the American Jewish community, I was left rather suspended. The lack of a responsive audience was as frustrating as the dearth of royalties" ("The Writer" 527). The novel did garner sympathetic reviews (see Lechlitner, Ehrlich, Trilling, and "A Zionist Colony"); however, the few critics who have addressed the novel more recently generally consider it a melodramatic Zionist novel, to its detriment. Bell dismisses *Yehuda* as a "sentimental tale" (66), while Guttmann characterizes the protagonist, Yehuda, as an "improbable man" (109).

Given the anti-Zionist mood in America, *Yehuda* would have been a courageous work even if it were merely "an optimistic and generally positive view of settlement life and the Zionist ideal" (Rubin 144). And the overall structure of the novel gives one good reason to interpret *Yehuda* in these terms. Levin takes pains to depict the idyllic Palestine that Yehuda and the other members of his *kibbutz* enjoy. The novel opens as Yehuda finishes a satisfying day of work in the fields and pauses to gaze, in awe, upon the majestic land—*his* land, Levin suggests. A great, almost ineffable joy often overcomes Yehuda while he works in the fields alongside his comrades. Levin, for example, describes Yehuda's happiness as he observes the progress of Sholom: "This was one of his comrades. Together they would bring about a new life, a new life!" (*Y* 162). Yehuda and his friends often burst into song, "The nation Israel lives! The soul of Israel lives!" (*Y* 356). Though Yehuda's ambition to gain worldwide acclaim as a concert musician dogs him throughout the story, he resolutely chooses the plow over the violin by the end of the novel. Yehuda gets his chance to prove his talent when the esteemed violinist, Yussuf Brenner, travels to the *kibbutz* to perform. However, Brenner's arrogance convinces Yehuda that he will play only for his comrades and, we are to believe, this will be enough:

> In the hot midafternoon Yehuda looked out over the plain. Never before had the clean air so joyously filled his body. He felt air vibrate within him, as it must vibrate in a songfilled violin. The whole plain danced in the white afternoon heat, wavered and beat under the glow of the sun. . . . After a while he would go down to the cabin and get his violin, and play his music. (*Y* 374)

There can be little doubt that Levin intends the reader to frolic in the Zionist current. That said, I would argue that the strength of *Yehuda* does not lie in its melodrama, but in Levin's perspicacious dramatization of the problems that beset the very first Israeli *kibbutzim* and continue to plague the increasingly unpopular *kibbutz* system today. To Levin's credit, several details of novel do *not* support the affirmative ending above.

First, several episodes in the novel indicate that the socialist ideals of a *kibbutz* cannot be so easily reconciled with individualist aspirations. Levin, to be sure, would like the reader to believe that *kibbutz* life harmonizes with and enhances Yehuda's individual talent. In one scene, Yehuda sees his comrades as fellow musicians who accompany him: "Rambam is a cello. Feldman, here, a deep trombone, pump-pum-pum. And Zahavey a fiddle that screeches and squeaks..." (*Y* 19). But an overwhelming number of details illustrate that the communal life stifles Yehuda's talent, a talent he must realize to gain fulfillment. He bemoans the severe limits on his practice time and must acknowledge the "strange stifling death that surrounded his music here" (*Y* 82). When an American Jew, Mr. Paley, visits the *kibbutz* and encourages Yehuda to pursue his artistic aspirations, Yehuda hopes that Paley will "pluck him from this place" (*Y* 120). Yehuda attempts to rationalize his dream by convincing himself of his altruistic motives; he resolves to send the bulk of his earnings back to the commune and reflects, "Such a comrade would be worth more to the commune than twenty pairs of hands on the farm!" (*Y* 157). However, the prospect of personal fame, not of helping the commune, invades Yehuda's dreams. He envisions himself "on the stage of some vast auditorium the walls of which were festooned with inconceivable elegancies, the pillars of which shone gold" (*Y* 171). Yehuda wishes he were like Sholom, unselfishly idealistic and "good" to the core. "To him," muses Yehuda, "ideals did not seem manners intellectually adopted, in him ideals flowed as some sweet substance in the blood" (*Y* 127). What one realizes, however (despite Levin's contrived ending), is that Yehuda cannot be like Sholom. He possesses great ambition which cannot—and probably should not—be stifled.

In addition to this main plot of the novel, Levin constructs several subplots to emphasize the often irreconcilable tension between individual aspiration and the socialist ideal. Relying so heavily upon others proves more than several characters can bear. Weary of the plodding inefficiency of communal farming, Aryay aspires to succeed on his own as a farmer: "One day ... he would do what he wanted to do. He would go out and *be for himself*. That was what he was yearning for: *his own* small fields to fence around and to tend perfectly so they were cleanly sown in neat rows ..." [emphasis mine] (*Y* 143). The socialist ban on private property turns one character, Sonya, into an irrepressible kleptomaniac. Before the novel ends, she makes off with a whistle and a fountain pen, and artlessly sells the commune's chickens to buy herself silk stockings (a bourgeois, capitalist symbol if there ever was one).

Although the *kibbutz* members ostracize Sonya for her behavior and, ultimately, impel her to leave the commune, several of her friends realize the validity of her individual needs. Says Yehudit, "Well, what if a girl wants silk stockings—!" (*Y* 249). Levin's Mr. Paley, an American Jewish visitor to Yehuda's *kibbutz,* also recognizes the pragmatic shortcomings of the socialist dream. He muses that this dream of "building the land of Israel . . . was one of those romantic dreams people dreamed. It was all right to live like a lumber jack for a few months sleeping on a cot in a shack and eating meals off tin plates on a raw wooden table, but after all what was civilization for if not to enjoy the fruits of it . . ." (*Y* 164).

Through the case of Yehuda and his violin, Aryay and his envisioned fields, Sonya and her stockings, and Paley's prescient observations, Levin anticipates the serious tensions between communalism and individualism that would take its toll on the *kibbutzim* in Israel. Today, no one would dispute that—while Israelis might laud the communal ideals of the first Jewish settlers in Palestine—individualism is the order of the day in the Jewish state. As one Israeli recently observed:

> Ideology brought Jews here; ideology also denigrated shopkeepers and praised those who went out to settle the land. It glorified not the rugged individual, but the rugged group—the commune, the underground, the army unit, the nation. . . . Today, forty-six years after its founding, Israel is like an ex-revolutionary shopping in the mall. Individualism and the desire for personal comfort, no longer weaknesses, quietly have become values. (Gorenberg 20)

Incredibly, Levin recognizes and dramatizes this individualist spirit which percolated even in the heyday, so to speak, of Palestine's communal phase. He anticipates (though unintentionally, perhaps) the contemporary, individualist ethos of the Israeli. To be sure, Levin's Sonya would be right at home in the shopping malls of Israel today.

Certainly, the irrepressible individualist urges of several Israeli *kibbutzniks* would not emerge as the only weakness of the *kibbutzim.* For the socialist credo of Israel's communes stifled not only individualist expression, but religious expression as well; socialism, in effect, became the religion on the *kibbutz,* thus replacing Judaism. This element of the *kibbutz* system has proven a shortcoming, as a number of members of *kibbutzim*—alienated from their Jewish roots—have abandoned their respective communes to reclaim the religious element of their identity. Hugh Nissenson, in *Notes from the Frontier* (1968), and Tova Reich, in

Master of the Return (1988), address this weakness of the Israeli *kibbutz* (see Chapters 4 and 8). Remarkably, however, Levin engages this religious weakness of the *kibbutzim* as early as 1931 in *Yehuda.*

Levin addresses the tension between religion and socialism through creating a Chasidic commune close by Yehuda's (more common) socialist *kibbutz.* Yehuda's love interest throughout the novel, Yocheved, lives at this religious commune and her religious precepts raise Yehuda's socialist hackles. He wishes to shake Yocheved out of her "archaic" religious convictions:

> We are socialists! Do you understand what that means! Have you ever read the books of Karl Marx! It seems you never even heard of him! . . . Here in our new land, we must find a new way of living. We must live as brothers. We must do away with exploitation. We must make everything perfect. See, everyone will work! Everyone will be equal. The teacher, and the ploughman, and the book-keeper, and the stableman, all will know how to work. (*Y* 43)

Yehuda, indeed, is nothing if not a good socialist. And one might be tempted here to see little narrative distance between Levin and his protagonist. After all, the novel ends in fatty affirmation of these socialist precepts as Yehuda looks forward to working the fields the next day with his comrade, Pinsker. However, just as several details suggest that Yehuda's individualist, musical ambitions will not be as easily suppressed as Levin insists in the concluding pages, several details also undermine Levin's ultimate affirmation of the irreligious, socialist ethos.

While Yehuda can exhort Yocheved, until blue in the face, regarding socialism's timeliness and, conversely, Judaism's obsolescence, the Sabbath rituals Yocheved's family observes provoke Yehuda's unwelcome nostalgia for his previous, religious life. Yocheved's preparation of the Sabbath cakes, for example, reminds him of his loving, religious childhood home: "These were the cookies that Yehuda very much liked, for his mother had made them and given them to him every Friday night and Sabbath day, but since his going away from home he had not seen or tasted them. . . . their taste immeasurably gladdened him" (*Y* 133–134). Later, Yehuda visits Yocheved's commune during their celebration of *Simchas Torah,* the Jewish holiday celebrating God's law. As Yocheved's father fervently sings in celebration of God's gift of the Torah (the Law), Yehuda must admit that religion possesses an enduring timeliness all its own: "The song of the old man seemed to say, here is my principle, that is all the principle one needs" (*Y* 206). Yehuda, significantly, cannot resist singing along with Yocheved and her father.

Now, one might argue that Yehuda's nostalgia for a certain food and song does not indicate his longing for religion; Yehuda does not, at any rate, long for religion at the end of the novel. But, regardless of Levin's contrived ending, one cannot separate the above food and song from their religious associations. The religious significance of the *Simchas Torah* song, of course, speaks for itself; Yehuda affirms the principle of God's law when he sings along with Yocheved and her father. In regard to the Sabbath cakes, Yehuda does not so much long for their flavor as he longs for the mother-love, embodied in those pastries that he enjoyed as a member of a traditionally religious family. In stressing the childrens' communal upbringing at Yehuda's *kibbutz*, Levin implies that the socialist precepts of the commune do not afford them the close-knit family life Yehuda cherishes in retrospect. Yehuda insists to Yocheved at one point that his *kibbutz* "set[s] aside" the "foolishness of religion," but "respect[s] the sincere devotion of our fathers" (*Y* 233). What the above details suggest, however, is that Judaism has far more to offer its adherents than "foolishness" and that a mere "respect" from those fortunate enough to realize this will not be enough, in the long run, to quell the religious stirrings of several *kibbutzniks*.

Levin details several other complications of *kibbutz* life which deserve brief mention because Levin's sentimental moments, unfortunately, garner more attention today than his realistic dramatization of Jewish life in Palestine/Israel. Levin, for example, faithfully depicts the almost incessant infighting that the socialist system of communal rule invites. Members of the *kibbutz* fight over nearly everything: whether or not it would be against principle to hire outside workers during the busy harvest, whether they should buy a new motor to work the water pump or fix the old one, whether two, three, or ten women should watch the children during the day, whether or not they should send some men to work in a nearby factory to earn money . . . the list goes on and on. Amid such squabbling, one wonders that anything ever gets accomplished at the *kibbutz*.

Levin also dramatizes the tensions between Yehuda's commune and neighboring Arabs—tensions that, of course, continue today between the Jewish state and surrounding Arab states. Illustrative of the sharp divide between the two cultures, Levin depicts an Arab donkey-path to

Haifa which "crossed through [Yocheved's] fields, and then went on through the fields of the commune. The path was like a long needle stuck through both stretches of land" (*Y* 42). The imagery scarcely needs elaboration. Arab and Jew, Levin suggests, intersect violently with one another in Palestine. Indeed, Arab raids and Jewish counter-raids, one learns, are simply a fact of life in the Middle East. Levin, interestingly, exposes the fruitlessness of such antagonism during one episode when the men of the commune take their only vehicle to attack neighboring Arabs. While the vehicle is gone, a pregnant member of the *kibbutz*, Aviva, loses her baby in delivery because she cannot reach the hospital.

Levin's dramatization in *Yehuda* of the problems that plagued even the earliest *kibbutzim*—heretofore largely neglected—does not render the novel any less a Zionist text. Rather, his serious scrutiny of the *kibbutz* system (marred only occasionally by sentimental affirmation) actually qualifies the novel as a Zionist text—that is, if we are to understand Zionism as a genuine commitment to Israel's political and spiritual condition (Polish 261). This important point deserves clarification, as casual readers of Levin's early Zionist literature often read his novels as "uncritically Zionist." A truer understanding of Zionism exposes the above quotation as the oxymoron it is, as Zionism—at its very core—is a critical and fluid orientation of inquiry. As I stated in the introduction to this study, a leading Jewish magazine, *Midstream*, aptly defines Zionism as "a questioning of the Jewish *status quo*, and a steady confrontation of the problems of Jewish existence." Levin's *Yehuda*, then, deserves recognition as the first significant American Zionist novel not merely for its portrayal of Palestine as a viable alternative to Jewish life in the Diaspora, but for Levin's visionary, even prophetic, account of the troubles lurking beneath the idyllic exterior of Palestine's earliest *kibbutzim*.

After the disappointment of *Yehuda*, Levin focused his creative energies upon American Jewish life and published his most popular novel, *The Old Bunch*, in 1937. Palestine would remain on his mind, however, and he returned there for a third visit just after the publication of *The Old Bunch*. During World War II, Levin worked as a war correspondent for the Overseas News Agency and the Jewish Telegraphic Agency. Just after the war, Levin described his chief duties as a correspondent:

> [M]y chief assignment was to write about Jews in battle, and surviving Jews in Europe. In the last weeks of the war, I chased up and down

the entire European front, trying to reach each concentration camp as
our armies approached it. I became saturated with the tales of the
survivors . . . ("The Writer" 529)

A fellow correspondent later noted Levin's fascination with the horrific
accounts of the Holocaust survivors (see Gendel). The plight of these
survivors reinforced Levin's Zionist convictions and Palestine once
again demanded his artistic attention. He thus published his second
Zionist novel, *My Father's House,* just after the Holocaust in 1947 (and,
oddly, after the story's film version, as well). The novel revolves around
a group of Holocaust survivors who heroically defy the British blockade
and reach Palestine by boat to make a new life for themselves. Levin
focuses, specifically, upon one young survivor, David (or Daavid), who
clings to the belief that his father somehow also survived the Holocaust
to meet him (as he promised) in Palestine. The child scours great
expanses of Palestine in his stubborn effort to locate his father.

Given the highly emotional inspiration behind the novel—Levin's
firsthand contact with Holocaust survivors—and the startlingly brief
period of time between inspiration and artistic product, one should not
be surprised that *My Father's House* suffers from melodrama and sentimentality even more than *Yehuda.* One of the novel's few reviewers
notes the fairy-tale atmosphere of the book and likens the commune
where the Holocaust survivors settle to a Girl Scout camp (see Bullock).
Guttmann more recently dismisses the novel as a "tenuously allegorical
book about a juvenile refugee sententiously welcomed home to Israel,
the House of his Father" (109). Rubin also concedes that, "Taken literally, Levin's view of Palestine and the Jews who have arrived to claim the
land of their fathers is too joyful, too idealistic, and too enthusiastic to
approach reality" (68).

Like *Yehuda,* Levin's second Zionist novel, on the surface, cries out
for such criticism. While Levin thankfully resists the temptation to allow
David to find his father alive in Palestine, he manipulates the plot in other
melodramatic ways so that it conforms neatly (alas, too neatly) to his
vision of Palestine as a vehicle for Jewish regeneration and rebirth after
the horrors of Europe. I will not recount the plot in its entirety (one might
refer to Rubin for a close reading). Rather, a few details will suffice to
illustrate the melodramatic shortcomings of the novel. One can pretty
much glean the tenor of the novel during the first episode, as David and
fellow Holocaust survivors successfully reach Palestine's shore aboard

the *Hannah Szenesch*. When they near the shore, one Jewish member of the crew knows it because "He can feel the shore. He is from here" (*MFH* 7). Levin insists upon this spiritual connection between Jews and Palestine throughout the novel. He, for example, depicts communal life there as an idyllic fulfillment of biblical prophecy. One comrade of *Makor Gallil* tells David and the other new arrivals, "Everything comrades ... the milk, the honey, everything, just as it says in the Torah. It flows" (*MFH* 37). Another leader of the *kibbutz* tells them that

> They were all needed in Palestine, all, there was work for everyone, builders were needed, and cobblers, machinists, electricians, farm workers, and teachers. Here in the settlement, he said, they would learn to speak Hebrew; those who already spoke a little would learn more. And they could remain, and find their places, and be at home. (*MFH* 37)

David's search for his father also unfolds sentimentally. When he first runs away from *Makor Gallil*, he does so with his young Arab friend, a donkey, and a flute. The scene, of course, smacks of Spenserian allegory; Levin urges the reader to interpret David's journey as a symbolic quest of the Jewish son to locate his roots (his father) in Palestine. This first attempt must end after the donkey unexpectedly gives birth to a foal. The Arab boy gives David the foal to keep at the *kibbutz*, but David must return the foal to his mother as it refuses to eat. Levin's message is clear. David, like the foal, needs nurturing. Consequently, he escapes from an orphanage (the members of the *kibbutz* decide that David should stay there for at least a short time) to seek out his father once again. On the road, friendly Jews and Arabs alike assist him. David finally makes his way to Jerusalem and the Search Bureau for Missing Relatives. There, a small yellow book lists survivors and huge stacks of boxes list those who perished in Europe; David, of course, discovers that his whole family was murdered during the Holocaust.

The shocking revelation provokes David's psychological regression to infancy, but Levin, of course, insists by the end of the novel that David (and other survivors) can be reborn in Palestine. The love that surrounds one survivor, Miriam, at the *kibbutz* finally pierces her protective shell late in the book. As several comrades rejoice in a circle of song upon the birth of their new youth settlement, "The circle carried [Miriam], forced her into its swing. ... Her arms were intertwined, and she scarcely knew who was on one side of her and who on the other. Then the words were coming from her, too, joined with all the others" (*MFH* 187). For his part, David's rebirth occurs once Avram (improbably) uncovers a rock in the fields with David's family name, Halevi, inscribed upon it. The rock proves to David that he has, indeed, reached the house of his father and he can begin his regeneration: "David knelt and touched the stone. He traced out the letters—Ha-le-vi. . . . 'That was the name of my real father,' Daavid said. . . . He had found all of his fathers, in their place" (*MFH* 192).

My Father's House would deserve critical attention based even upon the above superficial reading. David's very predicament, all too common in the wake of the Holocaust, makes Levin's novel the first significant Jewish-American work to argue convincingly for the pragmatic necessity of a Jewish state, given the dispossessed and psychologically scarred survivors of the Holocaust. Several of the details (the orphanage for child survivors, the sparse list of living relatives at the Search Bureau, etc.) strengthen Levin's Zionist argument—an argument that Leon Uris does not make until twelve years later when he fashions another group of Holocaust survivors who defy the British blockade to reach Palestine on an old fishing boat (see Chapter 3).

The greater strength of *My Father's House*, however, lies in its more realistic moments when Levin suggests just how deep the Holocaust survivors' psychological scars lie. For just as *Yehuda's* unrealistic, optimistic ending detracts from the more insightful elements of the novel, the affirmative conclusion of Levin's second Zionist novel, unfortunately, overshadows Levin's more discerning moments in the text. Levin suggests, early on, that Holocaust survivors will not so easily be able to begin a new life in Palestine. During the first episode in the novel, David learns that the ship they are on had a different name when it was an Italian fishing boat. He wonders, "if the ship could really have been changed from the *Guiseppa* to the *Hannah Szenesch*. For it was like people who carried false cards with false names. Marta [Miriam] said they remained the same" (*MFH* 10). David's casual thought takes on a greater significance after it becomes clear that he and his comrades are expected to change their names, too, once they reach Palestine. The new names signify, of course, a new identity for the Jewish survivors—one of strength, not victimhood. However, as Nahama encourages Marta/Miriam to change her name, David's earlier questions on the subject spring to mind: can one so easily assume another identity? Erase the past? Begin afresh? Just as David suspects that the Italian fishing boat will always be an Italian fishing boat, one suspects that Holocaust survivors, like David, will not be able to eschew their past as easily as they can shed their names.

Despite the affirmative ending in which Levin insists that such new beginnings are possible, much of the novel suggests otherwise. Levin suggests that Jewish suffering will likely persist as David encounters a group of Jewish children reenacting the biblical Purim story. The children sing, "Haman, Haman, hang him high, / Fifty cubits in the sky, / He said all the Jews should die! / Save us, Esther, Mordecai!" (*MFH* 160). Through the parallels between the Purim story and the Holocaust, Levin implies that the Holocaust cannot be viewed as an isolated event that can be left behind, but must be seen as part of the continual cycle of Jewish persecution. Moreover, in an earlier episode, Levin insists overtly upon the "presence" of the Holocaust in Palestine. On David's way to the orphanage, he spots a concentration camp, British-style:

> [T]hey came to a concentration camp. It was on the right side of the road. It was exactly the same as in Europe, with barbed wire and a tower, where he could see soldiers and machine guns, and there was a gate, with guards and pillboxes and machine-gun slits, and inside there were rows of barracks. The truck stopped. For a moment a terrible panic came over Daavid, a fear that they were bringing him here to give him over to this place. (*MFH* 101)

On one level, Levin offers here an accurate account of the British detention camps in Palestine, which surely would remind any Holocaust survivor of the Nazi concentration camps. Read on a more symbolic level, the scene implies that David and his fellow survivors cannot simply start over in Palestine; they cannot leave the concentration camps behind. The camps follow them to Palestine.

Additional details suggest that the concentration camps will dog the Holocaust survivors psychologically, if not physically. How readily, one might ask, will David shed his survivor guilt as one of the only children of Auschwitz to live? Will he ever forget the Nazi corporal's challenge to him, "With what will you clean my boots, little Yid? . . . With your tongue, you'll polish them!" (*Y* 55)? Miriam's story also causes one to question her dubious regeneration at the end of the novel. Her husband and child were both murdered at Auschwitz. One wonders how she managed to survive until she tells David that the Nazis allowed her to keep her hair; we then suspect, and additional details confirm, that she survived because the Nazis used her as a prostitute. Ultimately, these realistic depictions, as early as 1947, of the physical and psychological ravages of the Holocaust and the consequent necessity for a Jewish state make *My Father's House* a noteworthy Jewish-American Zionist novel.

Levin's 1951 short story, "After All I Did for Israel," rounds out Levin's early Zionist fiction and—like "Maurie Finds His Medium," *Yehuda,* and *My Father's House*—the story demonstrates convincingly how Levin anticipates the artistic concerns of Jewish-American writers who "imagine" Israel today. Levin strips the story of the melodramatic and sentimental elements that weaken the two novels. Four years after its publication in *Commentary,* Ribalow lauded the story as "the only 'unromantic' tale in a rather meager but interesting list of stories about Zionism or Israel" ("Zion" 573). The story revolves around a philanthropic Jewish narrator who, like several assimilated American Jews of the time, harbors no deep Zionist convictions but, nonetheless, gives generously to the state of Israel. Levin puts his insider status as an American Jew to good use as his narrator conveys deliciously the predicament of wealthy Jews in America: "I give my share and more than my share anyway to the UJA and the Talmud Torah and all the appeals they've got—they tell you there's going to be only one campaign but every week there's another special appeal for a secret submarine or for some Kistadrut outfit or the Hebrew University, and you've got to give, or you're on the spot in the community" ("After" 57). The passage brings to mind Albert Vorspan's observation that a Jew must "enter an FBI Witness Relocation Program and adopt a new identity" to "disassociate effectively" from Jewish fundraising campaigns (31). Indeed, though the narrator wonders "if we really need them in Israel," he donates generous sums of money to the state since American Jewish fund-raisers effectively convince him of his obligation toward his fellow Jews ("After" 58).

The story ends with a dramatic twist when the narrator receives his comeuppance for his detachment from Israel; his son, Mickey, decides to reject his comfortable materialistic life in America and move to Israel instead to build up the newly founded Jewish state. The narrator reasons with his son, "we're Americans. We have Israel now just like the Irish have Ireland—but how many Irish kids want to go to Ireland to raise potatoes?" ("After" 62). Such reasoning, predictably, fails to convince Mickey to remain in America. The narrator laments, "My own son isn't interested in our life any more. . . . After all I did for Israel, this is how I get paid for it" ("After" 62). The story evokes a number of scathing quips like, "A Zionist is someone who believes that *other* Jews should have the right to live in Israel" and "American Jews will do anything for Israel, except live there." For Levin uses the story to dramatize both the complacency of most American Jews in regard to Israel and the alienation from Judaism that such complacency signifies. Moreover, as I suggest above, Levin's depiction of his narrator's detachment from Israel anticipates the concerns of Jewish-American writers today. In recent novels by Philip Roth and Anne Roiphe, assimilated American Jews (like Levin's narrator) plead with their more Zionist loved ones (like the narrator's son) to reconsider their "misguided" decision to make *aliyah* (see Chapters 6 and 7).

It is regrettable that Meyer Levin's squabbles with the Jewish-American literary establishment garner more attention today than his courageous and incisive early Zionist fiction. Not only did Levin take on a decidedly anti-Zionist milieu when he obdurately wrote this fiction, but he envisioned and dramatized several of the tensions that continue to divide American and Israeli Jews: individualism versus communalism, assimilation versus cultural confidence, materialism versus socialism. He also anticipated the problems that would plague Israelis, specifically: the waning of religion, the enmity of neighboring Arabs, the nagging torment of the Holocaust. Jewish-American writers who engage these tensions today owe Levin a great debt. Levin, for his part, always hoped that his cohorts would eventually follow his lead to write about Israel and about other topics from a distinctively Jewish consciousness. In 1978, just a few years before his death, Levin predicted that "The coming generation of American-Jewish writers ... will be young writers who will have been to Israel or will be involved with the revival of Jewish studies. They will be trying to see themselves in the light of this material as real Jews" (Levin, "A Conversation" 40). The surge today in the number of young, distinctively Jewish writers (writers like Tova Reich and Anne Roiphe, whom I discuss later, and others like Pearl Abraham, Steve Stern, Allegra Goodman, Melvin Jules Bukiet, Curt Leviant, and Rebecca Goldstein) bears out Levin's hopeful prediction. In her introduction to the most recent anthology of American Jewish literature, Nessa Rapoport heralds in the arrival of a "Jewishly educated and culturally confident" generation of Jewish-American writers (xxix), and Ted Solotaroff (in his separate introduction) notes the surge in Jewish-American fiction set against an Israeli background. So while it was Levin's sad fate to stand against the grain of the American Jewish literary zeitgeist, he would no doubt take comfort today that his fellow writers have, finally, come around.

Chapter 3

EMBATTLED URIS
A Look Back at Exodus

Meyer Levin, in his early Zionist fiction, fought against a virtual tidal wave of American anti-Zionist sentiment. Leon Uris faced a comparably strong wave of American Zionism in the 1950s; but, unlike Levin, he decided to ride *with* the wave when he published *Exodus* in 1958. This is not to say that Uris's Jewish characters were familiar, stereotypical ones on the literary scene. Consider the following joke which circulated in America shortly after Israel's extraordinary victory in the Six-Day War: "During the Six-Day War an Israeli tank collides with an Egyptian tank in the Sinai desert. The Egyptian jumps out of his tank yelling, 'I surrender.' The Israeli jumps out yelling, 'Whiplash'" (Telushkin 173–174). Now, I recount this joke not so much for its dubious entertainment value, but for what it reveals about the American Jewish perception of Jewish might during the tenuous early years of Israel's statehood. Indeed, the humor of the joke (if we can agree for a moment that it is funny) lies in the intentionally skewed presentation of the Israeli soldier as more a litigious *nebbish* (or weakling) than a fighter. In the wake of Israel's very real heroic fighting, the teller of the joke chides the Jewish soldier, "You can't fool me." While the joke may seem to have little to do with Uris's novel, it really has everything to do with it. For, in *Exodus*, Leon Uris seeks to do no less than extricate Jews, once and for all, from the prevailing stereotype of the Jew as weakling that the joke exploits for its comedic purposes. In the prefatory pages of the novel's paperback edition, Uris touts *Exodus* as a novel in which "all the cliché Jewish characters who have cluttered up our American fiction—the clever businessman, the brilliant doctor, the sneaky lawyer, the sulking artist . . . all those good folk who spend their chapters hating themselves, the world, and all their aunts and uncles . . . all those steeped in self-pity . . . all those golden riders of the psychoanalysis couch . . . all these have been left where they rightfully belong, on the cutting room floor . . . *Exodus* is about fighting people."

Who can deny that Uris's effort was a "success"? The novel achieved modest sales early on, but then sales skyrocketed and the novel became an international bestseller; it has since been released in more than fifty languages, has never been out of print, and remains a perennial favorite. Several initial reviewers bestowed their kudos liberally to boot. Harry Gilroy of *The New York Times Book Review* called *Exodus* a "passionate summary of the inhuman treatment of the Jewish people in Europe, of the exodus in the nineteenth and twentieth centuries to Palestine and of the triumphant founding of the new Israel," and Herbert Kupferberg found the novel "searing in its intensity and illuminating in its insight" (32; 5). Even the tough-minded Midge Decter let on that she found *Exodus* a relief from all the "nagging, whining, doubting of most current literature" ("Popular Jews" 358). To be sure, Uris's construction of the courageous and (most importantly) triumphant Jew to supplant the image of the Jewish victim appealed to scores of readers in the wake of the Holocaust amid America's increasingly Zionist milieu.

Exodus, in fact, advanced the Zionist phase in America, as it impelled several members of the Jewish-American community to support Zionism with renewed fervor. In one novel, Uris dramatized palpable glimpses of the historic European anti-Semitism that stimulated the Zionist ideas of Theodor Herzl and Leo Pinsker; he presented tangible, heroic *sabras* (Israeli natives) to Jewish-American lay persons of the late 1950s; and, herein, Uris played a crucial role in transforming, for countless American Jews, their nebulous affinity for the Jews in Israel into concrete, if illusory, feelings of connectedness to and responsibility for Israeli Jews. Upon reading an unfavorable review of *Exodus* in a Zionist journal, one of the journal's subscribers wrote in, "Never mind the literature; *Exodus* made me cry—and made dozens of hitherto indifferent women eager to join Hadassah" (Qtd. in Ribalow, "A Look" 19). In his recent guide to Jewish books, Barry Holtz aptly notes that "the rebirth of Israel came to life for many people when they read *Exodus*" (323), and Sol Liptzin comments in his important study, *The Jew in American Literature,* that "Uris performed a great deed of immeasurable propagandistic value for Israel and for American Jewry" (224). Uris's novel has also transformed Jews abroad into ardent Zionists. In 1987, Edwin McDowell reported in *The New York Times Book Review*

that two Jews in the Soviet Union were imprisoned for distributing copies of *Exodus* and one Russian reader of the censored novel commented,
"It gave us hope and pride when we needed it" (Qtd. in McDowell 13).
Indeed, Uris—a writer none too humble, who once said "if you ask me
I think I'm the greatest goddamned writer alive"—did not overstate
matters when he relished the "world-wide impact" of *Exodus* (Hendrickson B3).

That said, Uris's *Exodus* inspired, and continues to inspire, heated
criticism from discerning readers who take exception to the facile stereotypes that Uris constructs in the novel. One reviewer notes that *Exodus*'s characters "stand in roughly the same relation to the reality of
Israel as Scarlett O'Hara, Rhett Butler, and Ashley Wilkes do to the
American Civil War and Reconstruction South" (Blocker 539). Interestingly enough, both critics sympathetic to the Arabs of the Middle East
(like Jeremy Salt and William Darby) and those especially concerned
with the representation of the Jews (like Philip Roth, Joel Blocker, and
Ruth Wisse) continue to express their mutual distaste for the novel in
the pages of *Commentary* and the *Journal of Palestine Studies*—periodicals with antithetical political agendas. What I hope that my brief
adumbration of the critical responses to *Exodus* illustrates is the complexity inherent in any reappraisal of the novel. For as tempting as it
may be—given the novel's heavy doses of melodrama—to adopt the
highbrow perspective of it as exploitative trash, such an approach fails
to account for the political impact of *Exodus* and its enduring popularity. What is more, this approach smacks of an unsavory academic elit-
ism, as the critics who take this tack argue, implicitly at least, that "aver-
age" readers of the novel are simply duped by Uris's flashy rhetoric. After
a quarter-century of such criticism, it is time to reassess *Exodus*. While
my reading of the text largely supports the arguments of Uris's detractors, I hope to fill in the gaps in their scholarship by exploring more
carefully the implications of Uris's problematic construction of both
Arab and Jew; I will also analyze Uris's skillful depiction of several individual Jewish histories of persecution in Europe, which, I believe,
accounts more accurately for the novel's political impact.

Let us begin, then, with the compelling post-colonial argument
that, in *Exodus*, Uris promotes only vicious stereotypes of the Arabs. In
Jeremy Salt's recent article, "Fact and Fiction in the Middle Eastern Novels of Leon Uris," he attempts to set the record straight; the Arabs who
appear in Uris's novel, he contends, are certainly not the Arabs who

occupied the real Palestine at the time. Salt isolates passages in which Uris describes Arab men as lazy, filthy, barbaric, and sexually aggressive and then, referring to nineteenth-century European travel journals about Palestine, convincingly refutes Uris's characterizations. Even more recently, William Darby, calling *Exodus* "neither skillful nor unbiased," supports Salt's reading, as he bemoans Uris's narrative that "presents only heroic Jews and cowardly and ignorant Arabs, so that the possibility of seeing both sides as possessing legitimate rights and being composed of recognizable human beings is lost" (94–95). Darby contends that Uris breaches the limits of historical decorum through such characterizations of the Arabs, which permeate the novel.

Salt and Darby's arguments ring true enough. Upon their arrival in Palestine, Jossi and Yakov Rabinsky (who later take the Hebrew names Barak and Akiva Ben Canaan) gaze upon "dung-filled streets" with "swarms of giant flies" and wince at the "overwhelming stench" of an Arab village (*Exodus* 211, 213). Jossi also notes the "unscrupulous ethics of the Arab" when he attempts to buy land from them (*Exodus* 229). Importantly, this is not only their "first taste of the Arab world," but the reader's as well; and one finds oneself wondering, as the novel unfolds, if Uris will ever exhaust his arsenal of new and derogatory ways to depict Arabs (*Exodus* 211). He, for example, cannot resist drawing a parallel between Arabs and snakes, as he describes "Arab thugs ... slithering along the ground with knives in their teeth" (*Exodus* 279). What interests me, however, is not so much whether Uris relies on stereotypes in his characterization of the Arabs (he clearly does), but why and how he constructs these stereotypes. In Sander Gilman's influential book, *Difference and Pathology: Stereotypes of Sexuality, Race, and Madness* (1985), he argues that we form stereotypes of the Other to establish or reaffirm order and control. Moreover, he asserts that "the categories [into which stereotypes can be divided] reflect the cultural categories of seeing objects as a reflection or distortion of the self. The resulting basic categories of difference reflect our preoccupation with the self and the control that the self must have over the world" (Gilman 23).

Interestingly enough, the text of *Exodus* supports Gilman's framework concerning the construction of stereotypes. Uris's desire to exert control over the Arab in the Middle East certainly manifests itself in the Arab stereotypes he constructs; to put it more concretely, Uris's construction of the Arab affirms what he and other American Zionists no doubt wished to believe about the Arab in the Middle East. Specifically, he defines the Arab—as Gilman suggests—as either a reflection or (more commonly) a distortion of the Jew. In Kammal, the benevolent muktar of Abu Yesha, Uris creates a reflection of the Jew. Kammal emerges as the only "good Arab" in a novel populated by countless "bad Arabs." Like Barak Ben Canaan, Kammal is peace-loving, trustworthy, and gracious (he sells the land on which Barak builds Yad El); put simply, Kammal is everything that the Arab, as Uris defines him, is not. He even reflects the Jewish perspective of the Middle East conflict when he speaks with Barak: "there are no greater exploiters than the Arab effendis. . . . I have watched the Jews come back and perform miracles on the land. . . . the Jews are the only salvation for the Arab people. The Jews are the only ones in a thousand years who have brought light to this part of the world" (*Exodus* 258). Here, one winces at the mug's game Uris plays by promoting the Jewish perspective via the Arab—by presenting the Arab as a mere reflection of the Jew. One can almost hear Uris snicker as he types Barak's noble response to his self-effacing friend, "I know this is difficult for you to say, Kammal" (*Exodus* 258).

Thankfully, we see few other reflections of the Jew in Uris's Arabs. But, in accordance with Gilman's framework, Uris does consistently and explicitly contrast the Jew and the Arab to render an image of the Arab as a grotesque distortion of the Jew. In the early pages of the novel, Bruce Sutherland—the reluctant British General in charge of the Jewish detention camps in Cyprus—laments Britain's deference to the Arabs in the Middle East by offering this not so subtle contrast between Arab and Jew: "I can't seem to forget the Arab slave markets in Saudi Arabia and the first time I was invited to watch a man have his hands amputated as punishment for stealing, and somehow I can't forget those Jews at Bergen-Belsen" (*Exodus* 31). Given Gilman's framework, it is important that Uris not only describes the Arabs, through Sutherland, as morally corrupt and sadistic, but that he immediately contrasts this picture with a glimpse of the Jews in a concentration camp—victims of the kind of sadism associated with the Arab. Whether Uris implements this rhetorical strategy consciously or not, the passage encourages the reader to see the Arab as a morally base distortion of the innocent and persecuted Jew.

Uris also contrasts Jewish industriousness and ingenuity with the stagnancy of the Arab civilization. While he dramatizes the rapid flowering of the Jews' *kibbutzim* and *moshavim*, he takes pains to show that the Arabs "were experts in building on other people's civilizations" (*Exodus* 315). At one point, our hero, Ari Ben Canaan, must remind

Taha, Kammal's son and successor at Abu Yesha, of the benefits that his people have enjoyed from living alongside Ari's burgeoning Jewish *moshav*, Yad El:

> These stone houses in your village were designed and built by us. Your children can read and write because of us. You have sewers because of us and your young don't die before the age of six because of us. We taught you how to farm properly and live decently. We have brought you things that your own people would not give you in a thousand years. (*Exodus* 344)

The only other Arab village in the novel that doesn't reek of excrement is the Druse village of Daliyat el Karmil. The Druse, who hide the injured Ari from the British, are allies of the Jews, and this, of course, explains the splendor of their village. Kitty Fremont, the gentile heroine of the novel who rushes to Daliyat el Karmil to give Ari medical attention, observes that the village is "sparkling white and clean in comparison to the filth and decay of most Arab villages" (*Exodus* 435). The Arabs, then, are defined as a historically rooted culture—a distortion of the Jewish culture—to define in greater clarity the Jews' "advanced" status.

Uris even more notably defines the Arab as a distortion of the Jew through the contrast between the Arab and Jew as fighters. For while he depicts the Jew as a reluctant warrior, he invariably depicts the Arab as a bloodthirsty, savage murderer. Uris informs the reader, early on, that "when an isolated and unarmed Jew was found his murder was always followed by decapitation, dismemberment, eye gouging, and the most primitive brutalities" (*Exodus* 274). In the pages that follow, Uris abundantly provides specific cases to substantiate his claim. Consider, for example, the following descriptions of killing, Arab-style:

> Within an hour Ben Solomon had been killed and mutilated. He was decapitated. The bodyless head was held up by the hair and photographed with twenty laughing Arabs around it. . . . (*Exodus* 367)

> Two days later [Dafna's] body was dumped near their camp. Her ears, nose, and hands had been amputated. Her eyes had been gouged out. She had been raped over a hundred times. (*Exodus* 281)

While even the stolid Ari Ben Canaan cries at the end of the novel, reflecting upon the endless cycle of killing in which he has been forced to participate, one senses from the above descriptions that the Arab would lament only the end of such a cycle. Moreover, the latter description, which details the brutal murder and rape of Ari Ben Canaan's first lover, leads us to yet another characteristic of the Arab which Uris dramatizes as a grotesque distortion of Jewish behavior: sexual aggressiveness and perversity.

While all of the Jews in the novel experience fruitful relationships and engage in only consensual sexual activity (one thinks of Jordana Ben Canaan and David Ben Ami, who, during their lovemaking, serenade one another with quotations from the Song of Songs), Uris highlights only the perverse and downright violent features of the Arab relations between the sexes. Barak, indeed, finds the position of women in Arab society intolerable: "they were held in absolute bondage, never seen, never heard, never consulted. Women often sought quick and vicious revenge by dagger or poison" (*Exodus* 229). Uris, implicitly at least, asserts that this unhealthy Arab vision of women is an essential characteristic. For even Taha—whom Barak raises as his son after Kammal's murder—displays what Barak perceives as a perverse sexual desire for Jordana. Sensing the attraction, Barak reflects that Arabs, unlike Jews, commonly feel lustful toward very young women. Ultimately, Taha expresses this lust by challenging Ari, "If I am your brother, then give me Jordana. Yes, that is right . . . give her to me and let me take her to my bed. Let her bear my children" (*Exodus* 484). Taha does not fret over the fact that, based upon his reasoning, the bearer of his children would be his sister.

Indeed, that *Exodus* raises the dander of post-colonial critics like Jeremy Salt comes as no surprise given Uris's narrow representation of the Arab as either a "good" reflection of Jewish virtue or a "bad" distortion of that virtue. More intriguing, however, is the criticism from within the Jewish ranks concerning Uris's vision of the Jew (I should note that Joel Blocker and other Jewish critics, from the beginning, also recognized Uris's Arab stereotypes). Uris intends, after all, to rescue the Jew—as fictional character—from the rigid set of stereotypes he identifies in the foreword of the paperback edition. The rub, of course, is that he merely substitutes one stereotype for another as he portrays the *sabra*, Ari Ben Canaan, as the stolid and tough hero so familiar in the popular American Western movies of the 1950s and 60s. To be sure, Joel Blocker was onto something when he claimed that *Exodus* "was written with one eye on the movies" (539). By substituting *kibbutzim* for two-saloon towns and smatterings of Hebrew for Western drawls, Uris transplants the essential elements of the American Western to Israel.

Israeli and American Jews were quick to challenge Uris's image of the *sabra*. *Time* magazine quoted an Israeli Army Captain as saying, "Israelis were pretty disappointed in the book, to put it lightly. The types that are described in it never existed in Israel" (Qtd. in Roth, "Some New," 195). Uris irascibly replied, "Captain who? . . . Just look at my sales figures" (Qtd. in Roth 195). He offers a slightly more thoughtful defense when he asserts that "in truth, we have been fighters" (Qtd. in Roth 194). Philip Roth, however, takes Uris to task for this comment by tersely stating, "So bald, stupid, and uninformed is the statement that it is not even worth disputing" (194). One could have expected Roth's scathing critique of *Exodus* in "Some New Jewish Stereotypes," since Uris's attack on the Jewish-American fiction so populated with self-pitying riders of the psychoanalytic couch was a thinly veiled attack against Roth's first collection of short stories, *Goodbye, Columbus*, published in the same year as *Exodus*'s paperback edition. Still, to Roth's (and the Israeli Captain's) credit, most of the Jewish settlers in Palestine during the first half of the twentieth century did not emigrate with "fighting" in mind, but with naïve aspirations to create an ideal, socialist community (Buber 9). As Robert Alter recently argued, "The earliest Zionist settlers toward the end of the nineteenth century and at the beginning of the twentieth century generally managed to shield themselves from any perception that they were thrusting themselves into historical circumstances that would lead them—that would compel them—to use armed force" (Alter, "Enemies" 28).

Uris challenges Alter's informed assessment of the early Zionist settlers' character through his depiction of Ari Ben Canaan, which summons forth the image of Gary Cooper in *High Noon*; one would hardly think of casting a young Moshe Dayan or Yitzhak Rabin for the Ari role. Uris constantly reminds us that "Ben Canaan seemed to show no traces of human emotion" (*Exodus* 42). "Ari Ben Canaan," we later learn, "was a machine. He was an efficient, daring operator. Sometimes he won, sometimes he lost" (*Exodus* 320). Or as Kitty Fremont reflects,

> Ari Ben Canaan comes from a breed of supermen whose stock in trade is their self-reliance. Ari Ben Canaan hasn't needed anyone since the day he cut his teeth on his father's bull whip. His blood is made of little steel and ice corpuscles and his heart is a pump like the

motor in that bus over there. All this keeps him above and beyond human emotions. (*Exodus* 379)

I cannot claim to speak for all readers of the novel, but Ari's super powers and steely determination—while straining plausibility—begin to grate against the nerves. Take, for instance, Ari's call to arms: "Give me something to shoot at those tanks and those destroyers! All we've got is our guts and what we believe in. We've had the hell knocked out of us for two thousand years. This is one fight we're going to win" (*Exodus* 180). Perhaps my overexposure, as a child, to both television and the movies should have inured me to such melodrama; but it takes only one or two passages like the one above to make me throw up my arms and say, enough already.

True, one would be hard pressed to challenge the critiques of Uris's canned representations of the *sabra*. However, Philip Roth dismisses Uris's construction of the Israeli Jew too readily as the novelist's means to court the popular reader. Ruth Wisse argues, as well, that Uris "exploited the idea of Israel's victimization at the moment of its greatest *trendiness*" by "reducing the complexity of Jewish history to a pulp fiction formula"[emphasis mine] (149). That Uris was interested in sales figures and movie contracts is clear enough; but does his construction of the modern Israeli Jew indicate something more significant about the nature of the Jewish-American perspective on Israel in the late 1950s? I believe so. Just as Uris's ambition to churn out a bestseller fails to account for the complexity of his Arab representations, it fails to account fully for his construction of the *sabra* and for the appeal of that construction. In Robert Alter's article, "Sentimentalizing the Jews," published seven years after the publication of *Exodus*, he offers the following observation about Jewish-American fiction and sheds a good deal of light on Uris's artistic vision:

[T]he American writer of Jewish descent finds himself utilizing Jewish experiences of which he is largely ignorant, and so the Jewish skeletons of his characters are fleshed with American fantasies about Jews. The result is a kind of double sentimental myth: the Jew emerges from this fiction as an imaginary creature embodying both what Americans would like to think about Jews and what American Jewish intellectuals would like to think about themselves. ("Sentimentalizing" 72)

Alter, I should note, was not thinking about Uris's novel when he wrote this canny passage. In fact, the novels to which Alter refers are more along the lines of Bernard Malamud's *The Assistant* and Edward Wallant's *The Children at the Gate* than *Exodus*. Alter takes exception to the portrayal of self-consciously "Jewish" protagonists as the *American* heroes of moral virtue, since the writer's real immersion in a distinctively Jewish culture, more often than not, extends only as far as a familiarity with "*gefilte fish* . . . crass bar-mitzvahs . . . and a mastery of several pungent Yiddish synonyms for the male organ" (71). However, this strategy of the Jewish-American writer to forge a new ethos (illusory but eminently palatable) for the American Jew applies even more explicitly to Uris's novel about the Israeli Jew. For Kitty Fremont's evolving relationship with Ari Ben Canaan bespeaks Uris's desire to "form" the Israeli Jew from a recognizably American perspective and thus create a heroic (albeit sensitive) alternative to the weak Jewish victim of Hitler's Holocaust.

Ruth Wisse comes close to the mark when she notes that "the main plot of the book, about the evolving love of the American Gentile nurse Kitty Fremont (who is 'as American as apple pie') for the Israeli-born Ari Ben Canaan, makes the validation of the Jews dependent on the approval of Gentiles" (148–149). Wisse, though, relegates Kitty to a largely passive role as one who "comes to appreciate" the *sabra* and the Israeli cause (149). The tenor of this comment applies more accurately to the Gentile Airline pilot, Foster J. MacWilliams, who agrees reluctantly to pilot a flight to transport a group of primitive Yemenite Jews to their new homeland, Israel. While Kitty is as American as apple pie, Foster summons up equally evocative metaphors of Americanness, like college football Saturdays and "big dough" enterprises. Upon witnessing the Yemenites' jubilation once they see Israel from his plane, Foster marvels "they didn't make this much fuss when we beat Georgia Tech in the Cotton Bowl" (*Exodus* 569). At first, Foster cannot fathom the ardor of the primitive Jews who yearn for Israel. Nor can he appreciate the selfless dedication of the Israeli volunteer, Hanna, who assists him on the flights (when he learns that she works for free, he tells her, "I don't dig you at all") (*Exodus* 568). Evidently, however, he comes to appreciate the Israeli cause and cannot resist accepting more and more dangerous missions: "He kept swearing that each trip was his last, right up to the time he married Hanna and took an apartment in Tel Aviv" (*Exodus* 570).

That Kitty's perspective toward Israel resembles Foster's is true enough. Fremont, like Foster, embraces the Jewish cause in Israel from an early perspective of institutionalized, if not virulent, anti-Semitism. In the beginning of the novel, she explains to her friend, Mark Parker, why she won't tend to the Jewish children in a Cyprus refugee camp: "I suppose Jewish children are pretty much like any others but I'd just rather not get mixed up with them" (*Exodus* 18). She later tells Mark "I've worked with enough Jewish doctors to know they are arrogant and aggressive people. They look down on us" (*Exodus* 52). Indeed, Kitty begins the novel as a prosaic, if lovely, American and, after 600 some odd pages, comes to resemble the biblical Ruth—the Moabitess in the Old Testament who tells her Israeli mother-in-law, "thy people shall be my people." Kitty decides to stay in Israel with her *sabra* lover, Ari Ben Canaan, and join the good fight.

Unlike Ruth (and Foster MacWilliams), however, Kitty does not merely come to accept the virtue and benevolence of the Israeli. Rather, as I have already implied, she actively assesses and reshapes the character of the modern Israeli Jew. Moreover, Uris's active "character-building" of the *sabra*, Ari, from Kitty's perspective reflects the pervasive desire on the part of American Jews during the early years of Israel's statehood to forge an appealing Israeli ethos that would bolster the image of the Jew in the Diaspora; this desire, in fact, persists today. I will return to this intriguing issue shortly, but first let us explore, specifically, how Kitty takes it upon herself to shape Ari's character. At one point in the novel, Harriet Saltzman, an elderly American Hadassah leader living in Israel, defines the term *sabra* for Kitty: "A *sabra* is the fruit of a wild cactus you will find all over Palestine. The *sabra* is hard on the outside . . . but inside, it is very tender and sweet" (*Exodus* 327–328). This definition of the native Israeli strikes Kitty as accurate enough; it is "a good description" she tells Saltzman (*Exodus* 328). However, Kitty remains unsatisfied by this most salient characteristic of Israeli natives, their interior, inexpressive sweetness and tenderness. For the latter half of the novel, Kitty thus takes it upon herself to free Ari's tender emotions from his hard, outer shell, beneath which they lie entombed. In short, she helps him to cry and, herein, she (and, through her, Uris) reshapes the ethos of the *sabra* as stolid, yes, but as a—by now clichéd—"sensitive-man" as well.

Well into her visit to Palestine, Kitty maintains her hard line, "I don't wish to become involved" (*Exodus* 349). She only travels to the region in the first place to extricate the young Karen Hansen from the volatile Middle East and take her to San Francisco. Kitty later learns that

Karen has no intentions of leaving the beautiful homeland for which she has yearned for so long in the Cyprus detention camp. Karen, it seems, needs her help less than she had realized. In contrast, Ari desperately needs her emotional guidance to become truly human, despite Kitty's initial belief in his self-reliance. She gives Ari his first lesson when she performs an emergency operation on his severely wounded leg without anesthesia. Once she cuts deeply into his flesh, "Ari shook violently. Mucus poured from his nose, and his eyes ran with tears of agony" (*Exodus* 440). To be sure, any surgery suggests a re-creation (one thinks of Mary Shelley's *Frankenstein*), if only a partial re-creation. Indeed, Kitty's makeshift surgery on Ari represents the most explicit shaping of the *sabra* by the Gentile American nurse. Now, this reading may seem a bit too ingenious. After all, Kitty merely does what she needs to do, as a nurse. She certainly does not want to make Ari cry tears of physical pain. That said, however, she does seem aware, before the surgery, that her razor blade, if not her love, might finally crack the hard outer shell of the *sabra*. She tells him forcefully before the operation (with, perhaps, a hint of satisfaction), "Start drinking this. When the bottle is empty, we'll get you another one. Get drunk . . . get as drunk as you can, because I'm going to hurt you like hell" (*Exodus* 439). She sobs after the operation on Ari's chest, feeling a strong connection with her patient whose tangible vulnerability she taps for the first time.

As Ari heals, though, and becomes outwardly less and less vulnerable, Kitty sees her work undermined and loses the feeling of connectedness with her *sabra*. From Kitty's American perspective, he is not the ideal Israeli anymore and she lets him know it:

> I just can't take it with the straight-faced unconcern of a *sabra*. . . .
> You're a mechanical animal, too infested with the second coming of
> the Israelites to be a human being. You don't know the meaning of
> giving love. You only know fighting. Well, I'm fighting *you*, Brother
> Ben Canaan, and I'm going to beat you, and I'm going to forget you
> in spades. . . . I want a man who knows what it is to cry. I feel sorry for
> you Ari Ben Canaan. (*Exodus* 445)

Though Kitty vows here to forget Ari, she cannot relinquish her subsequent opportunities to shape the *sabra's* outward behavior. When Zev Gilboa, a heroic soldier under Ari's command, dies in battle and Ari expresses to Kitty how hard it will be to replace him, she must say, enough is enough:

Is that what you were thinking . . . you'd have a hard time replacing him? . . . Is there nothing you cherish? . . . I thought this was a little different, Ari. You've known Zev since he was a boy. That girl, his wife, is a Yad El girl. She was raised two farms away from yours. (*Exodus* 508)

When Ari asks Kitty what she expects him to do, she answers, predictably, "Cry for that poor girl" (*Exodus* 508). Ari, every bit as predictably, refuses.

Kitty prevails, however, by the end of the novel. During the final few pages, Ari and Kitty learn that Karen has been murdered by Arabs at her *kibbutz*, Nahal Midbar, precariously located on the volatile Gaza Strip. This news, arriving amid the poignant Passover Seder during which Jews celebrate the biblical exodus, proves too much for Ari to bear and he leaves the Seder. The novel strikes its final crescendo as Ari walks toward Kitty, who follows him outside, and sinks to his knees before her. Uris devotes a single line to the passage, "Ari Ben Canaan wept." By contrast, Otto Preminger's movie version of *Exodus* concludes as Kitty, dressed in military fatigues and brandishing a rifle, joins Ari in what we know will be the fierce War of Liberation. Thus, Preminger emphasizes Kitty's ultimate "acceptance" of the Israeli cause. As I hope I have shown, this interpretation strays from the text, in which Uris emphasizes, instead, *Ari's* acceptance of his emotions, his recognition of his essential humanity. Kitty only accepts the Israeli cause—says "I will understand, always"—once Ari acts according to her standards of appropriate Israeli behavior.

As I have already indicated, Uris's shaping of the *sabra* through Kitty's American perspective reveals the pervasive American Jewish desire to forge a new, strong but sensitive Jewish identity in the wake of the Holocaust. What is more, Uris's construction of the "perfect" Israeli for consumption by a broad American readership embodies the American Jewish predilection for dictating Israeli behavior for the good of Jewish PR in the Diaspora. Midge Decter, a frequent contributor to Jewish periodicals, recently admonished these American Jews who "want Israel not only to be good but to *look* good, at whatever cost" ("American Jews" 32). "With such affectionate critics," Decter argues, "a country is hardly in need of enemies" (32). Indeed, this sentiment serves as the thesis to Edward Alexander's *With Friends Like These: The Jewish Critics of Israel* (1993), a collection of essays by American Jewish intellectuals who criticize the select group of "affectionate critics" to whom Decter refers. In the "Introduction," Edward Alexander, Cynthia Ozick, Norman Podhoretz, Marie Syrkin, and the eight other contributors collectively assert, "We believe that the Diaspora Jew who prattles about his 'right' and 'duty' to criticize Israel publicly is like the blind man who can direct others on their way, but cannot walk straight himself" (Alexander, *With Friends* 14). Most of the contributors to Alexander's collection are Americans; just imagine, then, how Israelis themselves have reacted to the determination, on the part of the American Jews in question, to influence Israeli behavior.

In Hillel Halkin's *Letters to an American Jewish Friend* (1977), he makes it quite clear that the American Jews' refusal to make *aliyah* calls their very "Jewishness" into question and thereby invalidates any attempt on their part to dictate the behavior of Israeli Jews. More recently, another Israeli, Matti Golan, needed to write a book-length letter addressed rhetorically to Elie Wiesel—*With Friends Like You: What Israelis Really Think About American Jews* (1993)—to fully express the collective indignation of his fellow Israelis with American Jews who want Israelis to behave only in ways that do not embarrass them, as if their monetary contributions entitle them to dictate Israeli policy. Golan's title suggests that Israeli/American tensions lie submerged and must be "exposed" by one of the few, like himself, "in the know." To my mind, however, this tension manifests itself today often and unambiguously; an American Jewish tourist in Israel need not arrive equipped with an uncanny intuition to recognize the strained expressions of kinship mustered by well-meaning Israelis. The love story of Ari and Kitty, in itself then, may seem a superfluous, canned theme, added by Uris only to court readers of popular fiction. One reviewer called the love story "tepid" and suggested that readers skip it ("Bestseller Revisited" 110). Fair enough. However, I hope I have illustrated that Uris's construction, at least, of the "tepid" relationship should not be missed because it reflects the essential "image-making" urge on the part of American Jews when it comes to the *sabra*.

Thus far, I have conceded that—to accommodate a fervently Zionist readership—Uris offers up Arab characters, blatantly stereotyped as dirty, unethical, and brutal; that he depicts the *sabra* as the clichéd hero of the popular American Westerns of the 50s; that the love story between Ari and Kitty falls flat (though I analyze, in each case, the significance of Uris's constructions). But if we are to agree with all of these critiques of Uris's novel, what accounts for the powerful boost the novel gave Zionism, and continues to give Zionism, worldwide? Most critics ascribe the novel's impact, implicitly at least, to its "trendy" fictional elements, which I have already discussed: the stereotyped representations of Arabs and Jews which undermine the Arab ethos and bolster a heroic image of the Israeli, and the love story between Ari Ben Canaan and Kitty Fremont. Consider, however, one Russian Jew's reading of the novel: "Its impact was enormous. . . . It was our first encounter with *Jewish history*. It gave us inspiration, and turned almost everybody who read it into more or less convinced Zionists" [emphasis mine](Qtd. in McDowell 13). This reader's emphasis on the "Jewish history" sections of the novel suggests that readers probably deserve a bit more credit for the process by which they arrive at their Zionist convictions and, likewise, Uris deserves more credit for the way in which he provokes these convictions. For the most compelling Zionist arguments in the novel are not to be found in Uris's adoption of clichéd fictional formulas; one Russian translation, in fact, eliminates the love affair between Ari and Kitty. Rather, as the Russian reader implies, the most powerful Zionist arguments manifest themselves in his seldom discussed accounts of the individual histories of several Jewish characters living in a virulently anti-Semitic Europe prior to Israel's creation (only one critic thus far, Harold Ribalow, has attempted to give Uris his due for these educational sections of *Exodus*). These accounts, which cut close to the bone of historical veracity, suggest convincingly the exigence of an independent Jewish state if the Jews are to survive unpersecuted as a people.

The Diaspora life of Simon Rabinsky goes a long way toward convincing one that his sons, Jossi/Barak and Yakov/Akiva, make the right choice when they decide to trudge on foot from the Pale, through Georgia and Turkey, to finally reach Palestine. Uris concentrates on the years just after the assassination of Czar Alexander II in 1881. The Jews, of course, were held responsible and "pogroms erupted and spread to every city of the Pale" (*Exodus* 200). The bootmaker Simon Rabinsky, like most of the Orthodox Jews living in the Pale during this period, refuses to emigrate to Palestine since he does not believe that the Jews are entitled to create their homeland anew: "The Messiah will come and take us back when he is good and ready" (*Exodus* 205). His strict adherence to biblical prophecy proves costly, as he falls victim to a fierce pogrom after he attempts to rescue the Torah from his burning synagogue:

> Simon pressed the holy parchment against his breast to protect it from the flames and staggered back to the door. He was badly burned and choking. He staggered outside and fell onto his knees. . . . Twenty of Andreev's students were waiting for him. . . . "Kill the Jew! . . ." Simon crawled a few yards and collapsed, covering the Sefer Torah with his body. Clubs smashed his skull. Hobnailed boots ripped his face. . . . When they found Simon Rabinsky he was beyond recognition. (*Exodus* 206–207)

Granted, Uris is not one to let the melodramatic potential of a pogrom scene slip through his fingers. That Rabinsky dies chanting the *Shema* (the most ardent expression of one's Jewishness) and clutching the Torah he just rescued can only be expected. But, to Uris's credit, such pogroms following the assassination of Alexander II are well documented and inspired the flight of scores of Jews, many of whom emigrated to America. America, however, remained out of reach for most of the poor Jews of the Pale. Through the tragic fate of the Orthodox Jew, then, Uris implicitly criticizes the Jewish anti-Zionist perspective which refuses to honor the sociopolitical necessity of a Jewish state in Israel.

Uris does not limit his historical focus to the persecuted Jews of the Pale just after the Czar's murder. Rather, he dramatizes case histories of characters living in various regions of the European Diaspora during other times before Israel's creation to emphasize the Jews' persecution in all countries of the European Diaspora. For example, he dramatizes the dismal fate of Dov Landau's family, who must scrounge for food in the Warsaw Ghetto during the Holocaust. When Dov's father, Mendel, joins the Polish resistance, the Nazis kill him quickly. His mother, Leah, and sister, Ruth, are later captured by the Germans and sent to Treblinka; both die horrible deaths. Ruth dies in the agony of childbirth, and her baby dies with her because she has no room in the cattle car to lie down. The Nazis murder Ruth in one of the early, crude extermination vans into which they channelled the carbon monoxide fumes from the exhaust. The Nazis eventually murder Dov's tough older brother, Mundek, by burning him alive with a flame thrower. After hiding in the Warsaw Ghetto sewers for months, Dov is finally captured and sent to Auschwitz. Through cleverness and determination, he manages to survive by working as a *Sonderkommando;* the Nazis gave these Jews the gruesome duty of removing the corpses from the gas chambers and crematorium.

The histories of the Landaus and Rabinskys make one wonder whether there were any prosperous Jewish families before the Holocaust. Indeed there were, and Uris dramatizes the travails of Johann Clement and his family to emphasize that Hitler's final solution targeted *all* Jews. Clement, living with his family in Cologne in 1938, would not consider his situation remotely similar to that of Simon Rabinsky or Mendel Landau. After all, "Professor Johann Clement is a terribly important man. Everyone at the university doffs his cap and smiles and bows and says, 'Good morning, Herr Doctor'" (*Exodus* 59). His life seems to be the epitome of a fruitful assimilated Jewish life in the Diaspora. Even as Clement witnesses the mushrooming of anti-Semitism later in 1938, he assures his wife that they are respected Germans first, and Jews second:

> My father and my grandfather taught here. I was born in this house. My life, the only things I've ever wanted, the only things I've ever loved are in these rooms . . . Just a little longer, Miriam . . . it will pass . . . it will pass. . . . " (*Exodus* 61)

The axe of Nazi aggression, of course, soon falls on all the Jews and Clement cannot delude himself any longer. Uris describes the German *Kristallnacht* in journalistic detail, and when Clement's daughter, Karen, comes home with a bloody face and with anti-Semitic epithets ringing in her ears, the professor manages to send her away to Denmark. Karen survives the war, thanks to the sympathetic Danish government and the benevolent Hansens who adopt her. However, Karen learns that her mother and two brothers were exterminated in the concentration camp, Dachau. The Holocaust convinces Karen that, despite her love for Denmark and the Hansens, the only real home for a Jew is in Israel. Once there, she locates her father, who had been persistently tortured by the Gestapo, but he suffers from psychotic depression and appears to Karen only as a shell of the father she once knew:

> She looked around for a moment and then she stiffened. A man was sitting on the floor in a corner. He was barefooted and uncombed. He sat with his back against the wall and his arms around his knees and stared blankly at the opposite wall . . . Karen took a step toward him. He was stubble-bearded and his face was scarred. . . . This is all a mistake, she thought . . . this man is a stranger . . . he is not my father . . . he cannot be. It is a mistake! A mistake! (*Exodus* 383)

To be sure, the deaths of Karen's mother and brothers, like the deaths of Simon Rabinsky and most of the Landaus, suggest the moral imperative of a Jewish state. However, through Uris's dramatization of Johann Clement's "survival," he argues, implicitly, even more forcibly for the Zionist cause. For, in the wake of the Holocaust, no country was willing to absorb the thousands of Jewish survivors, many of whom existed only as human wreckage, like Johann Clement. Several survivors returned to their European homes to find themselves dispossessed of their property and generally unwelcome. Uris presents an apt description of the homecoming that Poles in most regions offered the Jewish survivors of Auschwitz after the camp's liberation:

> One by one the Jews at Auschwitz ventured out to return to their homes. One by one they came back to Auschwitz with a final crushing disillusion. The Germans were gone but the Poles were carrying on for them. . . . the cities were covered with posters and the people screamed, "The Jews brought this war on us . . . the war was started so that Jews could make a profit . . . the Jews are the cause of all our troubles!" There were no tears for the dead but there was plenty of hatred for the few survivors. They smashed Jewish shops and beat up Jews who tried to return to their homes and property. (*Exodus* 144)

Again, it is worth noting that Poland's hostile reception of the Jewish Auschwitz survivors is well documented. Alan Dershowitz recently reminded us that "more than fifteen hundred Jewish survivors of Hitler's genocide were murdered *by Poles* in 1945 and 1946," and that the head of the Catholic Church in Poland, Cardinal Hlond, routinely blamed *the Jews* for provoking the pogroms and refused to condemn anti-Semitism (146). Indeed, Dershowitz's visit to his grandfather's Polish town illustrates how the Poles obliterated any remnants of their Jewish past after the war: "In the town my grandfather lived in, Przemysl, which was once a center of Jewish learning, publishing, and commerce, I could not even find the old synagogue or the Jewish cemetery. The official Jewish guidebook of Poland—published by the government—does not list Przemysl as among the cities or towns with surviving Jewish buildings, cemetaries, or archives, despite its long and distinguished Jewish past" (145). In stark contrast to Poland and other European countries, Israel, once founded, unconditionally granted citizenship and medical care to Jewish survivors, such as Johann Clement; the "law of return" remains the country's essential precept. It thus comes as no surprise that the largest number of Holocaust survivors still live in Israel.

Although readers naturally enjoy leaving a novel with a concrete, unclouded impression of its literary merit, I hope I have illustrated sufficiently how the text of *Exodus* resists such an unambiguous reading. On the one hand, Uris's excessive melodrama, his reliance on stereotypes, and his gratuitous inclusion of the love story—all of which tell us a great deal about the crucial role Israel played in the lives of American Jews during the early Zionist phase—deservedly inspire critical jabs, the most recent one offered just a couple years ago: "this is a book one ought to read with delight at a certain age (say 12 or 13), and then regard as unworthy a few years later" (Pinsker, "They Dream" 8X). On the other hand, such dismissals of the novel's worth (and there are several) leave one with the nagging sense that they have still not heard, as Paul Harvey likes to say, "the rest of the story." For Uris's novel would assuredly be a much sparser one if he deleted his short course in Jewish history that so enlivened the Zionism of Jews worldwide.

We can only speculate on the effect that Uris's novel had, and continues to have, on other Jewish-American writers. While the trendy fictional elements of *Exodus,* which Uris manipulated to exalt Israeli Jews and demonize Arabs, no doubt satisfied the expectations of several readers enthralled by America's Zionist phase, they also may have contributed to the reluctance, on the part of Uris's cohorts, to take on Israel as a major theme in their work. To be sure, *Exodus* showed Jewish-American writers exactly how their fictional approaches to Israel might misfire. Bernard Malamud may have had the novel in the back of his mind when he told an interviewer, "I'd rather write about Israel if I knew the country. I don't, so I leave it to the Israeli writers" (Qtd. in Field, "Israel" 50). Fortunately for us, the writers discussed in the subsequent chapters do not share Malamud's view. And today, nearly forty years after *Exodus*'s publication, I am not the only one who has recognized a recent surge of thoughtful Jewish-American novels about Israel.

Chapter 4

SAUL BELLOW'S
MIDDLE EAST PROBLEM

If any Jewish-American writer would have the courage to "imagine" Israel after the implicit cautionary tale of Leon Uris's *Exodus,* one would expect it to be Saul Bellow—by most accounts the preeminent Jewish-American writer of this century. So one should hardly be surprised that Bellow emerged at the height of America's Zionist phase (just after the Six-Day War in 1967) to explore Israel in his fiction with a more sensitive and perspicacious eye than had Uris some ten years earlier. To place Bellow's critical approach toward the Middle East even more squarely in its cultural context, allow me to paraphrase a story that Israeli Jews seem to like telling their American Jewish visitors: A toad, on the bank of a river finds itself face to face with a scorpion, its mortal enemy. The toad has escape on its mind, but then the scorpion asks its would-be prey, "will you take me across the river on your back, for I cannot swim." The toad replies, "Do you take me for a fool? You are my mortal enemy. If I let you on my back, you'll sting me and I'll die." The scorpion reasons with the toad, "Now why would I do such a foolish thing? If I sting you, you'll drown and I'll surely drown with you." Convinced by such sound reasoning, the toad allows the scorpion to crawl onto its back and begins swimming across the river. Half-way across, though, the toad feels the scorpion's fatal sting penetrate its soft flesh. The toad cries out, "How could you do such a stupid thing? Now we're both going to die!" As they begin to drown, the scorpion answers, "Welcome to the Middle East."

Now, why do Israelis tell this story to their Western visitors? On one level, the story amusingly informs the American that the "civilized" logic of the West fails to account for human behavior in the Middle East. Interpreted this way, the story seems innocuous enough. However, as Jacob Neusner suggests, the recent predilection of American Jews to criticize Israeli policy (Saul Bellow once implied that Western moralists flock to Israel in the same concentration that skiers flock to the Swiss Alps) has angered Israelis, who refuse to kowtow—and rightly so—to the wishes of their wealthy benefactors (110). Indeed, the Israeli story-teller almost always seeks to convey through the story a not-so-subtle admonishment to the American listener: "Don't feel entitled to judge the moral standards of my country! Your Western vision of morality is necessarily myopic when you look toward the Middle East." Who takes this admonishment to heart, you ask? All those, I believe, who accept, almost instinctively, that the scorpion serves as an apt metaphor for the Arab in the Middle East, as does the toad for the well-intentioned Jew; the Israeli storyteller, I hazard to guess, rarely needs to elaborate upon the story's symbolic import.

I am not sure whether an Israeli has ever told Saul Bellow the above story. In any case, Bellow has thankfully never been one to think his Western moral framework inapplicable. It should come as no surprise that Bellow—a writer whose most resonant literary influences include the Old Testament and the great nineteenth-century Russian novels—refuses to hedge moral issues. Bellow recently told an interviewer that the "raising of moral questions" remains the most important purpose of literature (Kakutani 28). Though most contemporary writers cringe at the suggestion that writers are, to any degree, "moralists," Bellow stands foursquare against this view. I must admit that I glean a certain amount of satisfaction when he expresses his old-fashioned but, to my mind, satisfyingly precise view of the writer's social role: "he should be a legislator and . . . should perform a *moral function*, and . . . he should provide emotional, spiritual stuff—those are rather old fashioned ideas, but I don't think that people have really given up old fashioned ideas—they just scoff at them, while in reality they continue to live by them" [emphasis mine] ("Literature" 7). Even more recently, in his "Summa-tions" to the 1987 International Saul Bellow Conference, Bellow reaf-firmed his artistic precepts by asserting, "Readers . . . expect authors to be instructive, informative, edifying, revelatory, even prophetic, and writers put themselves out to meet these expectations" ("Summations" 185). Indeed, Al Ellenberg places his finger squarely on what drives Saul Bellow, who continues to write prolifically as he nears his eightieth year. Says Ellenberg, Bellow "cannot be just a writer; he is committed to an aggressive moral diffidence" (15).

Still, that Bellow embraces the moral function of writing is one thing; that he directs his energies toward the enigmatic Middle East is quite another thing altogether and something of a puzzle. After all, Bellow has long eschewed the label, *Jewish*-American novelist, claiming, "The whole Jewish writer business is sheer invention—by the media, by critics and by 'scholars'" (Qtd. in Pinsker, *Jewish-American Fiction* xi). He, elsewhere, states that he thinks of himself as a Midwesterner more than as a Jew when he writes (Ehrenkrantz 87). What is more, Bellow was skeptical of Zionism (to put it mildly) before the Holocaust. In Benno Weiser Varon's well-informed and intriguing essay, "The Haunting of Meyer Levin," he claims that any of Bellow's early Zionist inclinations were stifled, as "the young Bellow belonged to a generation of Jewish intellectuals who were corroded to the core by one form of Marxism or another" (13). Citing Norman Podhoretz's *Making It* (1967) for support, Varon continues that Zionism, to Bellow and his cohorts, was perceived as a virulent form of Jewish nationalism during the 1930s and 40s (13).

First things first. In regard to Bellow's Jewishness, which may appear suspect given his comments about "Jewish writing," even a cursory reading of Bellow's work reveals his very real commitment to his Jewish heritage. One thinks of the powerful Napolean Street passages in *Herzog* (1964), wherein Bellow richly describes the Jewish upbringing of Moses Herzog; or Bellow's opening remarks in his Nobel Prize address in which he proudly asserts his affinity, as a child of Jewish immigrants, for the "uprooted Pole," Joseph Conrad ("The Nobel" 16); or, perhaps, the first pages of *To Jerusalem and Back: A Personal Account* (1976) (hereafter referred to without the subtitle), as Bellow, en route to Israel, finds himself surrounded on the plane by Hasidic Jews and reflects, "there is nothing foreign in these hats, sidelocks, and fringes. It is my childhood revisited. At the age of six, I myself wore a tallith katan, or scapular, under my shirt . . ." (*TJAB* 1–2). Louis Ehrenkrantz astutely cuts through the fog of Bellow's semantics to see that it has always been "the commercialization of his Jewishness that Bellow fears, not the identification itself. He is no self-hating self-denying Jew" (87).

I think Bellow, himself, most cogently places his early anti-Zionist precepts into context. Reflecting upon the lure of Marxism earlier in the century, Bellow tersely states, "Matters were different sixty years ago" (*TJAB* 118). True enough. Ruth Wisse recently notes how prevalent Jewish-American criticism of Israel was during the heyday of the Communist campaign ("A Symposium" 75). Lionel Abel also offers a glimpse of the contagion of anti-Israel sentiment among the literary left during this heyday when he expresses how it took the constant Arab threat to Jewish lives in Israel, as illustrated by the Six-Day War in 1967 and the Yom Kippur War in 1973, to make him finally aware of "how bankrupt were [his] previously held Marxist-socialist views" (22). At any rate, Bellow abandoned his anti-Zionist sentiments at least by the time the Six-Day War began. He, in fact, travelled to Israel during the war and served as a correspondent for *Newsday* magazine. In a clear disavowal of his early Marxist views, Bellow says, "I often wonder why it should rend people's hearts to give up their Marxism. What does it take to extinguish the hopes raised by the October revolution?" (*TJAB* 44). As Leslie Field notes, "it is safe to say that the Saul Bellow who has protested so vehemently that he was an American writer and not a Jewish writer, the Saul Bellow who rejected Meyer Levin and his Zionism, is not the same Saul Bellow who wrote *To Jerusalem and Back*" (58).

Today, who can question Bellow's commitment to the Jewish state? The directors of *Beit Hatefutsoth*, Israel's museum of the Jewish Diaspora, feature Bellow prominently in one of their displays, and the 1987 International Saul Bellow Conference was held in Haifa; the Israeli author A. B. Yehoshua and Shimon Peres, Foreign Minister at the time, were on hand to emphasize the importance of Bellow's writing to Israeli writers and readers. All told, we should probably be thankful for Bellow's initial skepticism toward Israel. For what lies at the root of this skepticism—Bellow's wariness of militarily powerful and aggressive nation-states—persists and combines with his devotion to Jewish life to make him one of our more thoughtful Jewish-American writers on Israel. We must remember that the moral scrutiny of Israel has always been central, not antithetical, to Zionism. "Zionism," as David Polish defines it, "has always concerned itself with two issues, the political condition of the Jewish people and its *spiritual* condition" [emphasis mine] (261). This definition in mind, Bellow proves himself a Zionist in *Mr. Sammler's Planet* (1970) and his non-fiction work, *To Jerusalem and Back* (1976), as he grapples with the moral dilemma that continues to face the Jewish state amid an Arab-dominated Middle East: can the Jewish soul survive the political and military exigencies that must be acted upon to ensure the Jews' physical survival in Israel?

Saul Bellow wrote *Mr. Sammler's Planet* in the wake of Israel's Six-Day War against the combined armies of Egypt, Jordan, and Syria. To fully appreciate, then, the sobriety and acuity of Bellow's moral vision in the novel, we must explore the contrary mood of the Jewish-American community during this time—the zenith of the Zionist phase in America. Thomas Friedman, perhaps, best encapsulates the zeitgeist in his recent book, *From Beirut to Jerusalem* :

> After the 1967 war, the perception of Israel in the mind of many American Jews shifted radically, from Israel as a safe haven for other Jews to Israel as the symbol and carrier of Jewish communal identity. . . . When the smoke cleared and the extent of Israel's victory became apparent, American Jews pored over the headlines, watched all the television footage of Israeli soldiers swimming in the Suez Canal, and said to themselves, "My God, look who we are! We have power! We do not fit the Shylock image, we are ace pilots; we are not the cowering timid Jews who get sand kicked in their faces, we are tank commanders . . ." (454–455)

Ted Solotaroff reaffirms Friedman's impressions when he contends that "since the Six-Day War the survival of Israel has been the paramount concern of organized Jewish life and probably the paramount source of Jewish identity" ("American Jewish" 33); Arthur Hertzberg adds that the American Jews' "identification with Israel" was their "religion" after the Six-Day War (*The Jews* 375); and Dennis Prager, a prominent Jewish-American intellectual, also illustrates the intoxicating effect of the Six-Day War: "During the Six-Day War, I walked to my college classes with a radio next to my ear. . . . I then fell in love with Israel itself during those days of my own youthful romanticism and Israel's own youthful and romantic days of 1967" (59; see also Pinsker, "They Dream" 8–X). Indeed, for many American Jews, Israel "could do no wrong" after 1967 (Spiegel 70).

    To his credit, Bellow was much too canny a writer and human being to be swept blindly away by the romance of Israel's military victory in 1967. For a man who once expressed how "horribly deprived" he felt because so many people whom he loved were killed (in various pogroms and the Holocaust, one presumes), wars—no matter the victor—take on a decidedly unglamorous aspect (Bellow, "Common Needs" 16). In short, killing is a serious business as far as Bellow is concerned. While it took Israel's incursions into Lebanon in the 1980s, the Pollard affair, and the *intifada* to impel most American Jews to scrutinize Israeli policy, Bellow realized the importance of such moral assessments early on. Thus, he rejects the facile, uncritically romantic approach to Israel as a theme, unlike, say, Leon Uris, in *Exodus*. Bellow's success in *Mr. Sammler's Planet* hinges, in fact, upon "his ability to undermine the expectations readers have developed [given books like *Exodus*] about Jewish subjects like the Holocaust or the state of Israel" (Wirth-Nesher and Malamut 59).

In Artur Sammler, Bellow creates an aging protagonist who feels duty-bound to examine the waning morality of his society; the physical decay of New York—with its smashed phone booths and dog excrement littering the streets—reflects the spiritual decay of its inhabitants. Amid this wasteland, we learn that Sammler, at "seventy plus," feels a particular urgency to sum up the human condition before he dies. He reflects, "If we are about to conclude our earth business—or at least the first great phase of it—we had better sum these things up. But briefly. As briefly as possible" (*MSP* 148). "Short views, for God's sake!" Sammler exclaims (*MSP* 148). Moreover, he believes that his miraculous survival of the Holocaust (he gropes and claws his way out of a ditch of human corpses) must signify a corresponding human assignment "to figure out certain things, to condense, in short views, some essence of experience" (*MSP* 274). M. Gilbert Porter recognizes that "getting a handle on the situation seems to be what the novel is finally all about" (164). While several critics have focused their attention on the role that Sammler's Holocaust experience plays in forming his moral vision (see Kremer, "The Holocaust," Alexander, "Imagining," and Cronin, "Faith"), none have explored, in any detail, the implications of Sammler's visit to Israel during the Six-Day War. One critic, Edward Grossman, even complains that Bellow manages the interlude in Israel "in the style of a thoughtful passer-by rather than as a novelist at home in the place and with the people who inhabit it" ("Bitterness" 9). What Grossman fails to recognize is how crucial a role Israel plays in restoring Sammler's humanity; concomitantly, Bellow uses Sammler's experiences in Israel and creates a psychologically disturbed Israeli, Eisen, to scrutinize the moral cost of Israeli aggression.

In order to understand and appreciate Sammler's vision of Israel (which does not, I hope to show, precisely reflect Bellow's perspective), we must first examine further Sammler, himself. We know that his Holocaust experiences have formed him into something less than human. Consider the following passage in which Bellow describes Sammler's incredible survival from a Nazi mass murder:

[H]e and sixty or seventy others, all stripped naked and having dug their own grave, were fired upon and fell in. Bodies upon his own body. Crushing. His dead wife nearby somewhere. Struggling out much later from the weight of corpses, crawling out of the loose soil. Scraping on his belly. Hiding in a shed. Finding a rag to wear. Lying in the woods many days. (*MSP* 92)

As John Clayton notes, "Sammler *has to* lack humanity in order to survive psychologically" after he escapes the above atrocity (246). Sammler's warped humanity manifests itself as he turns from victim to victimizer in the Zamosht forest after he crawls from the mass grave. Again, Bellow displays his penchant for crafting sentences that are terse yet pregnant with meaning:

There at very close range he shot a man he had disarmed. He made him fling away his carbine. To the side. A good five feet into snow. It landed flat and sank. Sammler ordered the man to take off his coat. Then the tunic. The sweater, the boots. After this, he said to Sammler in a low voice, *"Nicht schiessen."* He asked for his life. Red-headed, a big chin bronze-stubbled, he was scarcely breathing. He was white. Violet under the eyes. Sammler saw the soil already sprinkled on his face. He saw the grave on his skin.... "Don't kill me. Take the things." Sammler did not answer, but stood out of reach. "I have children." Sammler pulled the trigger. The body then lay in the snow. A second shot went through the head and shattered it. Bone burst. Matter flew out. (*MSP* 138–139)

Alas, for several years after this murder, Sammler "felt that he was not necessarily human" (*MSP* 117). He reflects that taking the defenseless German's life was an "ecstasy" at the time, since he believed that no God could possibly exist to judge him (*MSP* 141). Not until he rejoins society in New York does Sammler reconsider the moral implications of violence and thereby begin the process of regeneration and redemption. No stranger to either end of a gun, Sammler feels well-qualified to critique Hannah Arendt's thesis on the Banality of Evil, which Margotte Arkin, his niece and apartment-mate, espouses. Says Sammler to his misguided niece, ". . . life is sacred. To defy that old understanding is not banality. There was a conspiracy against the sacredness of life. Banality is the adopted disguise of a very powerful will to abolish conscience. Is such a project trivial? Only if human life is trivial" (*MSP* 18). It is worth noting that others such as Cynthia Ozick, Ruth Wisse, and Amos Oz have taken Arendt to task for her theory—a theory that strays far from the Jewish precept of one's accountability for one's actions. Oz contends that the Nazis' decision to use showers to exterminate the Jews, far from banal, was "a frightfully *thoughtful* realization of an ancient, classic anti-Semitic metaphor. 'Purge the world of Jews'" [emphasis mine] (24). Moreover, I think we can safely deduce that Sammler (here, at least) speaks for Bellow, since the novelist elaborates on his protagonist's arguments, at length, in an interview with Robert Boyers (Bellow, "Literature" 16–17).

At any rate, this is the Sammler—a man with a pronounced emotional stake in violence—who travels to Israel for the first time in the early 1960s (before the Six-Day War) to rescue his daughter, Shula-Slawa, from her physically abusive Israeli husband, Eisen. Sammler does not stay long in the Holy Land, since he wishes to spend as little of Elya Gruner's money as possible; Bellow describes the visit in a scant two or three pages. However, this brevity in no way indicates the significance of the episode. For, herein, Bellow reaffirms his protagonist's sensitivity toward violence as Sammler accosts a gaucho. Seeing the coypus that the gaucho raises, then slaughters with a stick, Sammler wonders, "Didn't he mind doing this to his little flock? Hadn't he known them from infancy—was there no tenderness for individuals—were there no favorites?" (*MSP* 25). Though I count myself as an animal lover, it seems clear that Bellow uses this scene to dramatize Sammler's peculiar (or, at least, exaggerated) sensitivity toward killing. We must remember that these are not sheep or goats or cows toward which Sammler shows such concern, but aquatic rodents that look like household rats blown up to about the size of a raccoon. The gaucho, in fact, attempts to quell Sammler's anxieties by emphasizing the rodents' stupidity. During Sammler's first visit to Israel, then, Bellow provides us with a sense of the perspective through which he later dramatizes the Six-Day War.

During this second visit to Israel, Sammler observes the killing, not of rodents, but of human soldiers. "No Zionist," Sammler yet feels a duty to "send reports, to do something, perhaps to die in the massacre" of the Jews which seems imminent (*MSP* 142–143). Importantly, Bellow narrates the Six-Day War section just after his protagonist reflects upon his murder of the defenseless German soldier. This is important because the war enables Sammler to reexamine his act of violence through his vicarious participation in the stunning Israeli victory. Although Sammler suffers from severely limited vision, thanks to a rifle butt during the Holocaust, Bellow takes one line to emphasize that, in Israel during the war, "He had seen" (*MSP* 164). Put simply, Sammler sees from the war that killing one's enemies finally offers little by way of "ecstasy." While one might expect from Bellow a triumphant account, given the jubilation of the American Jewish community after the Six-Day war, his protagonist instead recounts for us the horror of killing. Take, for instance, Sammler's unglamorous description of the Arab corpses that lie rotting on the desert sand:

> [T]here were hundreds of corpses. The odor was like damp cardboard. The clothes of the dead, greenish-brown sweaters, tunics, shirts were strained by the swelling, the gases, the fluids. Swollen gigantic arms, legs, roasted in the sun. The dogs ate human roast . . . Poor folk! Ah, poor creatures! . . . In the sun the faces softened, blackened, melted, and flowed away. The flesh sank to the skull, the cartilage of the nose warping, the lips shrinking, eyes dissolving, fluids filling the hollows and shining on the skin. (*MSP* 250–251)

Though Sammler's affinity for his fellow Jews motivates him to light out for the battle zone, his journey culminates here as he acknowledges his connectedness to these enemy Arab soldiers. Sammler reflects that, perhaps, his instincts directed him to "visit the great sun wheel of white desert in which these Egyptian corpses and machines were embedded, to make his primary contact" (*MSP* 252). We must remember that Sammler felt no sympathy for the German soldier he killed in the Zamosht forest, and Bellow suggests that Sammler emerges from the experience with a diminished humanity. Thus, Sammler's sympathy for the dead Egyptian soldiers denotes the restoration, at least in part, of his humanity.

To be sure, some readers object to Bellow's apparent condemnation of Israeli might. After all, why does Bellow find it necessary to describe, in such detail, the Israelis' illicit use of napalm? Why give such short shrift to the Israeli war victims? Benno Weiser Varon vents his disgust when he observes, "Mr. Sammler, the Holocaust survivor, goes to the Six-Day War and sees *only* Egyptian corpses and Italian photographers" (14). Criticism of this ilk arises, I believe, from the common failure of critics to recognize the narrative distance between Bellow and his protagonist. Echoing critical consensus, Edward Grossman bemoans the fact that "when Sammler sees things in a certain implausible or far-fetched way, Bellow does not seek gently to dissociate himself. On the contrary, we get the feeling at these moments that we are not actually looking through Sammler's eye but through Bellow's eyes" ("Bitterness" 10). John Clayton asserts, as well, that "the reader is given nothing to identify with beyond Sammler" (247). Despite Grossman's and Clayton's impressions, Bellow does not use Sammler merely as a mouthpiece for his own views. Rather, as Gloria Cronin contends in her feminist critique of the novel—and as I will show also in regard to Bellow's Middle East perspective—there exists a "very real working space . . . between Bellow and those fictional characters like Sammler who bear the unmistakable marks of Bellow's own history" ("Searching" 99). Just as Bellow uses this narrative distance to scrutinize Sammler's misogyny, he uses it to examine his protagonist's abhorrence of Israeli aggression in the Middle East (I am convinced, by the way, that most of those who find Bellow self-indulgent or pedantic fail to appreciate the self-irony inherent in this working space, especially in such works as *Mr. Sammler's Planet, Herzog* [1964], and *Humboldt's Gift* [1975]).

Bellow uses the working space between himself and Sammler most significantly through his depiction of Eisen. Through Sammler's limited omniscience, Eisen emerges as a violent, "ugly Israeli." He refers to Eisen as one of those "smiling gloomy maniacs" (155) and later calls him a "madman" (167). Granted, Sammler's impressions have some merit. Eisen is brutal. His brutality emerges most vividly as he rescues Lionel Feffer, Sammler's friend, from the elegant black pickpocket:

> [S]hortening his grip on the cords of the baize bag he swung it very wide, swung with full force and struck the pickpocket on the side of the face. It was a hard blow. The glasses flew. The hat. Feffer was not immediately freed. The man seemed to rest on him. Obviously stunned. Eisen was a laborer, a foundry worker. He had the strength of his trade but also of madness. There was something limitless, unbounded, about the way he squared off, took the man's measure, a kind of sturdy viciousness. Everything went into that blow, discipline, murderousness, everything. (*MSP* 290)

Though Sammler asks Eisen to intervene, the Israeli's vicious assault on the pickpocket stuns and horrifies him. "What have I done! This is much worse!" he thinks. As Eisen prepares to levy a third crushing blow onto his victim, Sammler grabs his arm and cautions, "You'll murder him. Do you want to beat out his brains?" (*MSP* 291). Ultimately, Sammler sympathizes with the pickpocket and concludes that Eisen, a homicidal maniac, belongs in a mental hospital.

But it should come as no surprise that Sammler finds Eisen's violence repugnant. Sammler's sensitivity toward violence is, no doubt, compounded by the fact that Eisen, all too often, directs this violence toward Sammler's own daughter. Interestingly, however, most critics of the novel uncritically adopt Sammler's reading of his Israeli son-in-law. Lillian Kremer joins in Sammler's condemnation of Eisen's brutality by noting that "Eisen has become a madman himself. . . . Whereas Sammler's ordeal in suffering has added depth to his character, left him with the compassion to weep for a fallen enemy of his people, Eisen responds only to the law of the jungle: kill or be killed" (22–23). Irvin Stock also laments that "As a Jew, [Eisen] crushes skulls, when it seems reasonable to do so, without any crippling tremors of doubt or remorse" (90). Most recently, Ellen Pifer emphasizes Sammler's "horrified protests" when "his son-in law, Eisen, whose help he has sought, viciously attacks the black man" (20). While Kremer, Stock, and Pifer aptly note Sammler's distance from Eisen's perspective, I would suggest that they neglect Bellow's distance from Sammler. For despite his protagonist's abhorrence for Eisen's code of unmitigated violence, Bellow refuses to condemn this code outright. When Sammler begs Eisen to stop beating the pickpocket, Eisen gives his father-in-law a refresher course in survival: "You can't hit a man like this just once. When you hit him you must really hit him. Otherwise he'll kill you. You know. We both fought in the war. You were a partisan. You had a gun. So don't you know?" (*MSP* 291). Even Sammler acknowledges the soundness of Eisen's reasoning as his heart sinks. Like it or not, Bellow seems to be saying that the "law of the jungle" applies along New York's gritty streets just as it applied in Europe during World War II.

Moreover, Bellow uses this scene to assert his distance from Sammler in regard to Israel's use of force in the Middle East. After all, Eisen (whose name means "iron" in Yiddish) clearly symbolizes Israeli might. He does not assault the pickpocket with just any weapon, but with his bag carrying the Jewish symbols he fashions out of iron pyrite from the Dead Sea: "Eisen had made the usual Stars of David, branched candelabra, scrolls and rams' horns, or inscriptions flaming away in Hebrew: *Nahamu!* 'Comfort ye!' Or God's command to Joshua: *Hazak!*" (*MSP* 170). Hazak, significantly, is the command God gave to Joshua, which translates into English as "Strengthen thyself." Eisen's strength, then, as it manifests itself during his assault on the pickpocket, symbolizes a fulfillment of God's command. Some critics might argue that such a reading ignores the irony of Eisen's violence with the religious symbols; that Bellow, in fact, uses the scene to critique the violence of the Old Testament (Joshua is, arguably, the Old Testament's most violent book), or, contrastingly, to set our current debased expressions of strength up against the heroic manifestations of strength in the Old Testament. The text, however, gravitates away from these ironic readings.

In addition to Eisen's own convincing justification of his brutality, Bellow elsewhere condones Israeli might after the Holocaust via Eisen's plight:

> No longer a victim of Hitler and Stalin; deposited starved to the bones on Israel's sands; lice, *lunacy*, and fever his only assets. . . . Rising from negligibility, expendability, something that waited to be slaughtered with a trenching tool (Eisen said he had watched this before escaping from Nazi-occupied territory into the Russian zone—men too insignificant to waste bullets on, having their heads smashed by shovel blows); but rising and rising to heights of world mastery. . . . Hurray, Eisen, flying from peak to peak! [emphasis mine] (*MSP* 168).

One would be hard pressed to argue that Bellow, here, condemns Eisen's code of power which enables him to live in Israel. Bellow makes it clear that Israel gives Eisen some measure of dignity, perhaps for the first time. Eisen reflects, "Twenty-five years ago I came to the Eretz a broken man. But I wouldn't die" (*MSP* 171). Given the alienated and weak status of the Jew in the European Diaspora before, during, and after the Holocaust, who can deny the enormous appeal of the indomitable Israeli ethos that Bellow fashions in Eisen?

Indeed, Bellow reinforces his espousal of Israeli strength through emphasizing the importance of the state's survival to the dispossessed Jews in postwar Europe. The European Diaspora emerges as an altogether unfeasible option for the resettlement of Holocaust survivors. The Russians, who throw Eisen from a moving train after the war, treat him scarcely better than the Nazis. Eisen, whose toes must be amputated, rationalizes, "You know what Russians are when they have a few glasses of vodka" (*MSP* 24). Sammler, after the Holocaust, also receives an icy reception from the European Diaspora; he must hide in a mausoleum from the Poles after the Polish Partisans decide to "reconstruct a Jewless Poland" (*MSP* 140). Thus, through dramatizing an unsavory

European Diaspora, Bellow illustrates the pragmatic driving force behind Zionism: "how to save Jews through fulfilling the Zionist program" (Polish 261). Sammler notes that "that was one of the uses of Israel, to gather in these cripples" (*MSP* 155).

The disparity between Sammler's perspective and Bellow's does crystallize, I believe, into a reasonably cogent vision of the Middle East. Ultimately, Bellow uses Sammler's sensitive perspective toward Eisen's violence and the violence of the Six-Day War to illustrate the very real moral costs of Israeli might. War, Bellow implies, invariably diminishes the humanity of all participants, especially the victors (Golda Meir, too, understood this, as evidenced in her thoughts after the Six-Day War: "When peace comes we will perhaps in time be able to forgive the Arabs for killing our sons, but it will be harder for us to forgive them for having forced us to kill their sons") (Qtd. in Syrkin, "Phony Israel" 270). Simultaneously, Bellow uses the narrative gap between himself and his protagonist to argue that such moral costs, while regrettable, must be paid if the Jews are to survive as a people. William Phillips, the editor of the *Partisan Review,* perhaps, best expresses the quandary that dogs Bellow when he states, "You cannot build an ideal democracy, with an unassailable foreign policy, in one country, and a small and militarily vulnerable one to boot" (57). While the very ineluctable nature of the quandary offers some measure of comfort perhaps, Bellow refuses to let it lull him into political complacency. Hence, six years after publishing *Mr. Sammler's Planet,* Bellow focused even more squarely on this Middle East problem in his non-fiction work, *To Jerusalem and Back.*

There is a joke that Bellow enjoys telling, since it illustrates, for him, one of the essential and inextricable predicaments of the artist. The joke involves an American tenor who performs in Italy for the first time. After he finishes his first aria, the crowd showers him with applause and yells, "*Ancora, vita.*" The applause is even more deafening after he performs his encore, so he repeats the aria again, and then once again at the audience's request. Finally, after they shout "*Ancora*" a fourth time, the jubilant tenor must say, "Enough already! As a poor American from Kansas City I am deeply honored, but the Maestro is waiting and we must go on. How many times do you expect me to sing this aria?" Someone then shouts, "you gonna sing until you get it right!" As a fastidious reviser of his seemingly interminable manuscripts, Bellow empathizes with the plight of the tenor here. Bellow's self-imposed demand to "get it right" accounts partly for his long and prolific career (each novel, in one sense or another, one-upping the previous one). With this in mind, I believe we can view *To Jerusalem and Back* as his attempt to revise and polish his, at times, elusive vision of Israel as it emerges in *Mr. Sammler's Planet*. Bellow certainly did not believe that he got it all right in *Mr. Sammler's Planet*, as he explains to Jo Brans, "*Sammler* would have been a better book if I had dealt openly with some of my feelings, instead of filtering them through [Sammler]" (Bellow, "Common Needs" 14). Small wonder, given this self-critique, that Bellow adopts in *To Jerusalem and Back* the genre of the non-fiction journal which allows him, of course, to write in his own voice and thereby deal more openly with the feelings he suppresses in *Mr. Sammler's Planet*. Perhaps winning the Nobel Prize for Literature earlier in the year gave Bellow the necessary pluck to shed the protective coat of narrative distance.

One who reads *To Jerusalem and Back* today, nearly twenty years after its publication, cannot help but be struck by how relevant the book remains. True, Bellow did not have to fret over, say, the *intifada*, the recent peace accord between Israel and the PLO, Hamas suicide bombers, Baruch Goldstein, Yigal Amir, Israel's incursions into Lebanon in the 1980s or in 1996. (Bellow also, writing now, probably would not defer to Kurt Waldheim or Gore Vidal as uncritically as he does in the book, given what we now know about the former's Nazism and the latter's malicious accusations of American Zionists' dual loyalty) (see Rosenbaum and Vidal). However, the essential hoopla of 1976—Israel's controversial occupation of Arab territories seized during the Six-Day War—attracts even more headlines today; Prime Minister Yitzhak Rabin and his Labor Party, ousted by Menachem Begin's right-wing Likud party in 1977, once again find themselves in power; and it is even more difficult now than at the time Bellow observed to imagine Jerusalem without Mayor Teddy Kollek (though, after a twenty-eight-year incumbency, he lost his re-election bid in November of 1993). What is more, Bellow, being Bellow, flaunts a Middle East itinerary sure to provoke the envy of several heads of state. He lunches with Abba Eban, joins the Rabins for dinner, meets with the Israeli writer Amos Oz and several members of the Foreign Ministry, the list goes on and on.

Lest I praise too vehemently Bellow's non-fiction enterprise, I hasten to note that a good number of the book's reviewers find Bellow's account something of a disappointment. Most critics bemoan the impressionistic and, thus, cursory level at which Bellow engages his subject. Irving Howe warns that readers "may find [the book] frustrating, if only because one expects from a writer like Bellow more sustained argument, deeper probing. We don't get it" ("People" 1). Steven Lavine takes Bellow to task, as well, for his refusal to "synthesize his findings" ("In Defiance" 72); finally, Sanford Pinsker observes that Bellow's "Impressions, however penetrating, resist the esthetic control we associate with Bellow's fiction" ("Jerusalem" 37) and probably echoes the frustration of several readers in his more recent quip: "the same Saul Bellow whose distracted, brainy protagonists nearly convince us that they have the Big Answers turned out to be just as confused about the Middle East as anybody else" ("William" 397). Fair enough. However, I would add that Bellow, at the very least, earns his confusion (he weaves us through his own crash-course on the Middle East, citing such notable scholars as Elie Kedourie, Walter Laquer, Yehoshafat Harkabi, Jakov Lind, Bernard Lewis, Malcolm Kerr, Theodore Draper, among others). Indeed, what bothers Bellow is that most people living in the West acquiesce to the state of confusion too readily, without earning it. Says Bellow, "With us in the West wakefulness, for some mysterious reason, comes and goes. . . . Sometimes I suspect that I am myself under a frightful hypnotic influence. . . . I am forced to consider . . . whether we do not go about lightly chloroformed" (*TJAB* 84). He broods, "Do the senior members of the class really know the answers to these hard questions?"(*TJAB* 65). Thus, those who look to Bellow's book for concrete answers to the host of problems that beset the Middle East fail to appreciate Bellow's essential striving in the work: he wishes to stir complacent readers into active inquiry of their own. By offering only glimpses and impressions, he encourages readers to awaken and make judgments for themselves. Bellow, merely an "interested amateur—a learner" himself, as he claims, does not presume to offer a cogent political argument, but sets out, instead, to share his *personal* account of a brief trip to Israel, as his subtitle indicates (*TJAB* 164). As such, the value of *To Jerusalem and Back* lies not in Bellow's analysis per se, but in his bared voice through which he expresses one Jewish-American writer's emotional and intellectual stake in Israel.

As a writer of novels set usually in a stark urban landscape, Bellow does, thankfully, travel to Israel with a healthy dose of skepticism. Upon seeing signed photos of Hubert Humphrey hanging on every wall of the King David Hotel's barber shop, Bellow thinks, "Thousands of influential American Jews, big givers, stop at the King David. How ingenious of Humphrey to win the barber's heart and cover the walls of this shop with letters and photographs" (*TJAB* 31). Thus disinclined to trust ostensible motives, Bellow considers the arguments of both Israeli doves and hawks concerning the Occupied territories; he criticizes the strict Halakha, the Jewish law, through dramatizing the predicament of Justice Haim Cohn, who represented Israel in the U. N. Human Rights Commission but could not legally marry a divorcée in Israel; and Bellow has little patience for those Israeli Jews who foolishly "call upon American Jews to give up their illusions about goyish democracy and emigrate full speed to Israel. As if America's two-hundred-year record of liberal democracy signified nothing" (*TJAB* 14). Illustrating this tension between Israeli Jews and American Jews, Irving Howe recently observed that some Israelis are just itching to say, "Look here, *chaverim,* come live with us or stop calling yourselves Zionists; and if you choose not to come, then good-bye and good luck" ("American Jews" 73). Jacob Neusner corroborates Howe's sense of the current Israeli mood when he observes that "Israelis generally regard the loyalty of American Jews to America as similar to the loyalty of 'Egyptian' Jews to the fleshpots of Pharoah, and similarly reprehensible" (108).

At any rate, Bellow's bookish, skeptical approach to the Middle East and his erudition obscure the emotional investment in Israel embodied in his account. Two critics, in fact, note the "unsentimental" nature of the work (Grossman, "Unsentimental" 80; Cohen 21). However, like most literary Jews of his generation (one thinks of Alfred Kazin, Isaac Rosenfeld, and Lionel Trilling), Bellow literally read his way out of the ghetto. "I was getting through America by reading," says Bellow ("Summations" 187). It should not be surprising that he returns to books to navigate his way through the quagmire that we know as the Middle East. Moreover, Bellow's skepticism often gives way to his spiritual affinity for the Jewish state. Stepping onto an Israeli street, Bellow muses, "The air, the very air, is thought-nourishing in Jerusalem, the Sages themselves said so. I am prepared to believe it. I know that it must have special properties" (*TJAB* 10). Later, invoking I. B. Singer's transcendental Jewishness, he elaborates, "I, too, feel that the light of Jerusalem has purifying powers and filters the blood and the thoughts: I don't forbid myself the reflection that light may be the outer garment of God" (*TJAB* 93).

Now, I underscore Bellow's spiritual connection with Israel not at all to deride such deep and eloquently expressed feelings, but to emphasize the highly personal nature of the book, too often overlooked by critics. Bellow creates his most evocative passages during those times when the splendor of Israel moves him:

> A few Arab hens are scratching up dust and pecking. Not a breakfast egg comes to the table that isn't death-speckled. Parties of American girls come down the slope in their dungarees, with sweaters tied by their sleeves about the waist. Above, to the left, a Muslim cemetery. The great Golden Gate that will open when the Redeemer appears stands sealed. Just beyond, the Garden of Gethsemane. As its name indicates, it was an olive grove. Now pines, cypresses, and eucalyptus trees grow there below the domes of the Russian Orthodox Church. Opposite it there are olives still, which Arabs are harvesting with long poles. They hit the branches, they thresh the leaves with their sticks, and the fruit rains down. (*TJAB* 16).

Here, the multicultural richness of Israeli life stirs Bellow the novelist: the juxtaposition of ancient olive groves and modern American girls, the proximity of Muslim, Jewish, and Christian holy places. And all peoples, all endure amid the palpable threat of death, emblematized by every blood-stained egg eaten over the breakfast table.

Bellow admires the Zionists who settled in Israel to partake in and preserve the cultural richness he describes here. While Bellow implies in *Mr. Sammler's Planet* that Israel represents a necessary and viable alternative for the persecuted Jew in the European Diaspora, he conveys this message more straightforwardly in *To Jerusalem and Back*. He quotes an Israeli friend to illustrate the hope a life in Israel offers for a shtetl Jew in the European Diaspora: "I ask myself in what ways my life has not been typical. For a Jew from Eastern Europe it has been completely typical—war, death of mother, death of father, death of sister, four years in disguise among the Germans, death of wife, death of son. Thirty years of hard work, planting and harvesting in the kibbutz. Nothing exceptional" (*TJAB* 23). That a young Russian boy manages to emigrate to Israel and play the violin understandably moves Bellow to tears and rids him of his cheap disingenuous smile, peculiarly American. "Life in Israel," says Bellow, "is far from enviable, yet there is a clear purpose in it. People are fighting for the society they have created, and for life and honor" (*TJAB* 141). Bellow minces no words; Israel offers its Jewish immigrants dignity, plain and simple.

Bellow goes to considerable lengths to dramatize the unenviable predicament of the Israeli Jews. All serious talk in Israel, while it may stray toward peripheral issues, ultimately returns to the issue of survival. Early in his account, Bellow makes it clear how tenuous Jewish survival is in the region, "that one fact of Jewish life [remains] unchanged by the creation of a Jewish state: you cannot take your right to live for granted. Others can; you cannot" (*TJAB* 27). Reports of terrorist bombs going off eerily take their place amid the prosaic hustle and bustle of everyday life in Israel—"A new explosion outside a coffee shop on the Jaffa Road: six young people killed and thirty-eight more wounded" (*TJAB* 25). Bellow visits the sodden and charred site and a cab driver accosts him, "My friend was there. So now my friend is dead. . . . And this is how we live, mister! Okay? We live this way" (*TJAB* 43). Indeed, few Israeli families, Bellow insists, have been untouched by death: "you know that your hostess has lost a son; that her sister lost children in the 1973 war . . . many other families have lost children" (*TJAB* 27). The sheer number of tragedies Bellow cites on the Jewish side of the fence bespeaks his respect for the Jewish sacrifice in the region. That the very sentences above might just as easily have been penned in 1996 rather than in 1976 is tragic indeed.

Consequently, while Bellow may assess the moral costs of Israeli policy (as he does in *Mr. Sammler's Planet*), he often resists criticizing these policies largely because of his own relative insulation, as an American, from such violence. He takes pains to avoid exercising that "green unripe morality" peculiar to North Americans. When an amiable masseur describes how his unit in the Yom Kippur War left wounded enemy soldiers (for whom there was no transportation) to bake on the desert sand, Bellow resists judgment. Lavine begrudges Bellow for "witholding judgment on all but the most transparent issues," but, as Bellow notes, someone who comes from Chicago and will return to Chicago can only be so contentious ("On the Road" 1). Kenneth Jacobson implicitly refutes Lavine and sympathizes with Bellow's perspective in a recent *Tikkun* article. He, like Bellow, chastises American Jewish critics of Israel for their *chutzpah*, since "Israelis, not we, still have to live with the life and death consequences of their decisions" (Jacobson 348; see also Himmelfarb 43, and Neusner 110). Bellow's message remains all the more relevant today. He insists that a balance must be struck between two conflicting urges: the urge—rooted in Zionism—to assess Israel's moral condition versus the urge to suppress the public expression of these assessments given the potentially drastic political ramifications of such criticism.

Bellow unflinchingly expresses his frustration with those who upset this precarious balance. Those, for example, who hold Israel to an even higher standard of behavior than other countries—who insist that Israel be a "light unto the Nations"—find no ally in Bellow. Marie Syrkin echoes Bellow's sentiments when she says "I resent the demand, concurred in by many Jews, that Israel be judged by criteria applied to no other people" ("A Symposium" 74). Ruth Wisse offers a shrewd analysis of how the pernicious "light unto Nations" expectation evolved when she notes that "The admirability of Jewish achievement was . . . offered as evidence of Jewish national legitimacy—a fatal mixture, since it appeared to make the legitimacy contingent on the admirability" (*If I Am Not For Myself* 76). In *To Jerusalem and Back,* Bellow anticipates Wisse's concerns. Considering Sartre's statement that "We demand more from this state," Bellow insists, "since Israel's sovereignty is questioned and world opinion is not ready to agree that it is indeed a country like other countries, to demand more is cruelly absurd" (*TJAB* 136). To place Israel's actions in the Middle East in the proper perspective, Bellow calls attention to Lebanon's Civil War: "In Lebanon, ten minutes away by jet, armed gangs kill hundreds of people weekly. On your television set you can see murders committed. Corpses are tied to automobile bumpers and dragged through the streets" (*TJAB* 132). Bellow also quotes Malcolm Kerr's findings that the Jordanian army "killed more Palestinians in 1970 than Moshe Dayan's had done in 1967" (*TJAB* 156) and Marie Syrkin's observation (in reference to the Palestinian refugee problem) that "Nasser had no qualms about dislodging whole villages for his Aswan Dam, despite the objections of the inhabitants" (*TJAB* 158). One might add to the list Hussein's massacre of the Kurds in Iraq; or Assad's 1982 massacre of the Muslims in Hama, Syria; or the Algerian government's death squads, which continue to hunt down and murder dozens of suspected Islamic militants (Hedges A6). How rarely do the atrocities of these other Middle East countries inspire sustained and forceful criticism. Indeed, while discussing his latest novel, *Fima,* on a November 9, 1993, interview on National Public Radio, Amos Oz (a long-time supporter of Palestinian rights and a member of Peace Now) remarked that Western intellectuals still apply a more rigorous set of moral criteria to Israeli behavior than they apply to the actions of Israel's Arab neighbors.

The Arabs in these other countries come off rather poorly in Bellow's account. Perhaps to dispel misconceptions of Israel's oppressiveness in the region, he calls attention to the history of Arab aggression toward Israel and the refusal of the Arab states to tolerate a Jewish state in their midst. As in *Mr. Sammler's Planet*, Bellow emphasizes the horrific aftermath of Israel's victory in the Six-Day War by describing the rotting Egyptian corpses on a battlefield. However, Bellow argues that the Arab countries must shoulder the blame for provoking Israel into a pre-emptive strike. At times, Bellow presents the Arabs as downright barbaric. He, for example, recounts the eulogy that the Syrian Minister of Defense gives a Syrian war hero in which he exalts the soldier's cannibalism (the soldier, reportedly, took a hatchet to chop Israelis' heads off and devoured the flesh of one Israeli soldier in front of his comrades). The Defense Minister, Mustafa T'Las, asks the mourners, "This is a special case. Need I single it out to award him the Medal of the Republic? I will grant this medal to any soldier who succeeds in killing twenty-eight Jews" (*TJAB* 170). Bellow repeatedly stresses—though not to this degree—the Arabs' brutality and their unwillingness to coexist with Israel. He quotes a friend as saying, "The Jews have not been inflexible and negative. Concessions are continually offered. They are rejected" (*TJAB* 37). Prime Minister Rabin concurs, "The Arabs . . . are not interested in territorial concessions and will never be satisfied with them. They consider themselves owners and masters of this land" (*TJAB* 113). Elie Kedourie, too, states tersely, "They simply want the Jews out" (*TJAB* 144). Finally, Bellow himself concludes, toward the cynical close of his account, that "The root of the problem is simply this—that the Arabs will not agree to the existence of Israel" (*TJAB* 179). Given the present turmoil in the Middle East, one wonders to what extent Yasir Arafat's equivocal recognition of Israel in December 1988 (couched in legal "mumbo-jumbo," according to Michael Lerner, "convoluted language," according to Thomas Friedman), Israel's Peace Accord with the PLO in September 1993, and the encouraging dawn of a peaceful coexistence between Jordan and Israel dates Bellow's fears (Qtd. in Husseini 359; Friedman 403).

While Bellow's essential critique of the Arab states in 1976—their refusal to recognize Israel—strikes me as well-informed, Bellow does address the Palestinian issue in problematic ways which demand notice, given the recent post-colonial perspectives of Edward Said, Anton Shamamas, and others. Bellow acknowledges the moral problem inherent in the subordinate status of the Palestinian Israelis, but lapses into a morally strained argument of his own when he attempts to speak for a contented Palestinian population (*TJAB* 34). After begrudgingly acknowledging the injustice dealt to the Palestinian refugees, Bellow argues that Israel still deserves credit for miraculously transforming the Palestinians' land from a wasteland (he cites Herman Melville's and Mark Twain's accounts of Palestine's desolation) into a paradise. The Palestinians are fortunate, Bellow subtlely implies, that "In this unlovely dreamland the Zionists planted orchards, sowed fields, and built a thriving society" (it should be noted that, in the *Journal of Palestine Studies,* Jeremy Salt cites other nineteenth-century travel journals which refute Melville's and Twain's accounts of an Arab wasteland)(*TJAB* 159).

Bellow lapses into similar suspect reasoning when he tries to refute the argument that "the Arabs do all the disagreeable jobs and form an exploited class of bottom dogs" (*TJAB* 131). He claims, "this is probably not how the Arab laborers see themselves. Their wages have risen, and there is no precedent for the prosperity they enjoy" (*TJAB* 131). Defenders of the Israeli occupation often make arguments of this nature, that the Palestinians are "better off" under Israeli rule. One can readily enough see the allure of this reasoning, given the low standard of living most Arabs endured in Palestine before Israel's statehood and continue to endure in the Arab states surrounding Israel. As recently as 1993, Irving Louis Horowitz and Maurice Zeitlin reaffirm Bellow's argument by noting that "the class structure, in which a few sheikhs ruled the agrarian population, exploiting their labor and living comfortable lives in the cities on their 'earnings' from lands tilled by subsistence peasantry in the villages of Palestine, was, in fact, increasingly altered as the Jewish settlement and agricultural and industrial development impinged on the feudal ruling patterns" (69–70). However, given the pernicious history of this essential argument that Bellow—and, more recently, Horowitz and Zeitlin—put forward, its allure must be resisted. Several post-colonial critics such as Patrick Brantlinger, Chinua Achebe, and Tejaswini Niranjana note that the moral credibility of colonialist enterprises in Africa, Asia, and in the Americas lay rooted in the conviction, on the part of the colonizers, that they lifted native peoples from a debased state. That Bellow cannot resist such arguments no doubt prompts Noam Chomsky, being Noam Chomsky, to complain that Bellow, "the perfect victim of the propoganda apparatus . . ." (306) "produced a catalogue of What Every Good American Should Believe, as compiled by the Israeli Information Ministry" (299). In Bellow's defense, one should note that in his very acknowledgment of a Palestinian people and perspective, he distances himself from the first wave of contemporary Zionists who argued that Palestine was a "land without a people," or, as one Zionist put it in *Commentary*, that "[The Palestinians] had no political organization whatsoever. They had no national feeling" (Shammas 33; Johnson 33). At any rate, I doubt highly that Bellow frets much over Chomsky's bitingly sarcastic review of *To Jerusalem and Back* (one does not undertake a study of the Middle East with the hopes of making new friends or, for that matter, keeping all of the old ones).

Bellow's more polemical arguments, however, do bring to mind once again his joke about the American tenor from Kansas City. How would Bellow sing his aria about the Middle East today? In an interview, would Bellow now provide us with the Big Answers: Who really deserves control of the West Bank, the Gaza Strip, the Golan Heights, Jerusalem? Has Israel overstepped its bounds, given its democratic precepts, during its often violent law enforcement practices directed against disgruntled Palestinian protestors? Do the Israeli courts offer fair trials and fair sentencing to Palestinian suspects? How culpable is Israel for the scores of civilian, rather than Hezbollah, casualties in Lebanon during the 1996 skirmishes? (I must admit that I would conduct the interview with a certain trepidation; while I wouldn't say that Bellow has contempt for critics, he does usually utter the word scholar with quotation marks wrapped implicitly around it). I doubt that Bellow has the big answers to these big questions, despite having had nearly twenty years to reflect upon his initial perceptions as expressed in *To Jerusalem and Back*. If such cogent answers exist, not one political expert has divulged them.

The final pages of *To Jerusalem and Back* offer some comfort. As Bellow prepares to leave Israel, he reflects that he "never did learn the trick of lighting the oven" (*TJAB* 139). Perhaps I allow my "academic" proclivity for identifying symbols too free a rein (Bellow, himself, chastised readers for this tendency in an article, "Deep Readers of the World Beware!"), but I cannot resist interpreting Bellow's expressed inability to light the oven as his acknowledgment—expressed in half-sigh—that he could not shine a light onto the nebulous Middle East either. Such an admission should not disappoint. Bellow does shed more light than heat onto the region and he admirably refuses to provide false answers (artificial light, if you will) to the Middle East problem. One is reminded of the brilliance of his novels. Moses Herzog takes comfort in God's existence at the end of *Herzog*, but does not have all the answers to the prevailing nihilism of his day; Tommy Wilhelm cries redemptive tears at the close of *Seize the Day,* but remains a *shlemiel;* and, while Sammler recognizes that a human contract binds all people to a dutiful life, he cannot account, in "short views," for the spiritual drought that befalls New York in the 1960s. Bellow may affirm human potential, but he never falsely affirms human accomplishments. It is just this type of intellectual integrity that draws one back and back again to Bellow's work. In regard to the Middle East, who are we to ask Bellow to start fudging now?

Chapter 5

HUGH NISSENSON'S ISRAEL
In Search of a Viable Jewish Ethos in Israel

If you look carefully, nobody's face matches
exactly. The halves are always different.

—Hugh Nissenson

"Hugh who?" Regrettably, this is the response one often elicits upon mentioning the fiction of Hugh Nissenson. Indeed, Leila Goldman understates matters when she laments that Nissenson "has not achieved the renown he deserves" (195), as does Arthur Kurzweil when he notes that Nissenson, unlike Saul Bellow, "has not become a household name" (15). That a distinctively Jewish-American writer of only two novels, two collections of stories, and a short memoir does not command widespread attention should come as little surprise in a literary marketplace experiencing no dearth of new and substantial work. However, one should not underestimate the importance of Nissenson's fiction. For his first collection of stories, *A Pile of Stones* (1965), convinced astute readers that Nissenson—a writer wholly immersed in Jewish themes and spiritual introspection—was something special to arrive upon the literary scene. The collection won the 1965 Edward Lewis Wallant award as the year's most significant work of Jewish-American fiction. Robert Alter praised the writer's "imaginative integrity" and contended that "Nissenson is, as far as I can recall, the only genuinely religious writer in the whole American Jewish group" ("Sentimentalizing" 75). To be sure, Nissenson's relatively sparse literary output since *A Pile of Stones* leaves those of us who share Alter's impressions thirsty for more. Still, in *A Pile of Stones*, in *Notes from the Frontier* (1968), a memoir of Nissenson's experiences living on a *kibbutz* bordering the Golan Heights, and in his second collection of stories, *In the Reign of Peace* (1972), Nissenson imagines Jewish life in Israel more substantially than most Jew-ish-American writers thus far.

Two critics have emphasized the Hemingwayesque in Nissenson's approach to Israel (see Rosenfeld, "Israel," and Daiker). Granted, par-allels exist between the two writers, for Nissenson admittedly draws upon Hemingway's spare style and, also like Hemingway, deals with the tangible violence and death that loom threateningly about his characters; furthermore, these parallels between Nissenson and an American literary icon beg notice because they, thereby, implicitly vali-date the merit of Nissenson's work. However, Cynthia Ozick, Ruth Wisse, Alan Berger, and Lawrence Berkove come closer to the mark when they suggest the uniqueness of Nissenson's work by identifying his fiction as *midrashim*, revelatory commentaries of religious texts. For if we concede for a moment that Israel serves as "our author's bull ring or war zone, the primal site of the encounter between man and death," we must also recognize that Nissenson fashions his bulls out of more mystic stuff than does Hemingway (Rosenfeld, "Israel" 54). At stake in Nissenson's work is not merely whether his protagonists can muster up enough courage, or grace under pressure, to survive physi-cally, but whether his protagonists place their spiritual survival in peril by adopting a code of physical force rather than a code of passivity. In an interview, Nissenson illustrates subtly how his fiction about Israel pivots about this primary concern: "I am frankly enamored, in love, with Israel, as one would love a woman. I mean the country of Israel and also what that represents" (Kurzweil 18).

What, specifically, should Israel "represent" in a post-Holocaust world? Should the state represent a secular refuge for Jews in which they can build a socialist society, or should it represent a religious homeland for the Jewish exiles? Can Israel sustain both ideologies simultaneously? As the above epigraph, culled from *Notes from the Frontier*, indicates, Nissenson recognizes and reckons courageously with these two discor-dant halves of Israel's face: the secular side acquiescent to the militarism necessary to ensure the Jews' physical survival in the region, and the reli-gious side which proscribes violence since it may preclude redemption. As I will show, Nissenson doubts that secularism can satisfy the Jewish soul; but he also doubts that religious faith can weather the political realities in modern Israel. This ideological conflict persists in Israel and continues to plague American Jews who care deeply about the state's spiritual complexion, for Israel, after all, represents the spiritual core for

Jews everywhere. Indeed, Nissenson explores more than merely Israel's particular spiritual dilemma in his work. Like most Jews in the Diaspora, he looks toward Israel to gauge the "Jewish condition" in general. Put another way, Israel serves as the objective correlative through which Nissenson explores the conflict between the secular and religious stirrings of Jews worldwide.

To reduce the Israeli ethos to a secular/militaristic and religious/passive dichotomy may seem altogether too reductive. While the dichotomy accounts for most of the secular nonobservant Israelis, who represent roughly 50 percent of Israel's Jewish population, and the ultra-Orthodox non-Zionist Jews (or Haredim), who make up roughly 15 percent of the Jewish population in Israel, Nissenson's rigid framework does not account for approximately 35 percent of the Jewish population who are Orthodox but also serve in the military, or the several secular Jews who are pacifists. In more concrete terms, the Gush Emunim Jews (Settler Jews who represent approximately 5 percent of Israel's Jewish population) believe Israel should annex the West Bank and ground their militaristic ideology in their strict interpretation of religious scripture. Likewise, the secular members of Israel's Peace Now movement tout a largely anti-militaristic, if not passive, ideology. Still, while Nissenson does not place his finger on *the* dichotomy of Israeli identity, he does recognize one essential tension that contributes to the torn Israeli ethos and overtly considers the inherent moral implications of this tension. Some critics chide Nissenson for this overtness of his allegorical content. Wisse argues that he ungracefully imposes his "moral design upon his characters" ("American Jewish Writing, Act II" 43). Alter puts it a bit more colorfully, claiming that Nissenson's stories "read like neatly arranged laboratory situations for testing out a series of problems of faith and theodicy" ("Sentimentalizing" 75). But both Alter and Wisse agree with Harold Fisch, who lauds Nissenson for, at least, "seriously handl[ing] the religious problem of the modern Jew" (72).

Nissenson sets his sights on this essential dilemma of the modern Israeli in his first collection of fiction, *A Pile of Stones.* In the collection, Nissenson sets only two stories in Israel, "The Blessing" and "The Well." However, to look merely at these two stories to assess Nissenson's vision of Israel in the book would be insufficient because the stories set in Europe and America, which frame the Israel stories, color our reading of the middle two stories. Nissenson, a careful craftsman, arranges the seven previously published stories to effect an aesthetic unity. As an initial reviewer notes, "these seven little tales do indeed make a book" (Koningsberger 38). More specifically, Nissenson, story by story—via essential changes in setting, plot, and character—shifts the lens through which he views his unifying concern: the role of covenantal belief amid environments seemingly devoid of redemptive possibilities. While our president, Bill Clinton, likes to refer to a "new" covenant in America, the status of the original covenant, centuries old, between God and Abraham stirs Hugh Nissenson's imagination as he considers the Jews' physical and spiritual condition in the Diaspora and in Israel.

In the first two stories, set in Poland before the Holocaust, "The Groom on Zlota Street" and "The Prisoner," the covenanted status of the Jew, with all its burdens, emerges as an implacable element of Jewish life in the European Diaspora. In "The Groom on Zlota Street," Nissenson focuses on the plight of a poor Jewish family who manufacture and sell carriage whips. Nissenson renders the tale as a recollection of a narrator who reflects upon an episode in the lives of his father, his father's parents, and his father's cousin, Yecheil. The episode involves Yecheil, whom the narrator's grandparents graciously take in, although the carriage-whip shop "could barely support three as it was" (*APOS* 23). Since Yecheil can contribute little in the shop, the narrator's grandfather must send his nephew to peddle the whips along the unfriendly streets of Warsaw, where Russian soldiers routinely harass him by pulling his beard. Yecheil's daily predicament begs the question: why does he not shave his beard? The lesson of the story lies in the answer to this question, which Nissenson withholds until the story's last scene. In the opening pages of the story, the narrator simply emphasizes that Yecheil will not make any effort to look less the Jew, despite the fact that such action would surely curtail the persecution imposed upon him daily: "For as long as the boy [the narrator's father] had known him, Yecheil had made no concession to modernity. He dressed in a garbadine and skullcap, his ritual locks curled behind his ears, and a razor had never touched his beard" (*APOS* 16). The boy suggests to his father that they consult the rabbi; that perhaps he will, under the circumstances, grant Yecheil permission to shave his beard. The father, however, knows that an Orthodox rabbi would never grant such permission since "it was forbidden" (*APOS* 21). He, of course, refers here to Leviticus 19:27, "Ye shall not round the corners of your heads, neither shalt thou mar the corners of thy beard."

Perhaps sensing his younger cousin's inclinations toward assimilation and away from a covenanted life, Yecheil takes him to the Zlota

Street groom on Sabbath night. As Yecheil, with his cousin in tow, meets the groom on Sabbath night, we learn why Yecheil refuses to sell whips to him; the anti-Semitic groom will only buy one whip for every time that Yecheil allows him to pull his beard. Yecheil explains to his cousin why he bothers to return time and time again to the groom and, in the process, explains to the boy, and to us, what it means to be covenanted: "Because he gives me a choice . . . Yes . . . Don't you see? . . . because I have a choice. I refuse . . . Listen . . . You see, you were wrong . . . There's always a choice to be made . . . Remember that . . . Remember that and rejoice . . . Rejoice . . . Praise Him . . . God provides" (*APOS* 39). Since the narrator filters the story through his father's perspective, Yecheil appears, through most of the story, to be naïvely obedient to the Jewish law. Here, however, Nissenson rescues the Orthodox Jew from this stereotype as Yecheil illustrates to his cousin that he exerts free will. He emerges as uncannily perceptive, as well. His assertion to his younger cousin that "you were wrong" indicates that he realizes that his younger cousin perceives him to be a weak shtetl Jew, bound, without choice, to Jewish law. Yecheil brings his cousin to the groom to teach him (and us) that one accepts the covenant by choice. Indeed, Yecheil praises God in this final scene because God empowers him with the free will to observe the covenant—a timely lesson for the narrator's father who, at twelve, will be of age within the year to accept the covenant as an adult, in a Bar Mitzvah ceremony.

Clearly, a few tugs on the beard by Russian soldiers and the taunting of a brutish groom fall far short of seriously testing the Jew's allegiance to God's covenant. In the next story, though, Nissenson holds the strength of the covenant to a more rigorous challenge. Whereas Yecheil need not fret over events that seriously challenge his faith in God, the Jewish prisoner in "The Prisoner" witnesses a vicious pogrom which does shake his belief. As in "The Groom on Zlota Street," Nissenson filters the story through the perceptions of the narrator's father, during a crucial time in the father's religious formative years—a time when he fumbles through passages of the Old Testament to glean whatever knowledge and religious inspiration he can. Through him, we meet the prisoner whom the Russians plan on sending to Siberia for his socialist views. Although the Jews of Warsaw cannot alter the prisoner's fate, the narrator's father, acting on behalf of Warsaw's Jews, takes the prisoner food and inquires into his socialist principles. To explain why he has eschewed his faith in God and awaits a socialist revolution instead, which he believes will end human suffering, the prisoner describes in graphic detail the pogrom he witnessed as a boy:

> Don't look, the rabbi tells me. Shut your eyes, my son and pray. . . .
> But I look just the same. I can't tear my eyes away, so I see what they
> do to a fourteen-year-old girl, the daughter of the Jew who owns the
> mill on the edge of town. One of them sits on her head, while they
> take turns. All told, there are six of them, and when they're finished,
> and see that she's still alive, still fully conscious, they cut open her
> belly with a sickle, and stuff it with goose feathers from a pillow
> they've looted from a house across the street . . . (*APOS* 58)

Whereas Leon Uris, in *Exodus*, dramatizes similar pogrom scenes to emphasize the pragmatic necessity for a Jewish state if the Jews are to survive physically, Nissenson dramatizes the pogrom above to put a Jew's spiritual survival to the test. Can a Jew witness a horrific scene like the one above and still embrace God and the covenant? Nissenson initially implies no, for the prisoner ostensibly rejects the covenant and embraces socialism, seeing the imminent worker's revolution as a secular alternative to an illusory faith in the Messiah. Leila Goldman notes that "the reaction of the prisoner reflects Nissenson's own movement away from belief, and, of course, the reaction of countless [Holocaust] survivors" (191). Goldman offers an apt parallel here between writer and character. Nissenson has declared himself a "militant atheist" (Kurzweil 15). However, unlike Nissenson (evidently, at least), the prisoner ultimately discovers that his faith in God cannot be shaken off as easily as an outgrown coat.

Herein lies the power of the story. The further the prisoner attempts to extricate himself from a covenantal existence, the more his covenanted status burdens him. In this way, Nissenson's prisoner represents a Jewish revisioning of Flannery O'Connor's Hazel Motes of *Wise Blood*, whose defilement of Jesus's teachings cannot free him from the burden of faith. But whereas Flannery O'Connor sees evil as the absence of Godly intervention, Nissenson, through the prisoner, posits that evil, as well as good, contributes to God's design. During the final pages of the story, the prisoner tells the narrator's father and grandfather about the nightmare that plagues him in which he sees order and meaning in the sordid conditions of his prison cell and even in the evil pogrom he witnessed as a child: "the straw on the floor, even the dirt under my fingernails, each and every straw, and every one perfectly distinct, and . . . significant. Meaningful, each one . . . Yes, I could remember it all [the pogrom], but it was like the straws. The straws do you hear? All in order. . . . More. Good . . . No, holy" (*APOS* 62–63). As Lawrence Berkove notes, "the story suggests a mysterious sense of order and purpose beyond—even through—evil. The prisoner confuses his opposition to evil with his resentment at not being able to know the purpose of evil" (78). Thus, while the narrator's father does not understand the message inherent in the prisoner's nightmare, Nissenson suggests to the reader that the existence of human suffering, evidently, does not free the European Jew from a belief in God and the covenant.

In the three final stories of *A Pile of Stones*, set in America, Nissenson illustrates a waning of covenantal belief; the material benefits of assimilation in America prove tempting indeed. However, in each of these stories, Nissenson provides a frame of reference from which he also illustrates the persistence of covenantal belief in America. In "The Law," Nissenson, I believe, dramatizes this persistence most powerfully, as a narrator, Joe, reflects upon his younger cousin's determination at his Bar Mitzvah to recite his Haftorah (a portion of the Torah) in front of the synagogue congregation despite his severe stammer. As his popular American name indicates, Joe typifies the assimilated American Jew. He explains to his cousin, Danny, that he does not believe in God and was never Bar Mitzvahed. Moreover, Nissenson dramatizes Joe's alienation from his Jewish roots through Joe's decision to write his History Ph.D. thesis on the Alien and Sedition Act of 1798. Through Joe's Uncle Willi, a survivor of a Holocaust concentration camp, Nissenson emphasizes that President Adams's suspension of free speech, directed against approximately twenty-five British and French foreigners, has little to do with Jewish persecution in America at the time. Clearly, Joe has given little thought to the Jewish condition throughout American history. When Willi asks his nephew if there was any "particular repression of the Jews, as such" in America, Joe responds, "I never thought about it, to tell you the truth" (*APOS* 142). Joe's thesis, interestingly, summons to mind another history scholar in Jewish-American fiction, Moses Herzog, whose estrangement from his Judaism in Saul Bellow's *Herzog* also manifests itself in his uncompleted scholarly manuscript, *Romanticism and Christianity*.

Joe's estrangement from a covenantal existence compels him to investigate Willi's and Danny's affirmation of their Judaism. Joe, initially, does not understand why Danny insists upon subjecting himself to the mortifying experience of affirming God's Law in front of the whole synagogue congregation. He asks Willi whether a party might suffice alone, where Danny would not have to speak publicly at all. Through Willi's recollection of Heinz, a brutal Nazi guard at Bergen Belsen, he explains to Joe why Danny feels he must embrace formally God's covenant. The Ten Commandments, Willi explains, tormented the Nazi guard, and this taught Willi why the Nazis murdered the Jews: "they were murdering, humiliating us because whether it was true or not we had come to—how shall I say it?—embody, I suppose ... In some strange way, we had come to embody that very Law and in destroying us ... what all of them hated, somehow, was the yoke that we had given them so long ago. The Law that makes all the difference, that makes a man different from a beast" (*APOS* 155–156). Before the Holocaust, Willi cannot even recite the Ten Commandments. Ironically, though, Willi's Holocaust experience cements his faith in God's covenant, for the abomination—this most tangible rejection of God's Law—illustrates for him the importance of that Law. Though Irving Malin faults Willi for "tyrannically" commanding his son to perform the Bar Mitzvah (58), Nissenson emphasizes that Danny, who listens often to his father's reflections of Bergen Belsen, embraces the covenant of his own free will, as evidenced in his resolve to affirm God's Law at his Bar Mitzvah. Joe reflects that "he had *made up his mind* to assume the burden of what the reiteration of the Law of his Fathers had demanded from the first" [emphasis mine] (*APOS* 162). Ultimately, then, in the stories set in both Europe and America, Nissenson emphasizes the burden of covenantal faith which weighs heavily upon Diaspora Jews. As one reviewer notes, "the socialist dying in a Czarist jail and the stammering boy at a Bar Mitzvah in Queens are brothers in fate" (Koninsberger 38).

I offer the explications of the first two stories set in Europe and "The Law," set in America, because they provide contrast to the Israeli stories in the collection, "The Blessing" and "The Well." Whereas covenantal existence emerges in the European and American stories as almost ineluctable for the Diaspora Jew, what of the Israeli Jew and the covenant? Nissenson's opening description of a stark Israeli landscape in the first Israel story, "The Blessing," suggests that covenantal belief will be put to the test in the Middle East. Yitshaak, whose young son has just died of lymph node cancer, watches from his balcony as Rabbi Levinsky leaves his house of mourning:

[T]he air was stifling, redolent of plaster and the exhaust fumes of cars. The long tapering leaves of the trees, shaped like knife blades, were covered with dust. The heated air shimmered above the red-tiled roofs of the houses on top of the hill. Beyond them, to the west, beyond the highway to Haifa, and shining between the gaps in the sand dunes, the inert Mediterranean reflected the pale-blue sky. (*APOS* 67)

The stifling air, knife-shaped eucalyptus leaves, and the inert sea reflect the spiritual sterility of Jewish life in Israel. The rabbi, in fact, glares back at Yitshaak in reproval, as Yitshaak tells him that he will not attend his son's religious funeral because they will pray over his grave, "Blessed art Thou O Lord our God who art the true judge in Israel" (*APOS* 74). Yitshaak realizes that he cannot utter these words because he no longer believes them. How can a true judge in Israel strike down an innocent child? The Israeli's rejection of God upon witnessing human suffering contrasts sharply with the European Jew's inability, in "The Prisoner," to shake off the burden of a covenantal existence after witnessing a fair share of human suffering, as well. Through Yitshaak's aunt Esther, a survivor of Auschwitz, Nissenson further emphasizes this contrast between the European Jews and Israelis when it comes to matters of covenantal duty. Although she lost both her husband and daughter in the camps, she still maintains her faith in God and she tells Yitshaak, "one must struggle every day" (*APOS* 76). One also thinks of the American Jew in "The Law," Willi, who embraces the covenant despite experiencing the Holocaust firsthand at Bergen Belsen.

It is important to note that Nissenson does not interpret Yitshaak's rejection of faith positively. For Yitshaak laments his inability to affirm the covenant at his son's funeral. He clings to the possibility that Rabbi Levinsky will enliven his faith once again, clings to "the possibility that remained of hope and peace, the chance that if he spoke to the bearded old man just once more, one of his phrases, perhaps one final word that he loosed upon the desolation, would come back to roost with an olive branch" (*APOS* 73). Nissenson provides no indication that this will happen. While Nissenson's prisoner in the Czarist jail wishes to reject religious belief but cannot, Yitshaak wishes for just the opposite—he wishes to embrace God and the covenant, but cannot in Israel. The story ends as he bemoans his rebellious heart which excludes him from rejoicing in the eternal order that Esther blesses, embodied in the starry sky. Moreover, Nissenson implies that the Israeli setting, specifically, exacerbates Yitshaak's religious crisis. When Esther reminds Yitshaak of the traditional condolence meal they must serve, he muses, "'I remember. The meal of condolence . . .' It seemed so remote; all of the random memories of his religious upbringing seemed now to belong to another life; the dark Polish synagogue on Dizengoff Road with its slippery floor, the candles and fish on Friday night, the red velvet *tallis* bag that his father had given him on his thirteenth birthday" (*APOS* 71). Here, Nissenson overtly suggests the contrast between a religious, European-influenced Israel and the new, irreligious Israel. To my mind, then, we can read the story as a lament on the waning of religious Judaism in Israel—Judaism that manifests itself so strongly, by contrast, in Nissenson's stories set in the European and American Diaspora.

Nissenson returns time and time again to the problem of Israel's religious sterility. But before moving onto "The Well," *Notes from the Frontier,* and *In the Reign of Peace,* let me pause to emphasize that several Jewish-American intellectuals during the 1960s and 70s echo Nissenson's concerns, expressed in his short fiction at the time. That these intellectuals continue to explore the implications of the waning religious content of Jewish identity in Israel suggests the degree to which they depend upon Israeli Jewish life to set the spiritual tone of their own Jewishness in America. Shortly after *A Pile of Stones* was published, Judah Eisenberg expressed his surprise at the secular overthrow of religion in Israel. "It is all perfectly fine," he writes in an issue of *Midstream,* "to realize that many Israelis are non-religious—so are many American Jews—but it still often catches one unawares when a primary school class is marched off to a nearby synagogue to see the quaint cultural relics of Jewish folkways" (64). In the article that precedes Eisenberg's in the magazine, Roland Gittelsohn, an American rabbi, admonishes the Israelis, like Nissenson's Yitshaak, who have allowed religion to become such a relic, a mere vestige of the nation's body:

> Many Israelis—judged superficially, most Israelis—have sinned in ignoring the religious component of our corporate identity. They see religion as something tedious and outmoded because—to be truthful—the only kind of religion to which they have been exposed has in fact been tedious and outmoded. They see themselves as an ethnic collectivity, as a nationality not innately different from all other nationalities. They have mutilated the corpus of Judaism by excising one of its vital organs. (59)

Interestingly, this hubbub among Jewish-American scholars in the 1960s and 70s remains the hubbub of today. In a recent *Tikkun* article, "What Kind of State is a Jewish State?," Michael Walzer wonders whether Israel will continue on its course of becoming simply "an Israeli state, Jewishness a feature of its founding but a declining influence on its existence" (303). Like Gittelsohn, but offering significantly more elaboration, Walzer blames the Israeli ultra-Orthodox Jews' obdurate allegiance to the tedious and outmoded Halakha (Jewish law) for the waning of religion in the state. Such an uncompromising interpretation of scripture "reduce[s] the number of ways of being Jewish" and, Walzer suggests, sours today's Israelis to Judaism altogether (305). Alternatively, Thomas Friedman argues that a waning of ritual observance in Israel was inevitable anyway because, in a state brimming with Jews, "[Jews] don't need to join a synagogue in order to avoid assimilation or feel part of a community. . . . They avoid assimilation simply by paying taxes to a Jewish state, speaking Hebrew, and sending their children to state schools, which observe the Jewish holidays as national holidays" (475). Several Israelis today bemoan what they perceive as the moral decline of their country that has accompanied its rampant secularism. In a recent issue of *The Jerusalem Post International Edition,* Rabbi Yehuda Amital laments this moral decline: "More crime, more violence, more materialism. Could you imagine 26 years ago that Madonna would perform here in front of 100,000 people?" (Qtd. in Keinon 9). Secularism, indeed, yields bitter fruit as far as Amital is concerned.

While the intellectuals above continue to debate the reasons for the religious decline in Israel—some blaming the uncompromising ultra-Orthodox, others blaming the corruption of today's youth, while still others, like Friedman, view the decline as a natural step toward Israel's normalcy as a nation—Nissenson adds his own artistic wrinkle to the secular phenomenon as he explores the emotional cost of religion's ironic decline in the Holy Land. In "The Blessing," for example, Nissenson problematizes Gittelsohn's assumption that Israelis have simply ignored the religious component of their Jewish identity. If this were true in Yitshaak's case, he would not suffer such alienation from God's firmament at the story's close. Indeed, the tragedy of the story is that he *cannot* ignore the religious component that remains irretrievably lost to him in Israel. What is more, in Nissenson's other Israel story in *A Pile of Stones,* he suggests that the indigenous Arabs, who live close by the first Israeli settlers, may impel the Jews of Israel to adopt a militaristic code and, thereby, drift further and further from their Diaspora roots of religious passivism.

In "The Well," the members of a *kibbutz* face a difficult decision when a drought devastates the neighboring Bedouin village. Since the *kibbutz's* well could probably see them and the Bedouin through until the next rain, should they act upon their charitable impulses and allow the Bedouin use of their water? Our narrator, the elected secretary of the *kibbutz*, is reluctant to "become officially involved in Bedouin affairs at all," as, "time and time again, experience has taught us that when we so much as offer them any material assistance, much less demonstrate a willingness for a real peace, it is refused, and then taken for nothing but a display of weakness on our part" (*APOS* 89, 90). Still, Grossman's proposal to share their water with their Arab neighbors passes by almost two to one after he describes the misery in the Bedouin village. He tells the narrator, "You should have seen the camp. . . . They're rationing what water they have, and the kids have sores on their lips—the corners of their mouths . . . They surrounded me with tin cans, begging for water, as one would beg for alms" (*APOS* 97).

The past failures of such charitable acts notwithstanding, the narrator seems optimistic that this gesture on the part of his *kibbutz* may bring about a lasting peace with the Bedouin. His description of the friendship and physical resemblance of Grossman and Ali, the Bedouin Sheik's son, suggests that perhaps the Arabs and Israelis do not lead such discordant lives after all:

> [T]heir physical resemblance is striking. They are even the same height and, but for the slightly darker cast of the Bedouin's skin, might be taken for blood relatives, cousins, or even brothers, perhaps, with their high cheekbones, and long mustaches that emphasize their thin lips. . . . It is not hard to imagine that they are recalling the memories they have of shepherding together, near Halutza. (*APOS* 101)

Ultimately, however, the disparity between the Bedouin ethical code and the Israelis' proves insurmountable, despite the superficial kinship between Grossman and Ali. The Sheik of the Bedouin, Ahmed, taxes his people for the use of the *kibbutz* water. Thus, the poorest Arabs who need the water the most cannot drink from the well. Grossman confronts Ali about the impropriety, but to no avail. The Bedouin maintains that his father, as Sheik, has every right to tax his people as he wishes. Grossman thus retracts the *kibbutz's* offer and he and Ali engage in a fistfight. Nissenson illustrates the seemingly insurmountable tensions between Arab and Jew through Grossman, who tells our narrator how the fight began: "[Ali] blames us for everything.... There was nothing I could say. He says his father is right. We've taken their land, and now deny them water.... He called me a dog of a Jew" (*APOS* 114).

We should consider here how recent post-colonial critical perspectives apply to Nissenson's constructions of his Arab characters. Particularly compelling, I believe, are Tzvetan Todorov's reflections concerning Christopher Columbus's attitude with regard to the Indians in the New World. Relying largely upon Columbus's journal entries, Todorov notes that he either perceived the Indians as identical to himself or as an inferior distortion of himself. "What is denied," Todorov continues, "is the existence of a human substance truly other, something capable of being not merely an imperfect state of oneself" (42). Todorov borrows, perhaps, from Edward Said's earlier contention that colonizers often construct the other as a "contrasting image" to help define their own identity (*Orientalism* 2). One can easily apply Todorov's and Said's observations to Nissenson's "The Well." After all, the Bedouin do emerge as either identical to the Jew (dramatized above in the physical likeness between Grossman and Ali) or as distortions—contrasting images—of Jewish virtue. The Bedouin violence (the narrator describes the Bedouin attack on the *kibbutz* eleven years before) contrasts with the Jews' passivity, their polygamy contrasts with the Jews' monogamy, and their autocratic sheikdom contrasts with the Jews' social democracy.

Said most cogently expresses the main concern of post-colonial critics when it comes to such constructions of the other: "How does one *represent* another culture? Is the notion of a distinct culture (or race, or religion, or civilization) a useful one, or does it always get involved either in self-congratulation (when one discusses one's own) or hostility and aggression (when one discusses the 'other')?" (*Orientalism* 325). These questions should concern all serious contemporary readers. With regard to Nissenson's "The Well," one must concede that Nissenson's one-dimensional construction of the Arab as a mere contrast to Jewish virtue sheds little "useful" light on the Bedouin culture. In Nissenson's defense, however, he does not intend to plumb the depths of the Arab civilization in "The Well," but to suggest the inadequacy of a benevolent socialist ideology amid hostile Arab neighbors. As a matter of record, early Zionist settlements were constantly under attack by surrounding Arab villages; one can hardly fault Nissenson for dramatizing the Jewish perspective of such aggression. Moreover, the sociopolitical framework of most Arab cultures does contrast sharply with Israel's sociopolitical framework; virtual autocracies continue as the order of the day in several Arab countries (one thinks of Assad's Syria or Hussein's Iraq). While one would be hard pressed to argue that Nissenson even attempts to engage the Bedouin social and political system as a "distinct culture," his constructions are still "useful" in that he locates one source of the seemingly inexorable tension between Jewish and Arab leaders in the Middle East—the disparity between their visions of what we might call the social contract.

To Nissenson's credit, this tension persists today between certain Arab states and Western democracies. For example, several Americans who opposed the recent war against Iraq argued primarily that Kuwait, a profoundly undemocratic country, did not merit the protection of the world's most powerful democracies. And Kuwait's resistance to adopting democratic reforms in the wake of the war has been seen as something of a rebuke to the countries that fought, ostensibly at least, on Kuwait's behalf. Even within Arab cultures today, tension mounts as the autocratic precepts of the powerful few clash against the democratic impulses of the many. Two prominent Palestinian spokespeople, Dr. Haidar Abdel-Shafi and Hanan Ashrawi, have been openly critical of Yasir Arafat's strong-arm style and his refusal to listen to dissenting views from within the Palestinian ranks (Arafat, for example, disgusted by the pro-Jordanian editorial stance of the East Jerusalem newspaper *An Nahar*, simply censored the paper). Ashrawi and other key PLO members quit as a result of Arafat's inflexibility, his apparent concern over just whose face will appear on Palestinian currency. Says Abdel-Shafi, "There is a justified worry that if there is no acceptance of democratic practice, we could face an autocratic state" (Qtd. in Haberman 12). Dr. Iyad Sarraj, a Palestinian psychiatrist and director of the Gaza Community Mental Health Project, one-ups Abdel-Shafi's doubts that democracy will prevail in Jericho and the Gaza strip:

> The worst is yet to come. The worst is that we will be a complete police state: corruption, dictatorship, chronic pockets of violence. Oh yes, I think this is inevitable. The P.L.O. as a machine is not ready for government and definitely it is not ready for democracy. Democracy means accepting that the people in the street are allowed to pose a threat to the people in power, and the P.L.O. cannot even contemplate that idea. (Qtd. in Kelly 60)

Dr. Sarraj's fears are neither unjustified nor atypical among Palestinians. Many fear that a Palestinian civil war might be imminent. Given the present milieu, then, one can argue that when Nissenson dramatizes the oppressiveness of an autocratic Bedouin sheikdom, he addresses an essential tension within certain Arab cultures that exacerbates Arab-Israeli relations, as well.

In his memoir, *Notes from the Frontier,* Nissenson continues to explore the practical weakness of socialism amid autocratic and hostile Arab neighbors, but he also explores its spiritual cost and the spiritual cost of an eminently practical Israeli militarism. Nissenson divides his memoir into two sections, "Summer 1965" and "June 1967," in which he records accordingly his two trips to the *kibbutz* of Mayan Baruch, located perilously along the Syrian border. In the memoir, Nissenson examines two ideologies, socialism and militarism, that challenge religious adherence in Israel. Jewish-American intellectuals in the 1960s had already explored the practical failings of Israeli socialism. In "The Problems of Israeli Socialism," Ben Halpern notes that the socialist Zionists "outlined no more than vague visions of the tasks that came after victory" and based their strategy of settling Israel "on no more than sheer utopian commitment to communal brotherhood" (53). In *Notes from the Frontier,* Nissenson implicitly argues that the socialist ideology, regardless of its dubious practical merits, cannot sustain the Israelis' spiritual well-being. On the surface, the socialist prescription which one *kibbutznik,* Aliza Wolfe, touts so fervently (equal duties and rights for all), seems a welcome alternative to the bitter pill offered the Jews in Europe during the first half of the twentieth century. Aliza describes how her parents remained in Germany during the Holocaust because they thought their German citizenship would protect them, but were ultimately deported to Auschwitz and murdered. Another member of Mayan Baruch, Aaron Stern, emphasizes to Nissenson the moral righteousness of socialism in contrast to the moral corruption in which he was forced to partake as a white South African. Though he works tirelessly in the orchard, Stern celebrates *kibbutz* life since "exploitation is impossible" (*Notes* 50).

In contrast to the apparent timeliness of socialism, Nissenson portrays the religious *Saba* (Hebrew for grandfather) who lives on the *kibbutz* as a hopeless anachronism. He must omit portions of his daily prayers because he can never form a *minyan* (a group of at least ten Jewish adults required during certain prayers); since the *kibbutz* food is not kosher, he lives on the brink of starvation on what little kosher food his daughter can prepare for him; and, though he trains the young members of the *kibbutz* for their Bar Mitzvah services, it is abundantly clear that none of the children embrace the religious portent of the service (more on this below). There can be little doubt that when the *Saba* dies, the last trace of formal religious observance in Mayan Baruch will die with him.

That said, the straight socialist ideology which replaces religion on the *kibbutz* proves thin fare for the Jewish soul. Take, for instance, the socialist version of the Bar Mitzvah service. For Jews, this service traditionally represents a sublime initiation into the adult religious community—the moment when the Bar Mitzvah embraces God's covenant. Alternatively, the thirteen-year-olds at Mayan Baruch break into laughter during the religious ceremony and the parents maintain an "embarrassed silence" (*Notes* 164). For the Mayan Baruch youths, their Bar Mitzvah represents their acceptance of the prosaic duties of adult life on the *kibbutz,* not a covenantal acceptance. They must complete a list of tasks to prove that they are ready to assume this burden, and the list that Aliza's daughter, Ruthie, prepares curiously echoes the pragmatism of Benjamin Franklin's list of thirteen virtues with their precepts. Number four on Ruthie's list, "put in a full day of work, eight or nine hours, according to sex, in a chosen area of the kibbutz," would no doubt please Franklin, who prescribes resolve as number four on his own list: "resolve to perform what you ought. Perform without fail what you resolve." The spiritual sterility of the socialist Bar Mitzvah emerges most explicitly in Ruthie's completion of her first task, to write an essay on Moses. Consider a portion of her first draft:

> The repressive Egyptian feudal system needed a cheap supply of labor, which the Hebrews provided. They farmed the land and helped build the pyramids and temples. Originally primitive nomads, they had no class solidarity. Moses organized them. Brought up in Pharaoh's court, he was educated and had a higher culture, like Herzl in comparison with the eastern European Jewish masses. Moses made the Hebrews class conscious and aware that they were being oppressed . . . (*Notes* 93)

Barring extensive revision, Ruthie's essay exposes the antiseptic effect of socialism on religion. Missing from her analysis of this reluctant prophet is, of course, God, and Moses's sense of religious duty which motivates him, a stutterer, to adhere to God's command and lead the Jews out of bondage. With considerable mental agility and terseness, Ruthie reduces Moses to merely an effective socialist leader of the oppressed masses. Indeed, one senses that Edward Alexander had essays like Ruthie's in mind when he recently reflected, "The narrow, often religiously illiterate, culture of socialist Zionism produced a system of education that has worked to detach Jews from their Jewish roots and weaken the bonds that most profoundly attach people to life" ("American Jews" 23).

Nissenson's wife, Marilyn, senses this spiritual and emotional void that threatens the members of the *kibbutz* since they have adopted a socialist ideology to replace religion. She says, "Faith is something that all children should have, at one point" (*Notes* 67). Later, she comments that "Life can't be contained by any ideology. It's too complex, too diverse . . ." (*Notes* 135). Moreover, even the most devout socialists in the *kibbutz* eventually realize that the socialist ideology cannot adequately replace religion. Just after the Jewish forces liberate Jerusalem in the Six-Day War, most members of the *kibbutz* cry upon hearing the radio broadcast of the blowing of the shofar at the Western Wall. Even before the war, Aliza votes with Nat to include the traditional Bible reading at the Bar Mitzvah ceremony and later tells Marilyn that she would vote the same way again. Nat, for his part, asserts, "I come from a good socialist home where I was brought up as an atheist as a matter of course" (*Notes* 116). However, he campaigns to include the religious elements of the Bar Mitzvah ceremony because he "knows that religion has been the sum and substance of Jewish civilization for almost five thousand years. . . . It's what defined and preserved us all throughout the Dispersion. A commitment to adhere to the law, the morality of the Torah, no matter what" (*Notes* 117). While Nat embraces the essential precepts of socialism and does not believe in God, he also recognizes that the jargon of socialism (some of which Ruthie relies upon in her essay on Moses) lacks the tangible quality of religious commentaries, that no socialist diatribe on the "class struggle" can match Rabbi Yehudi's interpretation of "Justice."

One senses that the Jewish Israeli ethos will remain a confused one as long as the majority of Nat's cohorts lack his perceptiveness. He knows that the *kibbutz* errs in presenting socialism to the children as a complete break from religion, since the socialist principles—the sanctity of work, the return of exiles and the creation of a just society—are truly religious ideas. While others at Mayan Baruch may acknowledge their religious feelings, he alone knows why he experiences those feelings. After the Six-Day War, he explains to Nissenson why he does not believe that Israel should give back Jerusalem to the Arabs: "Why did the early Zionists, who were atheists, insist on returning here? . . . It had to be *Eretz*, or nothing. . . . It was as if they unconsciously assumed that a covenant between the Jews and God still existed . . . and sometimes I feel that deep down we feel the same way" (*Notes* 198). Indeed, only Nat realizes that religion serves as the foundation of Israeli socialism. He asks the crucial question that permeates Nissenson's work: "Is it possible to create a humane civilization without Him?" (*Notes* 198).

Just as the straight socialist precepts of Mayan Baruch cannot satisfy the members' spiritual needs, these precepts cannot physically protect them either. When push comes to shove, militarism—not socialism—ensures the physical survival of the Israelis on the *kibbutz*. As one would suspect, violence besets the Israeli *kibbutzniks* along the Syrian border just as surely as do blistered hands from incessant labor in the orchards and poorly prepared institutional food. Syrian raids on border *kibbutzim* and Israeli counter-raids take their place alongside the other routine events on the Syrian border. Small wonder that Nissenson examines closely the moral cost of such routine militarism. Like Bellow's fictional and non-fictional depictions of the Six-Day War, Nissenson's grotesque description of the bloated Syrian corpses that lie rotting on the Golan Heights after the war and his description of the meter's worth of one *kibbutz* member's remains whom the Israeli forces have napalmed by accident go a long way toward dispelling any romantic perceptions of Israel's victory.

Nissenson scrutinizes such Israeli militarism more thoroughly than Bellow through the recollections of Shlomo Wolfe, Aliza's husband, who offers Nissenson a glimpse of one of the more sordid military episodes that ensured Israel's victory in War of Independence of 1948. As an Officer of Palmach, the elite body of the Jewish Defense Force, Shlomo orders his troops to shell a mosque in Lod from which the Arabs are firing machine guns and throwing hand grenades. When the Arabs surrender and Shlomo looks inside the mosque, he sees that "the whitewashed walls were all pitted and splashed with blood. There was nobody—not a soul left alive" (*Notes* 32). Shlomo realizes that the UN will condemn their attack of a Muslim holy place so he orders eight Arabs who have surrendered elsewhere in the town to clean up the mosque and carry out the corpses from inside. Then, because the eight Arabs will surely expose the Israeli attack on the mosque to the international press, Shlomo orders a soldier under his command to murder the defenseless Arabs.

In a recent article, one Jewish-American intellectual, Sanford Pinsker, notes the "special burden of those who look at the Middle East from the smug safety of American soil" (400). This smug safety probably accounts for Nissenson's decision to resist overt judgment of Shlomo's decision (in this respect, he resembles Saul Bellow in *To Jerusalem and Back,* who also resists judging Israel's militarism since, as an American, he does not have to live amid aggressive Arab nations). But, in presenting Shlomo's recollection of the event—which obviously troubles Shlomo—and Nat's opinion of Shlomo's decision, Nissenson suggests that such Israeli aggression threatens to corrupt the Jewish soul and, thus, deserves careful inspection. Nissenson offers the massacre at the Lod mosque as a litmus test of militarism's viability as an element of the Israeli identity.

Shlomo, apparently, does not regret ordering the assassination of the eight Arab soldiers. He tells Nissenson that "because we had Lod, Tel Aviv was secure . . . hell, if I had to do it all over again, I would. It was necessary (*Notes* 33). Shlomo also extols the usefulness of a few enthusiastic killers who enjoy committing such murders and resents the Orthodox community of his childhood town who, "surrounded by a majority of armed, hostile Arabs, humiliate him" since they remain docile (*Notes* 26). Nat also opines that "when all is said and done, Wolfe was right. . . . He did the right thing. If it had been up to me, I would have botched it" (*Notes* 118). While it would seem that Nat embraces the militarism embodied in Shlomo's decision, we must ask why he believes he would have "botched it." The answer, I believe, lies in his earlier recognition that the Jews of Israel could only embrace militarism after they "denied God and decided to acquire power to redeem themselves"; by so doing, Nat contends, the Jews "were destined to become like everyone else. Murderers" (*Notes* 70). The militaristic code Israel adopts, then, according to Nat, stands foursquare against religion—more specifically, against the covenantal belief in the coming of the Messiah. Nat, we must remember, recognizes the importance of the religious component of the Israeli ethos. Thus, through Nat's sensitive perspective, Nissenson exposes the clash between these two essential elements of Israeli identity which would probably cause Nat to "botch" the execution Wolfe carries out. In an interview with Harold Ribalow, Nissenson straightforwardly notes the bitter irony of the situation in which the modern Israelis, like Nat, find themselves: they were forced to "torture and kill in order to accomplish their mission [of creating a Jewish state]" (Nissenson, "A Conversation" 154). Because Nissenson emphasizes the importance of the religious component throughout *Notes from the Frontier*, we are forced to question whether the practical benefits of Israeli militarism outweigh the spiritual cost of torturing and killing. As several religious citizens of a now overwhelmingly secular Israel suggest, perhaps Israel should not strive so hard to become like everyone else.

In his second collection of short stories, *In the Reign of Peace*, Nissenson examines, through a variety of fictional circumstances, this essential conundrum, which he addresses in his memoir and in *A Pile of Stones*: does militarism, a practical necessity, and the Jews' concomitant (as Nissenson sees it) rejection of religion undermine the redemptive possibilities in Israel? He also examines further the viability of Israeli socialism. Cynthia Ozick contends that "it is a limitation . . . that this second book of stories is no more than a continuation of *A Pile of Stones*, his first" ("Christians" 4). What probably frustrates Ozick more than anything else is that Nissenson comes no closer in the stories of the second collection to an unequivocal moral stance concerning the troubled Israeli ethos he exposes, torn between militarism and passivism, a secular life and a religious life. Brief explications of five of the six stories set in Israel may suffice to illustrate how Nissenson's earlier fictional concerns resonate in his second collection. I will examine one story, "Lamentations," in considerably more detail, for Nissenson, therein, so powerfully addresses the religious crisis that burdens modern Israel.

In the title story, a young Orthodox Jew shows a socialist *kibbutznik* a mouse being eaten alive by ants to help him visualize what the Messiah will redeem in the "reign of peace"; he, thereby, exposes the paltriness of the socialist alternative to religion. In four other stories, Nissenson shifts his focus away from the problem of socialism and toward the problem of militarism. A Jewish doctor in Palestine during the British occupation wonders in "The Throne of Good" whether any good can come from the violent tactics of his boyhood friend's nationalist gang and, in "Forcing the End," we are forced to consider the moral implications when a different militant nationalist group, "The Knives," murder an Orthodox rabbi who espouses passivism. In "Crazy Old Man," an elderly Orthodox Jew shoots an Arab prisoner during the 1948 War of Independence—commits a sin of violence—to prevent two native

Israeli soldiers from tainting themselves with the sin. Finally, another religious Israeli laments Israel's adoption of a militaristic code in "Going Up" after he "goes up" to the Golan Heights just after the Six-Day War and sees the Arab carnage. He also finds it difficult to celebrate Jerusalem's liberation when he considers the story of the Israeli paratrooper who cries at the Western Wall because he does not know how to pray.

The quotation from the Babylonian Talmud which Nissenson uses as an epigram, "The Son of David will come when one generation of man is either totally guilty or totally innocent," leaves one wondering whether Israel will hasten the coming of the Messiah with their guilt; and in the stories briefly described above, Nissenson suggests that Israel's militarism might lead the new Israeli generation toward such guilt. However, several of these stories strain credulity owing to the imprecise fit, as noted earlier, of Nissenson's strict secular/militaristic, religious/passive dichotomy. As in *A Pile of Stones* and *Notes from the Frontier,* Nissenson insists on presenting a consistent religious antithesis to militarism that, as Harold Fisch notes, strikes a false chord since it "doesn't always work that way" in Israel (72). In the wake of increased Settler militancy in the Occupied Territories, one might modify Fisch's comment to read, it doesn't always work that way, especially now.

Still, in "Lamentations," Nissenson presents credible Orthodox and secular characters and powerfully casts their respective ideologies against one another. In the opening scene, Nissenson dramatizes what militarism has wrought upon Israel. A twenty-three-year-old pregnant woman, whose boyfriend was just killed in a battle against the Egyptians, tells her boyfriend's friend, Yigael, that she plans on marrying Uri over his grave so that her child will have his name. The young Israeli woman will marry a corpse. Although the scenario seems implausible, Nissenson contends that he bases the story "on the fact that several Israelis had told me this actually had taken place" ("A Conversation" 156). Unbelievably, Yigael resents Elana's luck thus far in the Middle East: "At her age, he had already buried his father and at least three good friends" (*ITROP* 154). As in *Notes from the Frontier,* then, Nissenson takes pains to emphasize the harsh realities of war. However, also as in Nissenson's memoir, the religious alternative to militarism seems archaic in "Lamentations." The religious waiter at the restaurant where Elana and Yigael are eating, like the *Saba* in *Notes from the Frontier,* seems a relic of a bygone age in an antithetically modern and secular Israel. Yigael muses, "he seemed absurdly out of place among the soiled tablecloths, waxed-paper napkins, and potted palms with wilting fronds that stood about the room. With his straw-colored, untrimmed beard, his earlocks, the yarmulke on the bald crown of his head, he looked to Yigael as if he had wandered in here by mistake on his way to one of the dark, smelly synagogues in Mea Shearim" (*ITROP* 147–148). The traditional religious aspect of the waiter, indeed, seems absurd amid the artificial elements of the restaurant, with its potted palms and waxed-paper napkins.

Like Shlomo in *Notes from the Frontier,* Yigael harbors bitter feelings for religious passivists who view evil as part of God's design. He cannot keep contempt out of his voice when he speaks to the waiter and thinks, "He had met this type before—the kind who had undoubtedly been deported without protest, who at night in the barracks, had never failed to gratefully mumble the blessing over a crust of moldy bread. His yellowish, bloodshot eyes had seen in the heaps of naked corpses the will of God" (*ITROP* 150). Yigael, here, expresses his anger at those religious Jews who, even in the wake of the Holocaust and God's silence, maintain their faith and refuse to fight for the creation of a Jewish state. Yigael and Elana posit the obsolescence of such religious faith in modern Israel. After the waiter attempts to hurry them out of the restaurant so that he can close up and observe Tisha b'Av, Yigael notes the silliness of its observance: "Tisha b'Av makes no sense . . . Not any more. There's no need for it any more" (*ITROP* 153). Nissenson chooses an apt holiday through which his protagonist argues this point. For on Tisha b'Av, religious Jews commemorate the Babylonians' destruction of the Jewish Temple in Jerusalem. Since the modern secular Jews, like Yigael, have liberated Jerusalem, why still mourn its destruction? Elana recites a poem that encapsulates this secular Israeli view which all but supplants the waiter's religious views in modern Israel:

> There is no angel there.
> The boy must free himself
> And seize the knife,
> Bind up his father,
> Throw the altar down.
>
> There is no Covenant.
> The sacrifice we make
> Is for a portion promised us
> By no one but ourselves. (*ITROP* 153–154)

The poem, to be sure, embodies the ethos of the secular Israeli in most of Nissenson's work. Elana, Yigael and their secular cohorts in Israel see themselves as the Isaac-figure in the poem who must reject the covenant his father embraces, even when God instructs Abraham to bind Isaac down and murder him as a sacrifice. The secular Israelis reject God's covenant by reclaiming Israel themselves instead of waiting for the Messiah, as prophecied. As the poem suggests, they make a promise to *themselves* to reclaim their rightful portion, Israel. In contrast, the roughly 15 percent ultra-Orthodox Jews in Israel whom the waiter represents—by still mourning the destruction of Jerusalem—embrace the covenant and admonish secular Israelis for their eschewal of religious faith. When it becomes apparent to the waiter that Yigael does not celebrate Tisha b'Av, he accosts him, "You call yourself a Jew?" (*ITROP* 148).

When Nissenson pits the ultra-Orthodox Israeli against the unabashedly secular Israeli, he engages an essential tension of the Israeli ethos. And there is no shortage of Jewish-American intellectuals willing to offer their spin on Israel's identity crisis. If my sense of the zeitgeist is correct, most of these intellectuals have great difficulty appreciating the unwavering moral righteousness of the Haredim minority in Israel. Sanford Pinsker, who lived for a year in 1971 with a Hasidic sect in New York, comments with regret that "I no longer feel as sympathetic, as uncritically accepting, as I once did. There are, alas, Hasidic Jews who strike me as very foreign indeed—not because they sport broad-brimmed black hats and long, flowing *capote,* unkempt beards and ear-locks—but because they seek to impose their definitions of Jewishness itself . . . onto a secular majority" ("William" 408–409). Leslie Fiedler suggests poignantly his own estrangement from the Haredim: ". . . in Zion (especially when some Orthodox zealot screams at me to put out my Sabbath Eve cigar) I know that I am an American and doubt that I am a Jew" (8). One thinks of the waiter, above, who admonishes Yigael—a member of the secular majority—for not behaving as a real Jew ought on Tisha b'Av. Ruth Wisse foregoes Pinsker's and Fiedler's regretful tone and administers a healthy dose of vitriol, instead, when she considers the passivity of the ultra-Orthodox. Says Wisse, "exemption from national service in the name of the Lord, in a country that requires so much self-sacrifice from its citizens, corrupts the moral integrity of both religion and politics" (*If I Am Not For Myself* 105). Ruth Wisse's acerbic assessment of the passive Haredim in Israel, I believe, bespeaks the problem several (perhaps most) American Jews have in appreciating the perspective of those who unabashedly approach and chastise their secular protectors when they commit a transgression of the Sabbath. I say "protectors" because the military service of these secular Jews ensures that their ultra-Orthodox critics can live in a state in which they can safely and openly observe the Sabbath in the first place.

While an increasing number of American Jews scoff at the political actions of the Israeli ultra-Orthodox, Nissenson concerns himself largely with the spiritual implications of the beleaguered religious ethos in Israel. On this score, he does not afford his major characters an easy resolution. An outright rejection of the religious aspect of Israeli identity, Nissenson suggests, simply won't do, for emotional loss invariably accompanies such a rejection. One thinks of Yitshaak in "The Blessing," who loses a piece of his spirit when he loses the religious component of his ethos; or Nat and his fellow *kibbutzniks* in *Notes from the Frontier,* who sense this imminent threat to their spiritual selves and, thus, cling to some small shred of religious faith after the Six-Day War. Likewise, Yigael cannot turn a deaf ear to the religious component of his identity. The waiter's chastisement, "You call yourself a Jew?" stings him more than it appears. For as Yigael walks Elana home, he looks through a window of a small synagogue and "the sight held him: the Ark and the *bimah* draped in black cloth, the overturned benches, the fifteen or twenty men seated in a dim circle of light on the stone floor. Their shadows wavered on the wall" (*ITROP* 156). Though Elana urges Yigael to continue on since she wants to shower, he stands transfixed by the sight of the Ark (which holds the Torah), the *bima* (a synagogue pulpit) and, especially, the nasal sounding prayers which rise and fall with the wind. As Elana tries to hash out the details of her eerie wedding, Yigael must avert his face, "astonished by the tears that welled up in his eyes" (*ITROP* 158). Nissenson, then, wages the battle between the secular and religious ethos within Yigael, torn between two aesthetic forms: the Zionist poem, which appeals to Yigael's sense of justice and pragmatism, and the nasal prayers emanating from the synagogue, which penetrate the walls of his anesthetized heart. Nowhere does Nissenson so tersely and poignantly dramatize the torn Israeli identity.

Nissenson calls his story "a lament for the death of God" (Kurzweil 17). His assessment, however, brings to mind D. H. Lawrence's dictum, "trust the tale, not the teller." For while Nissenson's comment cuts close to the bone of the story's message, it demands qualification. In the final analysis, the story seems to be not about the death of God at all, but about the death of the modern Israeli's faith in God. Yigael would, no doubt, maintain a derisive distance from the synagogue if he truly believed that God were dead. Rather, he stands transfixed by the praying congregation and cries because, like Yitshaak in "The Blessing," he cannot regain his religious faith. He can peer through the windows of the synagogue, but he cannot participate in their prayers. Unfortunately, as in "The Blessing," religion seems irretrievably lost to the modern Israeli in "Lamentations."

All told, Nissenson dramatizes in his work an altogether unenviable predicament for the modern Israeli. For while he posits the importance of the religious component of the nation's ethos, he seriously doubts that religious faith can persist in Israel given the Jews' dependence on militarism for their survival; the sterile socialism that supplants religion on the *kibbutzim* exacerbates matters, as well. Nissenson, for the most part, shares the perspective of a prominent Israeli Orthodox rabbi, David Hartman, who says "You can't build a Jewish state on the basis of national pride alone. The Jewish soul requires spiritual nourishment. . . . [The Jews] need to feel that their families and lives are built around a Judaism that can live with the modern world" (Qtd. in Friedman 315). We can derive this much from Nissenson's work. He has openly, in fact, criticized straight Israeli nationalism "because it has no mythic base. It does not move you in an unconscious way" ("A Conversation" 151). The rub, of course, is that—unlike the Orthodox rabbi—Nissenson shows little faith in the viability of Israel's mythic base, Judaism, amid the welter of opposing influences in the volatile Middle East. I would add that Nissenson's cynical vision accounts for only the roughly 50 percent of Israel's Jews who are secular Zionists; as I have already implied, he does not consider the case of 35 percent of Israel's Jews who are religious Zionists. These modern Orthodox Jews *do* serve in the army and support the secular Zionist state, but do not see the secular state as a substitute for religion. They are able to balance the state's secular and militaristic ethos with their Orthodox precepts—a balance that eludes Nissenson's major characters.

In a *National Jewish Monthly* interview, Nissenson comments, "I'm dying to set a book in Jerusalem some day. There's something about that light and that ambiance that makes me want to capture it" ("A Conversation" 12). Evidently, other Jewish-American writers sense the fruitfulness of the Israeli setting, as well. As Ruth Wisse cannily observes, writers "who feel the historic, moral and religious weight of Judaism, and want to represent it in literature, have had to ship their characters out of town by Greyhound or magic carpet, to an unlikely *shtetl,* to Israel . . . to other times and other climes, in search of pan-Jewish fictional atmospheres" ("American Jewish Writing, Act II" 45). One of the most promising of these young writers, Nessa Rapoport, accounts for this recent trend and places her finger on the pulse of contemporary Jewish-American literature when she calls for a "Jewishly educated and culturally confident group of writers" (xxix). Indeed, the cultural confidence contemporary Jewish-American writers now enjoy goes hand-in-hand, I believe, with their increasing resolve to turn toward Israel as a setting through which to explore American Jewish identity (I am thinking of writers like Tova Reich, Anne Roiphe, Joanna Spiro, and Nessa Rapoport). Thus, whatever the limitations of Nissenson's approach (e.g., his one-dimensional constructions of the Arab, the reductiveness of his secular/militaristic, religious/passive dichotomy), his predilection for the Israeli setting anticipates the direction in which we can expect the increasing number of culturally confident, theologically oriented Jewish-American writers to follow. That Hugh Nissenson possessed this cultural confidence from the start of his career in the early 1960s is a testament to his theological imagination and intellectual courage.

Chapter 6

ZIONISM IN CHAIM POTOK'S *THE CHOSEN*, MESSIANIC COMPLICATIONS, AND CURRENT CRISES

Unlike the case of Hugh Nissenson, most readers (Jewish and gentile) are eminently familiar with Chaim Potok's work. His first novel, *The Chosen* (1967), was a huge commercial success. It carved a niche for itself on the best-seller list for thirty-eight weeks and was later made into a movie starring Rod Steiger and Maximilian Schell. Daphne Merkin aptly captures the hoopla surrounding the novel when she comments, "After all the countless portrayals in American fiction of wandering and assimilated Jews—from Malamud's S. Levin to Bellow's Moses Herzog to Roth's Alexander Portnoy—the literary public, at least a large and enthusiastic segment of it, would seem to be ready for Chaim Potok's version of the American Jew—one who has never left the traditional Jewish community" ("Why Potok" 73). Still, while the public embraced Potok's novel, several initial reviewers and critics remain unconvinced of the book's literary merit (the inverse, one might note, of the reception of Hugh Nissenson's work). Curt Leviant, calling the novel "pseudo-literary," notes the "flat, cliché-ridden prose" which accounts, in his estimation, for an "imaginative gap between the suggestive theme—an American Hasid caught between tradition and the secular culture—and its execution" (76, 77). In a review published by *Commentary*, Baruch Hochman asserts that the novel lacks "imaginative vigor," and labels it a "wish fulfillment fairy tale" (108). One critic's contention that the novel represents "neither high art nor trash" perhaps best encapsulates the lukewarm reception of the novel by the critics (Grebstein 27). To my mind, though, Bruce Cook offers the most provocative spin on *The Chosen* when he observes that Chaim Potok "is not in any proper sense a writer.... the text and the neatly bearded visage in the jacket photo suggest that Mr. Potok is a rabbi. If I am correct, he will continue to be a rabbi for many years, and he will never write another novel" (23).

What intrigues me about Cook's comment—utterly wrong-headed, of course—is how it accounts for the predeliction on the part of pro-Potok critics to emphasize the universal implications of the novelist's work (one should probably note, in Cook's defense, that he goes on to offer a more or less laudatory review). Given Cook's virtual dismissal of Potok as a serious writer based upon the novel's overtly Jewish content (and, evidently, Potok's "Jewish" appearance), should it really come as a surprise that defenders of the novel stress the universal or "American" elements of this distinctively *Jewish*-American novel? Sanford Marovitz, for one, feels the exigence of such a strategy. In "Freedom, Faith, and Fanaticism: Cultural Conflict in the Novels of Chaim Potok," Marovitz asserts that "the significance of learning the local in order to compre-hend the universal ... may be applied to Potok's American Jewish nov-els" (131–132). Marovitz continues, "In [Potok's] fiction, it is the strug-gle for meaning and self-knowledge in the multiple entanglements of twentieth-century cultural confrontations that is central, though the actors who share in that struggle are all Jewish" (132). Like Marovitz, who here relegates the Jewishness of Potok's work to a subordinate clause, Potok himself emphasizes the universal significance of his nov-els. Rebuking those who view him as merely a hyphenated American writer, those who, in Potok's words, "take a book about Jews and imme-diately slot it in a lower echelon," Potok argues, "... I am writing about my world in precisely the same way Faulkner wrote about Yoknapataw-pha County. And nobody in a million years will convince me that Yoknapatawpha County is more American than the world I am writing about" ("A Conversation" 87). Reflecting upon his career in a more recent essay, Potok adds that his particular world of Orthodox Judaism "can be any world: Christian, Muslim, Native-American, African-American, Hispanic, secular, Australian aborigine, others ..." ("The Invisible Map" 30).

Potok is certainly not the first ethnically distinct writer to insist upon the universal implications of his work. We must remember that both William Faulkner's and James Joyce's settings seemed to be remote locales, indeed, through which to explore the universal human condi-tion. Faulkner, thus, persistently touted the universal significance of his postage stamp of native soil. Likewise, James Joyce claimed that if he could get to the heart of Dublin he could get to the heart of all the cities of the world. Moreover, Potok's most notable cohorts on the Jewish-American literary scene—Saul Bellow, Philip Roth, and Bernard Malamud—have each rejected the label, "Jewish-American writer," largely since they consider themselves every bit as American a writer as, say, John Updike, to whom no one refers as a Protestant-American writer.

I belabor this penchant of minority-culture writers and their critics to emphasize the universal implications of their work not to dispute the validity of such claims. The essential dynamics of the culture war that Potok dramatizes in *The Chosen*—between two core cultures, Orthodox Judaism and secularism—do apply in varying degrees to countless other cultures in conflict with one another. However, in concentrating upon the universal implications of *The Chosen* and minimizing the culturally specific elements of the novel, we lose more than merely a Talmudic nuance here, a whiff of gefilte fish there; we neglect Potok's exploration of the essential tension, which persists today within the Jewish community, between secular Zionism and the messianic precepts of Judaism. As a Jewish-American writer who writes "as a Jew and because he is a Jew," as a writer who struggles in his fiction "to maintain the viability of Judaism as a living civilization," Potok cannot help but scrutinize this tension in his imaginative writing (Walden, "Chaim Potok" 19, 25). Critics thus far have only adumbrated the terms over which messianism and secular Zionism war with one another in the novel. In order to preserve the accessible dichotomy between Reb Saunder's Orthodoxy and the Malters' secular Zionism, critics rarely move beyond the following identification of the warring parties: "Reb Saunders supports a post-messianic Israel and bitterly denounces secular Zionism, while the Malters support the Zionist goals" (Kremer, "Chaim Potok" 235). Readers of Jewish-American fiction should take to heart the efforts of other minority-culture literature scholars who are beginning to celebrate rather than subordinate the differences of their culturally specific texts. For if we explore Potok's dramatization of the specific culture war between secular Zionism and messianism, we see that he complicates each position to illustrate the religious crisis that beset American Jews in the years following the Holocaust, when the case for a Jewish homeland suddenly gained significant political ground.

The overtly Zionist narrative perspective belies the extent of this religious crisis in the novel, upon which I will elaborate shortly. First, Reb Saunders—the *tzaddik* (righteous one) of an anti-Zionist Hasidic sect—comes off rather poorly for most of the novel. The silence with which he raises his brilliant son, Danny, seems utterly cruel. David Malter, the Zionist father of Reuven, tells his son, "There are better ways to teach a child compassion" (*TC* 253). Potok undercuts the Hasidic movement, in general, throughout the novel. He suggests that Danny's Hasidic sect stifles his spirit and his intellect in much the same way that the spider's web which Reuven sees imprisons its fly; when Danny reads about Hasidic Jewry in the library, he finds that a respected contemporary scholar regards certain aspects of their tradition "vulgar and disgusting" (*TC* 145); their rigid approach to Talmud also seems uselessly archaic compared to David Malter's exciting method of textual explication, which he teaches his son. Judah Stampfer criticizes Potok's harsh depiction of the Hasid, claiming that he makes them "seem darker, more rigid, and more unattractive than they really are" (495). Likewise, Curt Leviant notes that, "Reading this book one would assume that Hasidim have neither humor nor life-zest" (77).

In contrast to the humorless and implacable Reb Saunders, David Malter, the Zionist, emerges as an ideal father and erudite scholar. Potok, in fact, models David Malter after his beloved father-in-law, whom he describes as "a very beautiful and enlightened Jew and a very lovely human being" ("A Conversation" 86). What is more, Potok has been open about the depth of his own Zionism and resides in Israel for part of each year. "[A] sense of loyalty toward Israel" is one of Potok's criteria for judging a good Jew (Potok, "Judaism" 15). Small wonder that Potok so convincingly presents Malter's Zionist arguments. Consider the power of Malter's convictions in the wake of the Holocaust:

> The world closed its doors, and six million Jews were slaughtered. What a world! . . . Some Jews say we should wait for God to send the Messiah. We cannot wait for God! We must make our own Messiah! We must rebuild American Jewry! And Palestine must become a Jewish homeland! We have suffered enough! How long must we wait for the Messiah? (*TC* 186)

Spirited language indeed. However, beyond the vehemence of Malter's rally-cry, Potok addresses the essential conflict between the mainstream American Jewish Zionists and the ultra-Orthodox anti-Zionists. For, unlike Malter, the ultra-Orthodox anti-Zionists believe that only the Messiah can restore Israel to the Jewish people. Jody Elizabeth Myers offers a cogent working definition of messianism: "Jewish messianism," she writes, "in all its permutations, is a belief in *God's* ultimate responsibility for the Exile of the Jews and in the certainty that *God*, through a redeemer, will restore His people to greatness, inaugurating a new era in accordance with biblical prophecies" [emphases mine] (4). Ultra-Orthodox anti-Zionists, like Reb Saunders, remained unyielding with regard to these messianic terms even after the Holocaust, as Danny explains tersely to Reuven: "A secular Jewish state in my father's eyes is a sacrilege, a violation of the Torah" (*TC* 188). Alternatively, most American Jews after the Holocaust viewed the foundation of a secular Jewish state as a practical necessity, since the few Jewish survivors in Europe returned to their home countries only to find themselves dispossessed and generally unwelcome (in Poland, for example, more than fifteen hundred Jewish survivors of the Holocaust were murdered by Poles in 1945 and 1946) (Dershowitz 146).

As critics like Leviant and Stampfer suggest, Potok plays something of a mug's game when he dramatizes the strife within the Jewish community over Zionism; several narrative elements in the text (some of which I note above) encourage us to support Malter's Zionism. But despite David Malter's compelling arguments, Potok subtly engages the major philosophical weakness of the Zionist movement, as Malter appropriates messianic language to espouse secular Zionism. With Myers's definition of messianism in mind, notice that Malter, in the above passage, does not reject messianism outright, but insists that the Jews themselves will make their own Messiah. Several historians of the Zionist movement note this "secularization of the messianic ideal," as Arthur Hertzberg puts it in his landmark study, *The Zionist Idea: A Historical Analysis and Reader* (1960, 18). Potok himself observes that "much of this messianic energy got diverted into the creation of the State of Israel" ("Judaism" 16), and Jacob Neusner also suggests that "Zionism appropriates the eschatological language and symbolism of classical Judaism . . . ," that "Jews who had lost hold of the mythic structure of the past were given a grasp on a new myth, one composed of the restructured remnants of the old one" ("Judaism" 311, 315). David Malter epitomizes this salient characteristic of the secular Zionist movement as he preserves the terminology of religious messianism while rejecting its fundamental precept—that God, and God only, can restore Israel and initiate the ingathering of the Jewish exiles.

The question presents itself: why did the secular Zionists, like David Malter, preserve the language of a theodicy they rejected? In a recent essay, Eli Lederhendler places his finger on the rhetorical power of this strategy. Says Lederhendler, "messianism was a mythic factor that provided romantic nationalists with a much richer dimension of oratory and conviction than anything that could be derived (negatively) from the rise of modern antisemitism or (positively) from the fluctuating will of the people" (30). This appropriation of messianic rhetoric by secular Zionists such as Malter strikes Jody Elizabeth Myers as covert and, thus, ethically problematic; she regards it as a "tactic designed to show that Zionism and messianism are not opposed to, but are compatible with, one another.... In short, it is a strategy for minimizing the radical break from tradition" (8). Here, Myers implicitly challenges the viability of secular Zionism. For how can messianism, "purged of its miraculous elements," as Jacob Katz phrases it, sustain the religious Jews' spiritual needs (Qtd. in Lederhendler 17)? While Myers's critique of the Zionists' ostensible messianism may seem like much ado about relatively nothing, other contemporary scholars of Judaism and Jewish culture share her concerns. Yehudi Adam, for example, sees no reason to hedge the deceptiveness of Zionism's secular ideology, couched in messianic terms: "... it is a plain fact that Judaism and the ideology of political Zionism are mutually exclusive" (282). In a recent *New York Times* Op-Ed piece, Rabbi Alexander Schindler—a Zionist—laments that "we have slipped into the sloppy equation that says Judaism equals Zionism equals Israel" (Qtd. in Goldman 27). Finally, in a symposium on American Jews and Israel, a prominent professor of Ethics and Theology at the Jewish Theological Seminary, Seymour Siegel, targets this "false messianism" of the Zionist movement as the major spiritual dilemma facing Israel today:

> The main problem [in Israel] revolves around the messianic (utopian) character of the state of Israel.... False messianism portends a grave danger to the body politic of the Jewish people because it promises more than it can deliver—and convinces the people that fulfillment is at hand when it is out of reach.... A premature messianism seems to be at the root of our problem with the state of Israel.... Zionism saw itself first as secular messianism.... Zionism used the language of faith—but filled the old bottles with new wine. This had far-reaching and dramatic effects. (Siegel 67–68)

Jacob Neusner puts it this way: "If Zionism solves 'the Jewish probem,' it also creates interesting problems for Judaism" ("Judaism"

314). At any rate, the reflections of the above scholars sufficiently problematize the secular Zionist movement to show that the advent of the
"Zionist phase" in the Jewish-American community just after World
War II—that is, the American Jews' privileging of Zionism over traditional messianic Judaism as the primary source of their identity—was
not nearly as smooth and uncomplicated as it may currently appear.
While several Jewish-American intellectuals just after World War II were
busy proposing their own frameworks for an Israeli government (see
David Horowitz and Crossman), others were still determined to squelch
Zionism altogether (from the first Zionist conference in 1897 until the
1930s, the Reform Jews, who founded the American Council for Judaism, represented the greatest number of these anti-Zionists; however,
for the purposes of this chapter, I will limit my focus to the unique concerns of the ultra-Orthodox anti-Zionists). As I have mentioned in earlier chapters, Zionism remained a minority movement within the Jewish community even during the 1930s and early 1940s (see Laqueur,
Blau, and Kolsky). Indeed, Israel did not "become" the religion of
American Jews without considerable strife within the Jewish community and without a considerable spiritual cost (Hertzberg, *The Jews,*
375). The religious Jews, like David Malter and Reb Saunders, were
forced to decide between two unsavory choices: they could eschew the
messianic precepts of Judaism and embrace Zionism, or they could
reject Zionism, thereby turning their backs on the beleaguered Jewish
survivors of the Holocaust.

It is this choice, laden with emotional and spiritual baggage, that
Potok dramatizes in *The Chosen.* Through his depiction of the fierce
battle between the ultra-Orthodox anti-Zionists and the secular Zionists, Potok intimates the "far-reaching and dramatic effects" of Zionism's victory over messianism, to which Siegel alludes above. He foreshadows the ferocity of this ideological clash in the opening scene of the
novel, as Danny Saunders and his Hasidic peers compete against Reuven
Malter's more Americanized yeshiva in a softball game. I will not dwell
upon this scene since Potok, himself, has already elaborated upon its
symbolic portent in some detail ("A Conversation" 123; "The Invisible
Map" 41). Suffice it to say that Potok depicts the game as a *jihad,* or holy
war, between rival faiths. Reuven's coach inspires his team with "war-
talk": "The enemy's on the ground. . . . No defensive holes in this war"
(*TC* 12). Reuven, in fact, becomes a casualty of the battle; he almost
loses his eye when his Hasidic counterpart, Danny, belts a line drive at

him, hitting him square in the face. When Danny visits Reuven in the hospital, he admits to his injured foe (who will soon become his best friend and only confidant) that he honestly wanted to kill him when he stepped up to the plate to bat. He also tells Reuven that his father, Reb Saunders, would only allow them to form a softball team because "we had a duty to beat you apikorsim [a sinner or hypocrite] at what you were best at" (*TC* 71).

Reb Saunders's Hasidic sect, of course, call upon a variety of justifications for maligning the Malters' yeshiva community as "Jewish goyim": Reuven's yeshiva devotes too much time (half of each day) toward English subjects, they study the religious subjects in Hebrew rather than in Yiddish to boot (thus desecrating the holy language), and they do not interpret passages of the Torah—the Jewish law—literally. Still, the secular Zionism of the Malters and their cohorts pitted against the messianism of Reb Saunders's Hasidim emerges as the most divisive element standing between the communities in *The Chosen*. Potok dramatizes the depths of these fault lines dividing the Jewish community when Reuven—staying at the Saunders's home while his father recovers from a heart attack—attempts to suggest innocuously that, in the wake of the Holocaust, "a lot of people were now saying that it was time for Palestine to become a Jewish homeland and not only a place where pious Jews went to die" (*TC* 187). Reuven has the good sense at the Saunders's breakfast table not to implicate his father as one of these people. However, we can tell from the whimper of Danny's younger brother that Reuven has just crossed a dangerous threshold in front of Reb Saunders. Foreshadowing the veritable "war" that erupts shortly between the secular Zionists and the ultra-Orthodox anti-Zionists, Reb Saunders points a finger at Reuven "that looked like a weapon" and fires, so to speak:

> "Who are these people? Who are these people?" he shouted in Yiddish, and the words went through me like knives. "Apikorsim! Goyim! Ben Gurion and his goyim will build Eretz Yisroel? They will build for us a Jewish land? They will bring Torah into this land? Goyishkeit they will bring into the land, not Torah! God will build the land, not Ben Gurion and his goyim! When the Messiah comes, we will have Eretz Yisroel, a Holy Land, not a land contaminated by Jewish goyim!" (*TC* 187).

The several narrative elements of the text encouraging us to support David Malter's Zionist perspective tend to undermine the persuasiveness of Reb Saunders's anti-Zionist argument. Read this way, the novel's denouement unfolds melodramatically as the benevolent Zionist forces war against the misguided, and downright pernicious, anti-Zionist movement. I hope that my brief exploration of Judaism's messianic tradition and the problematic secular Zionist appropriation of messianic language discourages this melodramatic interpretation and reveals, rather, the tragic implications of the novel; indeed, two forces of good collide in *The Chosen*. True, we are likely to align ourselves resolutely with either the Zionists or the anti-Zionists; and most contemporary readers will gravitate toward the Zionist arguments. However, we must not discount the eminently valid anti-Zionist stance Reb Saunders articulates because, herein, Potok complicates Malter's Zionism to question seriously the spiritual viability of a secular Jewish state.

What we must understand when we consider Reb Saunders's ultra-Orthodox anti-Zionist position, is that the overt, messianic pretentions of the secular Zionists justifiably exacerbated fears within certain segments of the Orthodox community that the Zionist movement would desecrate a core belief of Judaism, messianism. At the very start of the Herzlian nationalist movement, anti-Zionists chastised the Zionists for their false messianism. The following condemnation from one ultra-Orthodox anti-Zionist group, voiced just three years after the first Zionist conference in 1897, illustrates the fervor and endurance of the messianic tradition in which Reb Saunders partakes in 1947:

> [We cry out] against the delusions of the new false Messiah, that appears in somewhat different garb than [the] messianic pretenders of the past, and that calls itself "Zionism" . . . the Zionists have come and have broken the age-old rules. They have replaced the efforts to win improvement in the material and spiritual status and conditions of our lives with an effort to achieve a complete and perfect Redemption . . . They intoxicate the masses with the heady wine of eternal salvation and thereby deflect their attention from daily needs . . . and mislead them with . . . the lie that Redemption is here at hand. (Qtd. in Lederhendler 16)

In protesting against the false messianism of the secular Zionist movement, then, Reb Saunders and his ultra-Orthodox cohorts partake in their historical struggle to denounce the false messiahs who would intoxicate Jews with the false hope of an imminent redemption. Jesus represents, of course, the most notable false messiah according to Jewish belief, but the case of Shabbetai Zvi of the seventeenth century is also instructive. He told his followers that he would confront the sultan of Turkey to reclaim Palestine, and roughly half of the world's Jews believed him. Zvi's actions, however, lacked a certain panache; he converted to Islam upon the sultan's threat of execution. Such messianic disappointments, no doubt, moved Rabban Yochanan ben Zakkai in the first century to suggest sardonically, "If you should happen to be holding a sapling in your hand when they tell you that the messiah has arrived, first plant the sapling, then go and greet the messiah."

Given the stock that the most devout Jews, such as Reb Saunders, place in the true messiah (one need only visit an ultra-Orthodox neighborhood in America and see the storefront signs and bumper-stickers reading "Moshiach—Be a Part of it!"), one should not be surprised that the anti-Zionist students at Hirsch College wage a fierce ideological battle against the Zionist students. Harsh epithets slung back and forth between the ultra-Orthodox anti-Zionists and the several Zionist splinter groups become the lunchtime routine in the school's cafeteria; a fist-fight even erupts between two students. Reuven recalls one vitriolic slur levied against a Zionist group: "Hitler had only succeeded in destroying the Jewish body, he shouted in Yiddish, but the Revisionists were trying to destroy the Jewish soul" (*TC* 214). It is important to reiterate here that the Holocaust only cements the anti-Zionists' opposition to a secular Jewish state. Says Reb Saunders, "Tell me, we should forget completely about the Messiah? For this six million of our people were slaughtered?" (*TC* 187). Later, he explains to Reuven, "My brother ... the others ... they could not—they could not have died for such a state" (*TC* 268). In Saunders's eyes, then, the founding of a secular Jewish state would be a desecration, not a partial vindication, of the six million Jewish lives lost in the Holocaust.

Saunders recognizes his duty to reach beyond his own sect to suppress the post-Holocaust Zionist inclinations of several Jews. Thus, he organizes a group of Hasidic rebbes into an anti-Zionist group called The League for a Religious Eretz Yisroel. They hand out leaflets that state in clear terms that "[a] Jewish homeland created by Jewish goyim was to be considered contaminated and an open desecration of the name of God" (*TC* 221). Potok dramatizes just how deeply Saunders's anti-Zionist convictions run when he forces Danny to terminate his relationship with Reuven after David Malter delivers a Zionist speech. Reuven reflects, "My father and I had been excommunicated from the

Saunders family. If Reb Saunders even once heard of Danny being any-where in my presence, he would remove him immediately from the col-lege and send him to an out-of-town yeshiva for his rabbinic ordination . . . *never* would he let his son be the friend of the son of a man who was advocating the establishment of a secular Jewish state run by Jewish goyim" (*TC* 217).

David Malter remains every bit as inexorable in his Zionism. He works incessantly on his speeches for rallies and finally collapses of a heart attack. When Reuven later tries to convince his father to "take it a little easy," Malter gives his son a short course on Jewish covenantal duty:

> There is so much pain in the world. What does it mean to have to suf-fer so much if our lives are nothing more than the blink of an eye? . . .
> I learned a long time ago, Reuven, that a blink of an eye in itself is nothing. But the eye that blinks, *that* is something. . . . He can fill that tiny span with meaning, so its quality is immeasurable though its quantity may be insignificant. . . . It is hard work to fill one's life with meaning. *That* I do not think you understand yet. A life filled with meaning is worthy of rest. I want to be worthy of rest when I am no longer here. (*TC* 204–205)

Reuven, like Danny, is nothing if not a good student and, as a good stu-dent, he applies his father's teachings toward his own Zionist activities. In anticipation of Israel's war of Independence shortly after the UN rat-ification of the Middle East partition plan, Reuven and several of his classmates help to load army supplies illegally onto ships which will deliver them to the Israeli forces. Indeed, neither Reuven nor his father seem ambivalent in their Zionism. When Israel declares its indepen-dence on May 14, 1948, both Malters weep openly.

To be sure, Potok narrates triumphantly—via Reuven—the birth of the Jewish state. Everyone loves an underdog, and Potok emphasizes Israel's underdog status when he describes how seemingly every Arab country in the region joins in on the attack to annihilate the Jewish state: "The Etzion area in the Hebron Mountains fell, the Jordanian Army attacked Jerusalem, the Iraqi Army invaded the Jordan Valley, the Egyp-tian Army invaded the Negev, and the battle for Latrun, the decisive point along the road to Jerusalem, turned into a bloodbath" (*TC* 241). Potok also encourages us to support the newly declared Jewish state through Reuven's descriptions of "Arab riots" (240). The violence waged against the Jewish community in Palestine frighteningly parallels the atrocities committed against the European Jewish community during the Holocaust. Even Saunders's anti-Zionist group grows eerily quiet after an "Arab mob" sacks a Jewish commercial center in Jerusalem (*TC* 227). As the number of Jews killed in the region increases, his League for a Religious Eretz Yisroel acquiesces to the Zionists since, "Their pain over this new outbreak of violence against the Jews of Palestine out-weighed their hatred of Zionism" (*TC* 227). The anti-Zionist student group at Hirsch College also relents once word circulates that a brilliant mathematics graduate from Hirsch has been killed in the Middle East war trying to get a convoy through to Jerusalem.

Potok, then, explicitly depicts the inner tensions that plague the anti-Zionists. These tensions emerge most poignantly as Reb Saunders suffers openly for the victims of the Holocaust. Tormented individuals abound in his own Hasidic community, and they routinely climb the stairs to Saunders's office to share their burdens with the rebbe. While Saunders can more or less successfully absorb the suffering of his congregation, the news of the six million Jewish victims in Europe proves too much for him to bear (we must remember that Reb Saunders discovers that the Nazis murdered his own brother). While staying at the Saunders's home, Reuven observes that "Danny's father was forever silent, withdrawn, his dark eyes turned inward, brooding, as if witnessing a sea of suffering he alone could see.... Dark circles had formed around his eyes, and sometimes at the kitchen table I would see him begin to cry suddenly ..." (*TC* 183). A concerned Reuven asks Danny why his father cries so frequently and Danny responds, "Six million Jews have died ... He's—I think he's thinking of them. He's suffering for them" (*TC* 189). Saunders's unflinching opposition to a Jewish state should not obscure the emotional cost of his decision. We can only wonder how many tears Saunders sheds for the few Jewish survivors of the Holocaust. After all, he must realize their desperate need for a safe haven in a Jewish state, though this realization does not impel him to eschew his messianic precepts and support the Zionist cause.

The case for David Malter's inner tensions with regard to his Zionism is less obvious. That Potok's triumphant account of Israel's birth enforces the melodramatic reading of the Zionist struggle within the American Jewish community is true enough. One might interpret David Malter's defeat of Reb Saunders's anti-Zionist group in terms no less heroic than Israel's defeat of the combined Arab forces. But we should not ignore the spiritual cost involved in David Malter's rejection of messianism. While less observant American Jews had little trouble abandoning a seemingly nebulous messianism for a palpable secular Zionism, Myers aptly contends that a "familiarity [with the messianic tradition] often made the shift from messianism to Zionism all the more painful" (8). As an Orthodox Jew, eminently "familiar" with Judaism's messianic precepts, David Malter cannot reject messianism so easily. In subtle ways, Potok does dramatize the inner conflict that festers as Malter, a religious Jew, "compartmentalize[s] [his] religious outlook in order to deal most rationally with the problems at hand" (Myers 8).

Malter, for example, refuses to deride the messianism of Saunders's Hasidic sect. When Reuven finally loses patience with Saunders's anti-Zionism and calls him a fanatic, Malter gives the Hasidim their due: "Reuven . . . the fanaticism of men like Reb Saunders kept us alive for two thousand years of exile" (*TC* 219). Malter, in fact, repeatedly expresses to Reuven his respect for the anti-Zionist's messianic perspective. And why should he not respect this view? As an Orthodox Jew who dutifully observes the Sabbath and the kosher laws, who prays with the traditional tefillin, who adheres as closely as possible to the covenant between Moses and God (he attempts explicitly to emulate Moses's dutiful life), Malter surely realizes that his secular Zionism represents a departure from the covenant—that his pictures of Zionists like Theodor Herzl and Chaim Weizmann, which bedeck the hallway of his home, defy a central element of Judaism. What is more, Malter's flagging health throughout the novel suggests that his rejection of messianism torments him more than it superficially appears. Reuven, ultimately, describes his father as a "shell of a man" (*TC* 228). We must wonder to what extent Malter's rejection of messianism contributes to the steady disintegration of his core.

Potok emerges, finally, as no less prescient than Seymour Siegel of Zionism's shortcomings as a theodicy. While one would be hard pressed to dispute the Zionism of the novel, Potok foreshadows some of the complications that would arise within the American Jewish community after the Jews embraced a secular movement—albeit deceptively so—as its principal source of identity. Interestingly, David Malter realizes that secular Zionism will not be enough to satisfy the spiritual needs of the American Jewish community. Since Potok so dramatically renders the Zionist struggle in the novel, one easily overlooks Malter's insistence that the Jews "rebuild Jewry in America" (*TC* 182). Malter considers this revitalization of American Jewry just as important as the establishment of a Jewish state, as Reuven implicitly suggests: "Occasionally he spoke of the importance of Palestine as a Jewish homeland, *but mostly* he was concerned about American Jewry and the need for teachers and rabbis" [emphasis mine] (*TC* 185). In the generous financial donations to Israel by affluent, secular American Jews, like Jack Rose, Malter foresees a "religious renaissance" in America (*TC* 206).

Like David Malter in *The Chosen*, Jewish-American intellectuals have emphasized the importance of religious Judaism in America to complement secular Zionism. Just three years after the novel's publication, Jacob Neusner notes—in an overwhelmingly Zionist essay—the "mythic insufficiency of Zionism that renders its success a dilemma for contemporary American Jews, and for Israeli ones as well" ("Judaism" 317). Neusner realizes that Zionism provides thin fare for the American Jewish soul. After all, one descends into absurdities upon suggesting that American Jews' spiritual yearnings can be satisfied through an identification with a country in which they do not even live. Says Neusner, "Zionism is part of Judaism. It cannot be made the whole, because Jews are more than people who need either a place to live or a place on which to focus fantasies. . . . Zionism provides much of the vigor and excitement of contemporary Jewish affairs, but so far as Jews live and suffer, are born and die, reflect and doubt, raise children and worry over them, love and work—so far as Jews are human, they require Judaism" ("Judaism" 323). Writing more recently, Yehudi Adam shakes off Neusner's kid gloves and takes on a more confrontational tone with regard to Zionism's detrimental effect on American Judaism: "Today, Zionism is identified with Judaism to such a degree that most Jews who are active in Jewish life consider it a duty of every Jew to be a Zionist. But the verdict of the future will be that the ideology of political Zionism was a deviation from the task and destiny of the Jewish people" (285).

These are, indeed, fighting words. But what explains Adam's combative tone when it comes to Zionism's undermining of Judaism? The answer, I believe, lies in what we might call the cunning of history. For, during the first years of Israel's statehood, several American Zionists, like David Malter, were convinced that the rallying together of the American Jewish community behind the Zionist banner heralded a concomitant "religious renaissance" that would take hold in America. As Israel nears its fiftieth birthday, we know that such hopes were dashed by the secular revolution that swept across the American Jewish community during the 1950s, which continues today. Alas, the Jack Roses, who readily enough parted with generous sums of money to support Israel (in the month, for example, just before and during the Six-Day War in 1967, American Jews donated over one hundred million dollars to the Israel Emergency fund of the United Jewish Appeal), never really made it to the synagogue, as David Malter hopes. Reuven's remark, "I can't see Jack Rose in a synagogue," proves prophetic indeed (*TC* 206). In *The Jews in America* (1989), Arthur Hertzberg documents the rampant assimilation that permeated the American Jewish community just after World War II and the founding of the Jewish state:

> In the spring of 1953 the United Synagogue of America, the central lay organization of Conservative Judaism, did a self-study of the leaders of the synagogues. . . . About one in three of these synagogue leaders attended "the main Sabbath services" of their congregations with any frequency. About one in five came often, and nearly half showed up infrequently or not at all. Essentially, this profile of the synagogue leadership is not different from the results of a questionnaire about synagogue attendance among the laity as a whole. . . . The private religious habits of the leaders of the congregations were equally revealing. The Sabbath candles were lit in three-quarters of their homes, but three out of five did not make a sufficiently festive affair of the family dinner to chant the kiddush, the prayer over wine which is ordained by ritual custom. Only one-third of these board members kept a kosher home. . . . Only twenty-eight percent of the board members usually took their children on the occasions when they went to Sabbath services; as many as fifty-eight percent went by themselves, leaving their children the option to go shopping, to play in Little League baseball, or to attend ballet classes. (325–326)

Most disturbing, perhaps, is this last detail concerning the complacent manner with which Jewish parents during the 1950s directed their children's Jewish education. Hertzberg continues, "What the mass of parents wanted, apart from a decent performance at bar mitzvah, was that the school impart to their children enough of the sense of Jewish loyalty so that they would be inoculated against intermarriage. . . . Once that inoculation had supposedly taken hold, the Jewish child could then be launched on his next task, to succeed in being admitted into a prestigious college" (*The Jews* 332). The "inoculation" against intermarriage to which Hertzberg refers turned out to be so much placebo; the intermarriage rate among Jews has risen to nearly 50 percent today (some polls estimate an even higher percentage). What is more, "all the demographic indexes show a disastrously small birthrate and an ever-aging population, probably the oldest of any group in the United States" (Hertzberg, *Jewish Polemics* 134).

Jacob Neusner accurately predicted in 1969 that the "secular revolution," charted above by Hertzberg, would impose a "lingering crisis of identity" upon American Jews ("Zionism" 37). As he and David Malter (and Potok, I believe) recognize, American Jews cannot forge a viable ethos out of secular Zionism alone. Concern for Israel might have been enough to cement the American Jewish community during the initial, tenuous years of the state's existence. The rub: "the tension caused by persecution which was a constant feature of the situation of Jews in Europe and which found its expression in Zionist analysis, no longer exists" (Rotenstreich 8). This assertion might smack of hyperbole. The enduring political exigence of Zionism manifested itself in the 1991 Israeli airlift of nearly 15,000 imperiled Ethiopian Jews, and in the earlier mass immigration of Russian Jews to the state, which continues today with less intensity. But it is just as true that as Israel achieves normalcy as a nation (that is, as its existence becomes less tenuous), American Jews find that they need not channel all of their spiritual energies into the Middle East problem (increasingly, in fact, American Jews broach the topic of Israel in order to criticize the state's politics). At any rate, what the increasing rate of assimilation tells us—among other things—is that a whole generation of Jews find themselves coming of age in a post-Zionist milieu, and equipped with precious little *Yiddishkeit* needed to round out a meaningful Jewish life.

In "Zionist Education: The Essential Conflict," Solomon Goldman documents this waning of Zionism within the American Jewish community by noting a disconcerting trend, beginning in the 1970s and continuing today: Hebrew schools presented Zionism to students as a form of charity and deprived them "an intellectual understanding of Zionism, the nature of the Jewish people, nationalism and religion" (25). To combat the rapid assimilation of American Jews, Goldman proposes that American Jewish communities reinstill Zionism as the core of the education system. Egon Friedler also contends that a Secular Humanistic Judaism can provoke a "neo-Zionism ... committed to recover the Herzlian values of the Jewish State without theocratic pressures" (17). Both Goldman and Friedler, then, envision a reinvigorated

Zionism as part of a new *Yiddishkeit* that will give estranged Jews a sense of belonging once again to Jewish culture.

Speaking as one for whom Zionism achieved this goal in no small measure, I do not doubt the positive role that a reinvigorated Zionism can play for the next generation. That said, what Potok suggests in *The Chosen*, and what the past several years of assimilation confirm, is that the new *Yiddishkeit* cannot consist of Zionism alone, despite Friedler's perspicacious recognition that "theocratic pressures" will not carry the day either; indeed, a restoration of the "old" *Yiddishkeit*—what David Malter, no doubt, has in mind when he anticipates a religious renaissance—is too much to ask for amid our contemporary milieu in which Jewish adolescents are just as likely to clutch tickets to a Madonna concert during the Jewish High Holidays as they are to clutch tickets to their local synagogue.

This is not to say that Potok chronicles in *The Chosen* the last gasp of American Judaism as Danny Saunders, without beard and *payos* (earlocks) in the last scene, strolls down Lee Avenue toward an overwhelmingly secular life. For, if I may entertain one possible remedy for the religious crisis that Potok dramatizes in his novel, Hebrew literacy represents a fruitful avenue through which to reestablish a viable American Jewish ethos. As Alan Mintz aptly notes, "Jewish culture is embodied *by* Hebrew and embedded *in* it" (46). Consequently, he believes that "the quality of American Jewish life as it evolves into the future *depends* on Hebrew cultural literacy" (44). Unfortunately, precious few American Hebrew schools today emphasize Hebrew literacy. Rarely do thirteen-year-olds understand more than a smattering of the Hebrew words they utter so proficiently at their bar or bat mitzvahs. Although English translations of Hebrew religious texts and Israeli novels are currently the rage, "Judaism and its culture are not 'naturalized' into English without something substantial being renounced" (Mintz 4). To be sure, the English language serves as a vehicle through which to approach these texts; but it also functions as a filter through which a multitude of Hebrew-specific connotations cannot pass. Proficiency in Hebrew would allow American Jews to lift the filter of English and engage their culturally specific texts at an intimate level. Moreover, Hebrew literacy can also strengthen the bonds between American Jews and Israeli Jews during these times of increasing tensions between the two communities. As one Israeli expressed to me during my recent visit to the Jewish state, "Imagine if you could visit my country and we could speak to one another in Hebrew." The allure of this thought, no doubt, prompted Steven Spielberg to promise—while speaking about his film *Schindler's List* in Israel—that he would soon return to the country to study Hebrew.

I introduced Chaim Potok's *The Chosen* by suggesting that the culturally specific elements of the novel would lead us to a more fruitful interpretation. *The Chosen*, I continued to argue, emerges as a more complex and thoughtful novel once we explore the textual elements through which Potok subtly problematizes David Malters's Zionist movement; for, herein, Potok adeptly depicts the religious crisis that faced American Jews just after the Holocaust when they were forced to choose between Zionism and messianism. True, he dramatizes the significant triumph of Zionism, but not without anticipating the unfortunate ramifications of this triumph, as well. I espouse the same basic principle that inspired this interpretation of the novel—the celebration of the culturally specific—to conclude. Indeed, a celebration of the most pervasive, culturally specific element of Judaism, Hebrew, just might provide American Jews with the spiritual nourishment that Zionism cannot provide alone.

Chapter 7

PHILIP ROTH'S NERVE IN *THE COUNTERLIFE* AND *OPERATION SHYLOCK:* A CONFESSION

"Jewish Mischief" and the Post-Colonial Critique

In literary (i.e., canonical) terms, Philip Roth is far and away a more established Jewish-American writer than Chaim Potok (Saul Bellow once quipped that Philip Roth, Bernard Malamud, and he were the Hart, Schaffner, and Marx of Jewish-American fiction). Still, Roth has also been the target of numerous attacks from Jewish-American intellectuals and lay people who take exception to his "distorted" depiction of American Jewish life. From synagogue pulpits, in articles, in letters to magazines that publish Roth's stories and to Roth himself, his critics have accused him of no less than self-hatred and anti-Semitism. The late Irving Howe's "Philip Roth Reconsidered"—in which Howe, citing Roth's "thin personal culture," contends that Roth "grossly manipulate[s]" his characters—undoubtedly represents the most scathing scholarly attack on Roth's work (73, 70). Howe and others considered the writer's work, laden with goldbricking Jewish soldiers, adulterous Jewish husbands, inordinately materialistic Jewish daughters, and lascivious Jewish sons, in short, "bad for the Jews," and they refused to let it go unchallenged (Roth refuted the comments of some of these others in a 1963 essay, "Writing about Jews," but, in 1993, curiously empathized with their concerns in a *New York Times Book Review* article entitled, "A Bit of Jewish Mischief"). To be sure, then, Roth's Jewish mischief, as he calls it, has ruffled more than a few feathers in the Jewish-American community; one Roth scholar tellingly dedicates his study of the writer's fiction, "For my mother, who hoped I would write about somebody else" (Pinsker, *The Comedy that "Hoits"*).

I belabor Philip Roth's lukewarm reception by the American Jewish community since I believe that two of Roth's recent novels, *The Counterlife* (1987) and *Operation Shylock: A Confession* (1993), both set largely in Israel, problematize the essential arguments of Roth's detractors. For, as I mention briefly in the introduction to this study, scholars of Jewish-American fiction have noted the curious and disconcerting reluctance of most Jewish-American writers to engage Israel seriously in their work. In an essay praising Roth's focus upon Israel, Robert Alter comments, "It was not that serious American Jewish writers should have been obliged to be Zionists or to produce highbrow versions of *Exodus* but only that the creation of Israel represented a fundamental alteration in the facts of Jewish existence, so that a fiction that simply ignored the momentous challenge of renewed Jewish autonomy could scarcely be thought to probe the problematic of modern Jewish identity" ("Defenders" 55). Theodore Solotaroff also notes in the introduction to his recent anthology of American Jewish fiction that, "American-Jewish fiction, with the exception of Philip Roth's *The Counterlife* [*Operation Shylock* had not yet been published], has been slow, and perhaps loath, to explore the more vexed subject that has been set by the occupation of the West Bank and Gaza . . ." ("The Open Community" xvi). It strikes me as ironic, indeed, that Philip Roth—a Jewish-American writer persistently maligned by the Jewish-American community—has emerged as the most courageous voice to probe this gap in Jewish-American fiction. That Roth, in *The Counterlife* and *Operation Shylock*, has engaged Israel with far greater intellectual rigor than any other contemporary Jewish-American writer (with the possible exception of Tova Reich) must be a source of great confusion for those critics who have long chastised Roth for his flippant, irresponsible treatment of his Jewish subjects.

Why, though, have other Jewish-American writers been "slow, and perhaps loath" to focus their imaginations squarely upon Israel and the concomitant political issues of the Middle East? I have explored some possible explanations in the introduction—primarily the elusive "strangeness" of Israel to Jewish-*American* writers. But as Alter implies, Leon Uris's *Exodus*, replete with virulent stereotypes of the Arab and equally wrongheaded stereotypes (though perhaps less pernicious) of the Israeli Jew, went a long way, as well, toward discouraging Jewish-American writers from engaging Israel seriously in their work. Uris, writing amid the excitement of the "Zionist phase" in America, proved that it was all too easy for the *galut* [exiled] Zionist to fall back on the comfortable stereotypes of the Arab, and of the Israeli Jew, when seeking to write about or merely discuss Israel. This rhetoric, which insidiously stacks the moral cards in the Israeli hand, pervades the casual conversations of Zionists, often in the form of jokes. I offer one as an example: "You know what a moderate Arab is, don't you? One that runs out of bullets." Jewish-American novelists, also, have found it difficult to avoid this rhetorical mug's game when writing about Israel. Leon Uris's *Exodus* seems politically correct compared to more recent pulp-fiction style vilifications of the Arab in such novels as Peter Abraham's *Tongues of Fire* (1982), Lewis Orde's *Munich 10* (1982), Chaim Zeldis's *Forbidden Love* (1983), and Alfred Coppel's *Thirty-four East* (1974).

Edward Said proves helpful in explaining why the few Jewish-American writers who depict Arabs in their fiction persist in demonizing them: "I do not believe that authors are mechanically determined by ideology, class, or economic history, but authors are, I also believe, very much in the history of their societies, shaping and shaped by that history and their social experience in different measure" (*Culture* xxii). Now, Said, as a post-colonial critic, does not forge a new critical paradigm here, but simply reaffirms a precept that Ralph Waldo Emerson so eloquently articulated in a much earlier essay, "Art":

> No man can quite emancipate himself from his age and country, or produce a model in which the education, the religion, the politics, usages and arts of his times shall have no share. Though he were never so original, never so wilful and fantastic, he cannot wipe out of his work every trace of the thoughts amidst which it grew. The very avoidance betrays the usage he avoids. Above his will and out of his sight he is necessitated by the air he breathes and the idea on which he and his contemporaries live and toil, to share the manner of his times, without knowing what that manner is. (290)

Put another way, a tension permeates even the best art, for artists simultaneously function as social critics and social products, as arbiters and inheritors of culture. This tension, I believe, emerges in both of Roth's Middle East novels to suggest the enormity of the Jewish-American *tsores* [troubles] today in our "post-Zionist" milieu when it comes to Israel and the Middle East problem. Both *The Counterlife* and *Operation Shylock* mark a new and welcome current in Jewish-American fiction about Israel in that Roth creates thoughtful Jewish and Arab voices openly skeptical of Israeli policy on the West Bank; Roth, the preeminent craftsman of Jewish mischief, refuses to look toward Israel with a myopic eye, bedazzled by Masada, the Western Wall, and all other things Jewish. Still, there remain several narrative subtleties (subtleties that emerge most prevalently in *The Counterlife*) which deconstruct these voices and reinscribe stereotypes of the Arab. As Paul Brown notes (in discussing the colonialist function of stereotypes, in general), these stereotypes contribute to a "discursive strategy . . . to locate or 'fix' [the] colonial other in a position of inferiority" (58). Roth, then, as social critic, gives voice to a multitude of Middle East perspectives and takes both Palestinian and Zionist perspectives to task. However, he occasionally reaffirms comfortable Zionist assumptions about the Arabs in the Middle East.

As a scholar of Jewish-American literature and a Zionist, it occurs to me that several readers might wonder why I embrace the methodologies of post-colonial critics to examine Roth's Jewish-American novels about Israel and the Occupied Territories. So let me say up front that I see no anomaly in scrutinizing a Jewish author's stereotyped construction of an Arab character or distorted depiction of the Middle East landscape, in general. For I resolutely believe that Israel's legitimacy as a nation does not depend upon the demonization of a whole race (indeed, I would not be a Zionist if I did believe that such distortions were necessary to preserve Israel's political viability). Roth deserves much credit for rescuing Jewish-American fiction about Israel from the realm of the conventional Zionist propoganda novel, a la Leon Uris's *Exodus*. To ignore the textual moments during which Roth unwittingly acquiesces to these conventions would be to participate in the very discourse that Roth endeavors to reject. Alternatively, through exploring the ways in which Roth both resists and reaffirms this discourse, we catch a glimpse of one Jewish-American writer's struggle to carve out a morally viable narrative perspective on the Middle East. As I have suggested, it is in this struggle itself that Roth betrays the Jewish-American ambivalence about the Middle East in general, and the plight of the Palestinians in the Occupied Territories, specifically.

One cannot begin to discuss *The Counterlife* without accounting for its enigmatic structure. The novel consists of five long chapters: "Basel," "Judea," "Aloft," "Gloucestershire," and "Christendom." From these five chapters emerge four incongruous fictions about two protagonists,

Nathan Zuckerman, the familiar, alienated fiction writer in Roth's oeuvre, and his brother, Henry, a dentist. In "Basel," narrated in the third person, Roth details Henry's decision whether to continue taking "beta-blockers" for his heart condition or undergo a risky cardiac operation instead. The rub: while the drugs effectively stabilize Henry's condition, they also render him impotent. Unwilling to forego any longer his routine of receiving daily *fellatio* from his young, gentile dental assistant, he opts for surgery and dies on the operating table.

In the next chapter, "Judea," Roth resurrects Henry and places him on the West Bank of Israel. After pulling through the cardiac operation just fine, Henry seems to forget why he undertook the risk in the first place. He rejects the stability of his family and the lascivious delights of his mistress in favor of a folding cot and a gun at Agor, the most militant Israeli settlement in the West Bank. In touch at last with his Jewish roots, Henry changes his name to Hanoch and becomes a loyal follower of Agor's powerful and charismatic leader, Mordecai Lippman. Nathan, who narrates "Judea" and "Aloft," visits his brother upon the request of Henry's/Hanoch's perplexed wife, Carol, but cannot shake Henry's inexorable faith in Lippman.

While the plot in "Aloft" (which details Nathan's eventful flight out of Israel) remains factually consistent with "Judea," Roth once again turns his own fiction on its head in the last two chapters. In "Gloucestershire," the heart problem belongs to Nathan and he does not stand up (so to speak) to the beta-blockers any better than Henry did in the first chapter. It is Nathan who opts for surgery and sexual fulfillment with a gentile woman; it is Nathan who dies on the operating table. However, he does not perish without leaving behind a manuscript—our final chapter, "Christendom"—in which he envisions his survival and arguably fruitful family life with his fourth Christian bride, Maria.

To be sure, Roth, as mischief-maker, quite consciously toys with his artistic medium and challenges our precepts concerning just what "the novel" should really be. Debra Shostak aptly notes that "Roth consistently thumbs his nose at his contract with the reader, thereby asserting his own authority as the author of his text" (211). This presumed contract greatly complicates the act of reading *The Counterlife*. Because the chapters contradict one another in such essential ways, it becomes all too easy to attempt absurdly to locate the "real" fiction. Maria admonishes such tendencies to equate art with life (or, worse yet, art with the artist) as she asserts her own purely fictional role. Fed up with the way things are going by page 357, she simply throws in the towel: "Dear Nathan, I'm leaving, I've left. I'm leaving you and I'm leaving the book . . . I know characters rebelling against their author has been done before, but . . . I have no desire to be original and never did" (*TC* 357). Roth's elusive postmodern touch has, indeed, frustrated certain critics who take their fiction seriously. Sanford Pinsker, for one, concluded that "whatever my feelings about Israel and the Middle East, they struck me as requiring more than a wisecracker like Philip Roth could provide" ("William Faulkner" 400). In a separate article, "The Lives and Deaths of Nathan Zuckerman," Pinsker vents some good-humored frustration in noting that Roth's revival of Henry passes for "experimentalism" although the producers of the television show "Dallas" brought back Bobby Ewing using the same "trick" (54).

Pinsker's canny dig rings true enough on its consciously superficial level. However, given the great many ambivalences of Jewish-Americans when it comes to Israel and their role as Jews in the Diaspora, Roth's constant shifting of perspective serves a serious function. At one point in the novel, Nathan offers us a glimpse into this function of Roth's narrative framework. Says Nathan, "the treacherous imagination is everybody's maker—we are all the invention of each other, everybody a conjuration conjuring up everyone else. We are all each other's authors" (*TC* 164). In this light, the novel seems a lot less like "trendy" hocus-pocus, and a lot more like a serious attempt to do justice to the manifold voices and perspectives informing Jewish life—voices that meet and often clash, especially when questions of Israeli policy crop up. In approbation of Roth's narrative structure, Robert Alter comments that "the dimensions of the question [of how a Jew should live] can be seen only by following out a collision course of opposing ideas" (55). Mark Shechner also recognizes the appropriateness of Roth's maze-like structure by noting that the Jewish experience is a maze, as well (229).

What voices, then, does Roth construct to define the Arab and the Arab-Israeli conflict, in general, in the "Judea" section of the novel? How does the narrative framework serve to deny and affirm the comfortable stereotypes of the other? And, finally, how does ambivalence function in the novel to call certain colonialist perspectives into question while legitimizing others? Let us now try to answer these difficult questions.

Roth's choice of Nathan as the chapter's narrator represents the most salient feature of the narrative resistant to comfortable Zionist pieties about the Middle East conflict. As I have already suggested, in earlier Jewish-American fiction about Israel, the narrative perspective is almost always unequivocally and passionately Zionist (Uris's *Exodus* and Meyer Levin's *Yehuda* come to mind). In stark contrast, Nathan Zuckerman offers us the perspective of a disaffected Jew at odds with the Zionist privileging of Israel over America. Indeed, Nathan's first trip to Israel in 1960 inspires him to assert his full fledged "Americanness" to the father of his Israeli friend, Shuki Elchanan:

> My landscape wasn't the Negev wilderness, or the Galilean hills, or the coastal plan of ancient Philistia; it was industrial, immigrant America—Newark where I'd been raised, Chicago where I'd been educated, and New York where I was living in a basement apartment on a Lower East Side street among poor Ukrainians and Puerto Ricans. My sacred text wasn't the Bible but novels translated from Russian, German, and French into the language in which I was beginning to write and publish my own fiction—not the semantic range of classical Hebrew but the jumpy beat of American English was what excited me. (*TC* 58)

Here, Roth engages one of the sore points that contribute to the current tensions between Israeli and American Jews. Several Israeli Jews noisily insist that the only real home for the Jew is in Israel, while most American Jews (of course) feel otherwise. Nathan, for one, redefines Zionism to include the vision of his Galician grandfathers who fled from Christian Europe to America. Says Nathan, "Insomuch as Zionism meant taking upon oneself, rather than leaving to others, responsibility for one's survival as a Jew, this was their brand of Zionism. And it worked" (*TC* 59). Nathan's grandfathers, then, had a Zionist idea of their own when they embraced America as homeland for the Jew, not Israel. Nathan pontificates eloquently about his homeland's pluralism and tolerance and, moreover, attacks Israel's "law of return" by boasting that America "did not have at its center the idea of exclusion" (*TC* 60).

Israel's law of return—which encourages all Jews to emigrate and restricts the immigration of other people—remains the most controversial element of Zionism. In 1975, the United Nations, under secretary-general Kurt Waldheim, equated Zionism with Racism (this resolution was repealed in 1991). Alan Dershowitz cannot seem to spill enough ink in defending the policy (see *Chutzpah* [1991]), while an Israeli journalist, Yossi Melman, takes a more critical look at the law of return (see *The New Israelis* [1992]). The latest skirmishes can be heard within the Zionist ranks. For example, after Israel recently announced its decision to bar immigrants with the HIV virus, Israelis such as Dan Yakir, an Israeli civil rights attorney, and Ephraim Gur, a member of the Israeli parliament, argued that the new policy violated the law of return. Several Israelis also object to the rapid influx of non-Jews from Europe and the Far East (a state-supported influx of workers who are more than happy to take on the menial labor jobs formerly reserved for Palestinian workers). Finally, in the wake of Baruch Goldstein's massacre of twenty-nine Palestinians in a Hebron mosque, Israeli journalists like Allan Shapiro are questioning whether Jews who incite racism should be denied the right to immigrate to Israel (Shapiro 6). On less contentious fronts, Joel Fleischmann of television's quirky/cerebral *Northern Exposure* recently rejoiced, "You [meaning Jews in exile for 2000 years] can always go to Israel." Nathan, then, asserts his distance from an essential and heated Zionist ideal (to make Israel a truly *Jewish* homeland) when he attacks the law of return.

Nathan's ambivalences concerning Israel remain strong some twenty years later as he returns to see his brother, Henry (or should we call him Hanoch now?). Upon visiting the Western Wall—the last remnant of the Second Temple and the most hallowed of Jewish places—Nathan feels as unspiritual as ever. While he observes a group of devout Jews praying (or *davening*) fervently, he thinks, "If there is a God who plays a role in our world, I will eat every hat in this town" (*TC* 96). He feels alienated from the Jews at the Wall and believes that he "would have felt less detachment from seventeen Jews who openly admitted that they *were* talking to rock than from these seventeen who imagined themselves telexing the Creator directly" (*TC* 96).

Nathan asserts his detachment from the Jews at the Wall more overtly when he refuses to join a minyan when asked by a young Chasid. To understand the significance of this act, one must understand that a Jewish congregation cannot even perform the Torah service without a minyan, a group of at least ten post-Bar Mitzvah Jews; and that this service celebrates (among other things) God's covenant with the children of Israel. Thus, Nathan's refusal to join the minyan can be viewed as a repudiation of Israel itself. That said, let me assert my hesitancy to place such symbolic weight into Nathan's act (my conditional tone was quite intentional). Indeed, I can no more imagine Nathan participating in a group card game, a group chat, or a group *anything*, than I can imagine him participating in group prayer. However, this episode does make it quite clear that Nathan visits Israel not to make *aliyah* in his idyllic homeland but, rather, to bail his brother out of such a ridiculous act of self-deception.

Given Nathan's alienation from Israel, we should not be surprised that he stands foursquare against those blind followers of the Jewish state who see the Arab only as a war-loving antagonist of the Jew. Nathan describes his Uncle Shimmy—who says "bomb the Arab bastards till they cry uncle"—as "Neanderthal" and "arguably the family's stupidest relative" (*TC* 41–42). Nonetheless, there is something unequivocally dissatisfying about Nathan's virtual apathy toward the Middle East. Thus, Roth creates a more serious countervoice to Shimmy's crude Zionist perspective in Nathan's friend, Shuki Elchanan. An Israeli journalist, Shuki asserts a more moderate Zionist position and would rather see Mordecai Lippman and his cohorts leave the West Bank to the Arabs. He even expresses remorse upon discovering that Nathan's brother has joined Lippman's settlement on the West Bank. Herein, we receive our first real glimpse of Lippman through Shuki's eyes:

> Well, that's wonderful. Lippman drives into Hebron with his pistol and tells the Arabs in the market how the Jews and Arabs can live happily side by side as long as the Jews are on top. He's dying for somebody to throw a Molotov cocktail. Then his thugs can really go to town. (*TC* 83)

Here, Roth turns the "Neanderthal" discourse of Shimmy on its head. The Jew, represented by Lippman, emerges as the aggressor of the Middle East; the Jew wields a pistol and anxiously hopes for violence; and the Jew invades the peaceful Arab realm of a Hebron market. Shuki reflects that Jews of Lippman's ilk are at least equally infatuated with the gun (representing heroic Hebrew force) as they are with the Jewish beard which has long stood for saintly Yiddish weakness. He asks Nathan, "Is your brother as thrilled by the religion as by the explosives?" (*TC* 84).

In Shuki, Roth creates a thoughtful Israeli voice which contrasts sharply to Nathan's mere estrangement from Israel. Shuki does not only oppose the aggressive methods of Lippman's colonialism, but takes Lippman to task on ideological grounds, as well. He sees the principle behind Lippman's desire to reclaim the West Bank as Judea—Israel's historical claim on the land rooted in the Torah—as self-serving and corrupt. Such an argument, according to Shuki, which places all of its stock in the Old

Testament, smacks of smug, religious piety completely out of touch with the exigencies of the contemporary political landscape:

> Everything going wrong with this country is in the first five books of the Old Testament. Smite the enemy, sacrifice your son, the desert is yours and nobody else's all the way to the Euphrates. A body count of dead Philistines on every other page—that's the wisdom of their wonderful Torah. (*TC* 84)

To be sure, Jewish fundamentalists find no friend in Shuki Elchanan. He continues, "if they want so much to sleep at the biblical source because that is where Abraham tied his shoelaces, then they can sleep there under Arab rule!" (*TC* 84). Shuki does embrace the Zionist idea, but not as defined by the "gangster," Lippman. He recognizes the hypocrisy inherent in any attempt by Israel, a state conceived as a refuge from European fascism, to police a steadily rising indigenous population, the Arabs.

It is significant that Shuki describes Lippman and his fanatical movement, modelled after the messianic Zionists of the Gush Emunim Jewish Settler movement, before Roth allows Lippman to speak for himself. Indeed, before we even hear him speak, we are convinced that he must be more than a little bit nuts. Shuki's portrait of Agor's leader, in fact, provokes Nathan to hurry to his brother's aid, thinking that if "Lippman was anything like the *shlayger* [whipper] he'd described, then it was possible that Henry was as much captive as disciple" (*TC* 89). Although false, Nathan's suspicions are not at all unreasonable. Lippman's very appearance goes a long way toward convincing one that he, if anyone, would be the type to exert his physical will over others.

Upon first seeing Agor's leader, Nathan reflects that his "wide-set, almond-shaped, slightly protuberant eyes, though a gentle milky blue, proclaimed, unmistakably, STOP" (*TC* 128). Nathan sees in Lippman's mangled body, from his crippled leg (an injury from the 1967 Six-Day war) to his smashed nose, evidence of those who have tried—and failed—to stop *him*. One need not wonder what the recently impotent Henry/Hanoch sees in Agor's militant defender of the faith; Lippman embodies power and potency, as Nathan will later reflect (*TC* 154). Roth, however, does not want his readers to be so easily taken in by Lippman and his fundamentalist precepts. Thus, he undercuts Nathan's initially heroic description of the leader by emphasizing his preposterous head of hair, which Nathan describes as a "bunchy cabbage of disarranged plumage" (*TC* 128–129). Lippman comes off, finally, not as an indomitable warrior, but as "some majestic Harpo Marx—Harpo as Hannibal" (*TC* 129). Not only are we predisposed to view Lippman as politically crazy (via Shuki), but now slightly ridiculous, as well.

Still, we cannot discount the power of Lippman's rhetoric. Through the exclamation points and italics riddled throughout the fifteen or so pages dominated by Lippman's voice, Roth offers a short course in the stylistic distinction between the *Jewish*-American novel, in general, and those of the Jamesian variety. At any rate, through Lippman's narrow lens of Jewish fundamentalism, the Arab emerges only as an immutable and inexorable counterforce to an ideologically pure Israel. Lippman would, no doubt, frown upon the September 17, 1993, accord between Israel and the PLO since, according to him, "the Arab will take what is given and then continue the war, and instead of less trouble there will be *more*" (*TC* 130). Though Lippman recognizes the conflicting political voices from the Israeli side of the fence, he can envision only a monolithic Islam bent on spilling Jewish blood:

> Islam is not a civilization of doubt like the civilization of the Hellenized Jew. The Jew is always blaming himself for what happens in Cairo. He is blaming himself for what happens in Baghdad. But in Baghdad, believe me, they do not blame themselves for what is happening in Jerusalem. Theirs is not a civilization of doubt—theirs is a civilization of *certainty*. Islam is not plagued by niceys and goodies who want to be sure they don't do the wrong thing. Islam wants one thing only: to *win*, to *triumph*, to obliterate the cancer of Israel from the body of the Islamic world. (*TC* 131)

Lippman refers specifically to Shuki Elchanan when he castigates the "goody" Jew concerned with issues of morality. These moral issues, according to Lippman, are irrelevant in the Middle East because the Arabs are ill-equipped to honor any such virtue. Their monomanic quest to reclaim Israeli land renders moral considerations obsolete. Consequently, Lippman can only make sense of Shuki by viewing him as a coward, kowtowing to the demands of the goy: "How he wants the goy to throw him just a little smile! How desperately he wants that smile" (*TC* 136).

Put simply, power, and who wields more of it, represents the only relevant issue of the conflict as far as Lippman is concerned. The Arabs, he would have us believe, forced Israel into a game in which only one can win—"those are the rules the Arabs have set" (*TC* 137). Henry/ Hanoch, a virtual mouthpiece of the Lippman ideology, asserts that "[Arabs] don't respect niceness and they don't respect weakness. What the Arab respects is power" (*TC* 119). Lippman, of course, does not shy away from exerting such power, whether voicing his resolve to Arab leaders in their own tongue or standing up to the disapproving Israeli government itself.

While Lippman's essential argument may ring true for some readers given the history of Arab aggression against the Jewish state, Roth undercuts the attractiveness of Lippman's politics here by dramatizing his alienation from the Israeli government (the government responsible, I should add, for seizing the Golan Heights and the West Bank in the first place). Lippman fears that Israel will attempt to placate the Arabs by dismantling the Jewish settlements on the West Bank and raves, "let their Jewish army come and stone us! I dare this Jewish government! I dare *any* Jewish government, to try to evict us by force!" (*TC* 136). Referring to the Jewish army as "their" army (Israel's, not his), Lippman distances himself from Israel. Some lines later, in an apparent attempt to convince us once and for all of his fanaticism and paranoia, he warns Nathan of the forthcoming American Holocaust of the Jews which will be carried out by, of all people, the blacks. According to Lippman, the blacks in the ghettos "are already sharpening their knives" (*TC* 139). Nathan pokes fun at Lippman's paranoia by asking him whether the blacks will accomplish the slaughter "With or without the help of the federal government" (*TC* 139).

Ultimately, the reader can only espouse Lippman's unwavering Middle East policy—*"we do not give ground!"*—by rejecting the perspective of the narrator, Nathan, who hardly seems moved by his antagonist's vehemence (*TC* 145). Just after Lippman's tirade, Nathan cannot keep himself from insulting his brother's ridiculous allegiance to the Harpo/Hannibal. Abandoning tact altogether, Nathan asks of his brother, "when are you going to stop being an apprentice fanatic and start practicing dentistry again?" (*TC* 155). He also wishes that he had told Lippman when he had the chance that "Maybe the Jews begin with Judea, but Henry doesn't and he never will. He begins with WJZ and WOR, with double features at the Roosevelt on Saturday afternoons and Sunday doubleheaders at Ruppert Stadium watching the Newark Bears. Not nearly as epical, but there you are. Why don't you let my brother go?" (*TC* 150). In thus playing Moses to Lippman's Pharaoh, Nathan calls attention to Lippman's enslavement of those around him, not only the enslavement of Henry/Hanoch but also of the Arabs whom he controls with his gun.

We should not underestimate Roth's achievement in bringing so many palpable Jewish voices to bear on the Middle East problem. There are those who doubt that such disparate Jewish voices even exist. In Edward Said's influential study, *Orientalism,* he interestingly succumbs to one of the "Occidental" tendencies he admonishes (to fix the "other" as morally inferior) when he defines Israelis as merely the bourgeois colonialists of the Middle East. Said argues that "the Semitic myth bifurcated in the Zionist movement; one Semite went the way of Orientalism, the other, the Arab, was forced to go the way of the Oriental" (*Orientalism* 307). Such a simple dichotomy does little justice to the complicated political issues that beset the Middle East evident in the heated debates within the Israeli camp. Only recently has Said acknowledged "the contribution of many Jewish, and even Zionist, groups and individuals . . . speaking out for human rights, and active[ly] campaigning against Israeli militarism"; and this acknowledgment rings more like politically correct lip service than real conviction amid an essay that overwhelmingly reaffirms his earlier views ("Reflections" 10). Even after Israel's courageous provision for Palestinian self-rule in Gaza and Jericho, Said curiously commented in the *New York Times* that "We want a real agreement with Israel. . . . They don't want any agreement at all" (Qtd. in Schemo A10). Moreover, Said refused to see Baruch Goldstein as the psychotic radical that he was, and instead asserted that he merely typified the "extraordinary violence latent in American Zionism" ("Hebron" 27). If nothing else, then, the contradictory Jewish voices in the "Judea" section of *The Counterlife* surely problematize Said's essential vision of a monolithic Israel.

It would be easy to end my discussion of *The Counterlife* here, on this unqualified note of Roth's resistance to Lippman's colonialist perspective. However, to do so would be to ignore the counter-elements of the text through which Roth reaffirms—wittingly or unwittingly—Lippman's arguments. As I have already implied, several elements of the narrative reinscribe the conventional views of the Arab and, thereby, implicitly affirm an Israeli moral rectitude. Roth's use of pathos represents the most subtle of these narrative modes. Try as he might to hold the "Neanderthal" view of the Arab up to scrutiny, Roth cannot help but espouse this view of a war-loving, sadistic antagonist of the Jews, as well, via this rhetorical technique.

There are a precious few moments that shape Nathan's impressions of Israel. Interestingly enough, most of these moments are emotionally charged with the element of Israeli suffering and sacrifice caused directly by Arab aggression. In a taxi, on the way to visit his brother at Agor, Nathan observes a group of Israeli soldiers sunning and listening to music on the side of the road. He unflinchingly comments to the driver, "Easy going army you have here" (*TC* 106). In response, the driver shows Nathan a picture of his son in army fatigues, whom Nathan describes as "an intense-looking boy" (*TC* 106). When Nathan says innocuously enough, "Very nice," the driver tersely replies, "Dead ... Someone is shooting a bomb. He is no more there. No shoes, nothing ... Killed ... No good. I never see my son no more" (*TC* 106). The driver's laconic delivery only intensifies the scene's pathos, and Nathan, of course, stands admonished for his blithe judgment of the army's lack of seriousness. Moreover, the Arab—undoubtedly the "someone" responsible for the bomb—does not emerge from the scene unscathed either. Indeed, the reader must see the Arab as responsible for the driver's grief by randomly killing his mere "boy" of a son.

Roth represents the Arab not only as a senseless murderer of children, but as downright sadistic. The barbarity of the Arab emerges most vividly as Nathan recalls Shuki's description of his brother's torture at the hands of the Syrians during the Six-Day War:

> After the Syrian retreat, they found him and the rest of his captured platoon with their hands tied behind them to stakes in the ground; they had been castrated, decapitated, and their penises stuffed in their mouths. Strewn around the abandoned battlefield were necklaces made of their ears. (*TC* 70)

The passage hardly needs elaboration. In short, it unequivocally strips the Arab of any moral high ground. What moral claim (on land, on human rights issues, on *anything*) can such sadistic people make? One need only read the passage to understand why Shuki's son, Mati, feels a duty to give up his beloved piano for military service.

Such moments of pathos leave the strongest impression on Nathan, and Roth takes care to emphasize these scenes, just in case we have not remembered them as well as his narrator. Nathan reminds us of his "impressions fostered by what little I'd heard from [Shuki] about his massacred brother, his disheartened wife, and that patriotic young pianist of his serving in the army . . . nor could I forget the Yemenite father who'd driven me to Agor, who, without any common language to express to me the depths of his grief, nonetheless, with Sacco-Vanzettian eloquence, had cryptically described the extinction of his soldier-son" (*TC* 112). Through Nathan's reflections, Roth underscores these scenes in which the Arab emerges as the violent and sadistic aggressor of the Middle East.

Moreover, Roth gives the Arab no voice in the text to counter the pro-Zionist pathos. In fact, the only Arabs who are ever specifically represented in the novel are the harmless restaurant owners in Hebron where the Zuckerman brothers eat. Nathan comments that "The Arab family who ran the place couldn't have been more welcoming; indeed, the owner, who took our order in English, called Henry 'Doctor' with considerable esteem" (*TC* 120). The restaurant owner's respectful salutation to Henry/Hanoch, "Doctor," (filtered indirectly through Nathan's perspective) represents the only word uttered by an Arab in the novel. Essentially, then, Roth defines through *The Counterlife* two kinds—and only two kinds—of Arabs that exist in the Middle East: the "bad" Arabs who murder Jewish children and men (though they torture the men first) and the "good" Arabs who speak a polite, subservient English to the American Jew.

Roth does flirt with the possibilities of depicting a significant Arab voice in Shuki's farewell letter to Nathan. Through his letter, Shuki joins the ranks of Roth characters who attempt to control Nathan's pen (one thinks especially of Judge Wapter's ten points in *The Ghost Writer* [1979]). Shuki begs of Nathan not to satirize Mordecai Lippman for fear that the fictionalized Lippman will make for bad Israeli P.R. in America. Herein, he suggests what an Arab voice might sound like:

By the way, you haven't met Lippman's Arab counterpart yet and been assaulted head-on by the wildness of *his* rhetoric. I'm sure that at Agor you will have heard Lippman talking about the Arabs and how we must rule them, but if you haven't heard the Arabs talk about ruling, if you haven't *seen* them ruling, then as a satirist you're in for an even bigger treat. Jewish ranting and bullshitting there is—but, however entertaining you may find Lippman's, the Arab ranting and bullshitting has distinction all its own, and the characters spewing it are no less ugly. (*TC* 183)

The closest we come to a significant Arab voice in the novel, then, is Shuki's allusion here to an altogether "ugly" one. Shuki calls this nebulous Arab "as bad if not worse" than Lippman and implores Nathan not to "mislead the guy in Kansas. It's too damn complicated for that" (*TC* 183). Interestingly enough, Roth's mere suggestion of a possible Arab voice evidently suits critics of the novel just fine. Most scholars have, up to this point, focused their efforts squarely upon the aesthetic implications of Roth's structure (see Shostak and Goodheart). Naomi Sokoloff comes closest to placing a finger on the absence of an Arab voice when she notes the absence of a moderate American-Jewish voice to counter Nathan's detachment from Israel (79). Sokoloff's recognition, however, of certain absent voices in the novel makes her omission of the absent Arab all the more conspicuous. What is more, the critics' refusal to acknowledge the absent "other" in *The Counterlife* raises interesting questions concerning their unconscious complicity in the anti-Arab strategies that Roth employs (also unconsciously, I believe) through his narrative.

That said, let me note that I do not presume to prescribe a short list of mandatory voices the Jewish-American writer must create when thoughts of Israel bestir the imagination (e.g., one Arab voice/one American voice/one Israeli voice). However, the conspicuous absence of the Arab in Jewish-American novels about Israel does have an effect, well worth our attention. In *The Counterlife*, the absence of Arab voices contributes to the anti-Arab elements of the text which not only solidify comfortable stereotypes of the Arab, but also valorize several Jewish perspectives in the novel that would otherwise remain suspect. Henry's/ Hanoch's religious awakening, for example, takes on a certain indisputable poignancy. While we may laugh at his ridiculous week-long worship of a challah as if it were sculpture, his convincing identification with the most orthodox sect of Israeli Jews—"I am not *just* a Jew, I'm not *also* a Jew—*I'm a Jew as deep as those Jews*"—emerges as heroic when pitted against the evil Arab empire (*TC* 68). Given Roth's depiction of the Arab, who can dispute the exigency of such Jewish awakenings? To survive, the Jew, it seems, must develop a "frame of reference slightly larger than the kitchen table in Newark?" (*TC* 155).

Mordecai Lippman offers this broader perspective. For while Roth undercuts Lippman's arguments (as I have explored above), we should not give short shrift to the actual persuasiveness of his rhetoric rooted in his unchallenged depiction of the Arab; they throw stones at school buses and roll hand grenades at his house while his children sleep (*TC* 132, 143). In the absence of an Arab counter-voice, Lippman's militancy seems an attractive alternative to the traditional Jewish role of victim. Even Nathan defends the viability of Lippman's politics in contrast to Shuki's moderation when he replies to his friend's letter: "It's Lippman, after all, who is the unequivocal patriot and devout believer, whose morality is plain and unambiguous, whose rhetoric is righteous and readily accessible" (*TC* 185). Indeed, while one may wish to dispute (and rightly so) Roth's affinity for the Mordecai Lippmans of Israel, one cannot deny that he also equips him with the most forceful arguments. Nathan must admit after his dinner with Lippman that Agor's leader rhetorically "outclassed" him.

I hope that I have illustrated the nagging attractiveness and repulsiveness of Mordecai Lippman's fundamentalist stance and Shuki Elchanan's more moderate Zionism—a tension I attribute to Roth's ambivalences concerning the Middle East problem. Ultimately, he can neither exalt nor condemn *any* Jewish perspective. Rather than a shortcoming of the novel, this element manifests itself as Roth's greatest stride toward a thoughtful Jewish-American imagining of the current Israeli landscape. That much said, however, the absence of an intelligent Arab voice strikes one, today, as particularly odd given the volubility of such voices amid the current political climate in the Middle East. Hanan Ashrawi and Faisel Husseini, for example, have made their way from the inconspicuous pages of the *Journal of Palestine Studies* to the nightly news. Perhaps recognizing the several muted voices in *The Counterlife,* Roth creates a significant Palestinian character (and several more Jewish ones as well) in his latest Middle East novel, *Operation Shylock: A Confession.*

There can be little doubt that *Operation Shylock* can be seen, at least in part, as Roth's attempt to probe further into the polemical Middle East perspectives he only touches upon in *The Counterlife.* To wit: Shuki Elchanan, at one point in *The Counterlife,* suggests that the Jewish Diaspora has fulfilled the function that the first Zionists had envisioned only a Jewish state could fulfill: "we are the excitable, ghettoized, jittery little Jews of the Diaspora, and you are the Jews with all the confidence and cultivation that comes of feeling at home where you are" (*TC* 82). In *Operation Shylock,* Roth pursues Shuki's "Diasporism" further. Philip Roth, the protagonist, travels to Israel simply to interview his friend, Aharon Appelfeld; while in Israel, though, he comes face to face with his double, who usurps Roth's identity to more successfully tout the anti-Zionist ideology of Diasporism. While this ideology can be seen as an elaboration of some of Shuki's Diasporist inclinations, it can also be seen as an elaboration of Jimmy Lustig's plan to destroy Yad Vashem in *The Counterlife*. Jimmy wants to destroy Israel's Holocaust remembrance Hall to preclude Jewish moral abrasiveness toward gentiles and, ultimately, to avert a second Holocaust; likewise, Roth's double has these same goals in mind, but sets his sights on dismantling Israel itself, to a great extent, to achieve them. Zionism, according to Roth's impostor, "has outlived its historical function" (*OS* 32). Resettlement in the European Diaspora—the "most authentic Jewish homeland, the birthplace of rabbinic Judaism, Jewish secularism, socialism . . ."—would avert a second Holocaust at the hands of the Arabs as well as accomplish a "spiritual victory over Hitler and Auschwitz" (*OS* 32).

Though it may be hard to imagine a more harebrained Middle East proposal than Jimmy Lustig's in *The Counterlife*, Roth manages to do just that in the Diasporism of Roth's impostor. Roth pokes fun, on several occasions, at the implausibility of the plan. When Roth suggests to his double that Europe might be less than elated to reabsorb thousands of Jews, the impostor replies,

> You know what will happen in Warsaw, at the railway station, when the first trainload of Jews returns? There will be crowds to welcome them. People will be jubilant. People will be in tears. They will be shouting, "Our Jews are back! Our Jews are back!" The spectacle will be transmitted by television throughout the world. (*OS* 45)

The hilarity of this fantasy aside, one need only visit Auschwitz in Poland and see what short shrift Jewish suffering receives on the guided tour to realize that Poland has yet to come to terms with its Jews. Alternatively, how many Jews have come to terms with Europe? Would Israeli Jews be anxious to resettle in the very European countries from which they recently fled? Says Roth to his double, "are they lining up, the Romanian Jews who are dying to go back to Ceausescus's Romania? Are they lining up, the Polish Jews who are dying to return to Communist Poland? Those Russians struggling to leave the Soviet Union, is your plan to turn them around at the Tel Aviv airport . . . ?" (*OS* 47). Roth does such a good job exposing the ridiculousness of Diasporism that one scholar responded in a *Tikkun* symposium on Roth's Diasporism,

"Do you really expect me to take 'Diasporism' seriously when Philip Roth doesn't propose it seriously?" (Dickstein 44).

My hunch is that Roth has received few letters from Israeli Jews inquiring further about Diasporism and one-way tickets to their respective European homelands. Roth, one hopes, took the advice of the *New York Times* reviewer who suggested that the author send his double on the promotional tour of the book in Israel. Still, we cannot dismiss Diasporism as blithely as the above scholar, for Roth uses the double's Diasporism to access and scrutinize legitimate Middle East concerns. The serious implications associated with the Diasporist ideology, not its obvious absurdity, make *Operation Shylock* a noteworthy book. For in the novel, Roth raises the stakes considerably from Jimmy Lustig's Yad Vashem plan. In Diasporism, Roth's impostor does not merely call into question the political shrewdness of Holocaust remembrance (as Lustig does in *The Counterlife*), but considers whether Jews have exploited the Holocaust to legitimize a colonialist state, Israel, that violently oppresses the indigenous Palestinian population.

Roth dramatizes this view most forcefully through George Ziad (or Zee), a Palestinian friend of Roth's from graduate school who mistakes him for his double in Israel. In Ziad, Roth creates a radical Palestinian voice which complements the radical Zionist voice of Mordecai Lippman in *The Counterlife*. Since graduate school, Ziad has immersed himself in the Palestinian cause and, thus, strikes up an immediate kinship once again with Roth, whom he thinks founded the Diasporist movement; few Arabs, of course, wouldn't love Roth's double who yearns to see the state halved of its Jewish population and returned to its 1948 borders. Ziad, like Lippman in *The Counterlife*, delivers a fundamentalist diatribe that spans several pages. By exposing what he perceives to be Israel's "mythology of victimization," Ziad implicitly refutes Lippman's perspective concerning Israel's claim to the Occupied Territories:

> This is the public-relations campaign cunningly devised by the terrorist Begin; to establish Israeli military expansionism as historically just by joining it to the memory of Jewish victimization; to rationalize—as historical justice, as just retribution, as nothing more than self-defense—the gobbling up of the Occupied Territories and the driving of the Palestinians off their land once again. What justifies seizing every opportunity to extend Israel's boundaries? Auschwitz. What justifies bombing Beirut civilians? Auschwitz . . . (*OS* 132).

Now, Roth intentionally blurs the line between fact and fiction in the novel and some initial reviewers of the book exhausted a good deal of page space promoting their spin on the conundrum; to my mind, however, passages like the one above suggest the relative fruitlessness of the "fact or fiction" debate. For the issues Ziad raises here are certainly real enough. True, Roth describes his friend's views as a "pungent ideological mulch of overstatement and lucidity, of insight and stupidity, of precise historical data and willful historical ignorance . . . the intoxication of resistance had rendered [Ziad] incapable of even nibbling at the truth, however intelligent he still happened to be" (OS 129). But, Ziad's essential claim that "the state of Israel has drawn the last of its moral credit out of the bank of the dead six million" cuts to the heart of the real life concerns of several Jews on the political left: that Israelis, and Americans, have exploited the Holocaust-related guilt of the world community to justify the state's actions for too long (OS 135).

Consider, for example, the case of Amos Elon, an Israeli journalist who persistently invokes the Holocaust to describe Israel's victimization of the Arabs; or Thomas L. Friedman, who laments the "Yad Vasheming" of Israel in From Beirut to Jerusalem (282); or consider the members of the Citizens' Rights Movement and the New Jewish Agenda—Jewish organizations on the far left—who also invoke the language of the Shoah to call attention to the plight of the Palestinians. Hilda Silverman, an Agenda leader, published an essay provocatively entitled, "Palestinian Holocaust Memorial?" In the April 17, 1994, edition of The New York Times, the editors of the liberal American-Jewish magazine, Tikkun, used a full-page advertisement to encourage the speeding up of the Middle East Peace Process and condemned the "distressing tendency in some sectors of the Jewish world, both in Israel and the United States . . . to act as if past Jewish suffering is the warrant for contemporary acts of insensitivity or even brutality." Finally, in Paul Breines's 1990 study, Tough Jews: Political Fantasies and the Moral Dilemma of American Jewry, he probes the basis for this "distressing tendency" and, in so doing, characterizes Zionism in a way that would, no doubt, please Ziad:

> Zionism is at once a decisive break with the traditions of Jewish weakness and gentleness and also not so decisive a break: it rejects meekness and gentleness in favor of the normalcy of toughness, while preserving the older tradition of the Jews as a special or chosen people,

which *depends on* imagery of Jews as frail victims. Zionism needs its
weak and gentle Jewish counterparts to give moral justification to
Jewish participation in the world of bodies, specifically, of physical
violence, including killing or even sadism. To put the matter most
starkly: the image of Jewish victimization vindicates the image of the
Jewish victimizer. (50)

An exclamation point here, a vitriolic comment there, and this passage
would appear as if it were lifted directly from Ziad's dialogue in *Operation Shylock*. How far, really, is Breines's coolly intellectual analysis of the
Israeli ethos from Ziad's pithy perspective, "Marlboro has the Marlboro
Man, Israel has its Holocaust Man" (*OS* 296). At any rate, my point is
that several left-wing Jews (in America and in Israel) seem to agree with
Ziad that Israel, by exploiting the Holocaust to justify its brutality and
colonialism, has "forfeited its claim to the Holocaust" (*OS* 135).
Although Roth, then, might undercut Ziad's credibility, the Palestinian
regardless puts his finger on the pulse of our present cultural debate
over the Middle East.

What is more, Roth's depiction of the contemporary Middle East
scene goes a long way toward salvaging George Ziad's credibility. Roth
includes several scenes in the novel, for example, that call into question
how humanely Israel treats the Arab Israelis. Indeed, Roth's double
espouses Diasporism not only to avert a second Holocaust of the Jews
but also to avert the more insidious and gradual moral decay of the
Israeli Jews precipitated by their treatment of the Palestinians. One does
not leave the novel certain of widespread Israeli abuses of the Arabs.
Still, we see enough heavily armed Israeli soldiers in the West Bank and
hear of enough blood-stained walls there to make us suspicious of
Israeli abuses of power. Roth also depicts part of a trial of Palestinian
children (who may or may not have been drugged and abused by the
Israeli police) accused less than convincingly of throwing Molotov
cocktails. Roth muses that the courtroom, with its Jewish flags, judges,
and lawyers was a courtroom "such as Jews had envisioned in their fantasies for many hundreds of years, answering longings even more
unimaginable than those for an army or a state. One day *we* will deter-
mine justice" (*OS* 140). Roth wonders, and so do we, how fair a trial any
Palestinian can expect in such a courtroom. To have even a chance, the
defendants must rely upon an Orthodox Jewish defense lawyer who harbors little sympathy for Palestinians and admonishes Roth (mistaking
him for his double) for his Diasporism.

Most disturbingly, perhaps, Roth dramatizes the ambivalence of an Israeli army lieutenant who must tell his mother each night, "Look, you want to know if I personally beat anyone? I didn't. But I had to do an awful lot of maneuvering to avoid it!" (*OS* 169). The soldier realizes that Israel cannot survive by acting out of a moral ideology, but when he looks at the Israeli government he wants to vomit (*OS* 170). Through all of these elements (certain to enrage many Jews), Roth presents a disturbing contrast, a gap, between what Israel was supposed to be, and what it has become. Roth's skeptical vision of the Israeli moral ledger prompted one American-Jewish writer, Daphne Merkin, to comment, "If I were living in Israel—if I were my sister, say, who lives in Jerusalem with her American husband and four American-born children despite ongoing doubts and criticism—I would despise this book. As someone whose emotional investment is safely tallied from these shores I merely dislike it" ("Philip Roth's Diasporism" 44). Indeed, we cannot dismiss Roth's characterization of Ziad as a blithe, "colonialist" depiction of the Palestinian. For the above elements of the novel, which raise the hackles of Merkin and several other Jews, lend a good bit of credibility to Ziad's maniacally rendered perspective.

Given what Roth sees in Israel, one should not be surprised that he cannot dismiss his double's Diasporism as merely "anti-Zionist crap" (*OS* 289). As Roth's impostor notes, the two Roths' identities are not wholly distinguishable; there is not one liar, one truth-teller, one honest Philip, one dishonest Philip, one reasonable Philip and one psychopath (*OS* 193). Likewise, there is not one "Diasporist" and one "Zionist" Roth. Roth must admit the "mad plausibility about [Diasporism]. There's more than a grain of truth in recognizing and acknowledging the Eurocentrism of Judaism" (Roth, as I noted earlier, suggested this Eurocentrism in *The Counterlife* through Nathan Zuckerman's redefinition of Zionism to include the vision of his Galician grandfathers) (*OS* 191). Roth dramatizes the melting of the two Roths' identities as Roth usurps the identity of his double and fervently espouses Diasporism to George Ziad and his family. He describes Irving Berlin—who turned Christmas into a holiday about snow and Easter into a fashion show— as the father of the Diasporist movement. Israeli nuclear reactors pale in comparison to Berlin's "nice" defusing of Christian enmity toward the Jews, as Berlin's songs did nothing to jeopardize the Jews' moral survival. Says Roth (the writer-character, not the impostor), "Better to be marginal neurotics, anxious assimilationists, and everything else that the Zionists despise, better to *lose* the state than to lose your moral being by unleashing a nuclear war" (*OS* 158). Roth undercuts his lecture by calling it "Diasporist blah-blah," but the moral issues he raises are compelling given the backdrop in the novel of a volatile West Bank where Israeli morality seems under threat constantly. At least one critic, Daniel Lazare, has noted Roth's courage in expressing these controversial sentiments "full blast" and welcomes Roth's celebration, in "Diasporism," of the assimilationist impulse over the nationalist impulse. Says Lazare, "Out of the nationalistic, embattled, ethnically-cleansed existence in Israel has come—what? The invasion of Lebanon, the West Bank and Gaza Strip settlements, and the Intifada" (42).

Granted, Lazare subscribes to the impostor Roth's Diasporism a good deal more than does Roth (the real-life writer, that is). The anti-Zionist plan of Roth's double to retake Europe as if Hitler never reigned for twelve years has its appeal (there is, in fact, a strong Jewish tradition of blotting out the names of enemies), but only a superficial, ideological appeal. The illusory outward health and vigor of Roth's double suggests the concomitant shallowness of Diasporism (though Roth's impostor looks like the "after" to Roth's "before" in a plastic surgery advertisement, he dies of cancer shortly after his trip to Israel). Roth, recognizing the superficiality of Diasporism, protests vehemently for Holocaust remembrance since "Those twelve years cannot be expunged from history any more than they can be obliterated from memory, however mercifully forgetful one might prefer to be. The meaning of the destruction of European Jewry cannot be measured or interpreted by the brevity with which it was attained" (*OS* 43). The anti-Semitism that culminated in the Holocaust still seethes close to the surface in Roth's Middle East and in Europe, making Diasporism impossible and Zionism essential. Roth feels the palpable anti-Semitic threat in a vile caricature of Menachem Begin standing over a pyramid of dead Arab bodies which he sees in the London papers; in the free and easy way with which Palestinians and their sympathizers (like some of the Jewish ones listed above) link the Israeli Occupation with Nazism; in the way the popular press dignifies stone-throwing "riots" by calling them "uprisings"; in the Iraqi Scud attacks on Israel during the Gulf War; and, most forcefully, Roth recognizes this threat in the assassination of Leon Klinghoffer while aboard the *Achille Lauro*. His murder, as Roth imagines it, convinces one of the Holocaust's enduring relevance and the consequent necessity of Israel. Despite any Diasporist urge for normalcy in a neutral Europe, the

Klinghoffer murder proves that "*there is no neutral territory*," not even on a cruise ship (328). Roth espouses Israel indirectly, yet convincingly, through the above details, which resonate in *Operation Shylock*. Roth may be critical of the Israeli government and military, but he falls far short of seriously endorsing "Diasporism"; he may be tempted to forget the Holocaust, but realizes the ineluctable moral and political urgency to remember (Roth, in fact, has reflected in interviews upon the enduring relevance of the Holocaust) (see Roth, "Interview" 136).

Let me hasten to add, however, that Lazare's espousal of the essential Diasporist/Palestinian arguments, *as Roth presents them,* illustrates the moral rigorousness of Roth's fictional approach. That one can read the novel as either Zionist at its core, or anti-Zionist (like Lazare), bespeaks the complexity of the Middle East crisis and suggests the concomitant inner tensions that plague thoughtful Jewish-Americans like Philip Roth. To my mind, there can be little doubt that Roth, at least to some extent, implicates both stone-throwing Arabs and gun-wielding Israeli soldiers as Roth (the protagonist) simultaneously observes from his hotel room Arab rock gatherers and armed Israeli soldiers heading toward the West Bank to have it out.

Philip Roth's precise moral perspective remains intentionally ambiguous in both of his Middle East novels to reflect the moral conundrum that is the Middle East itself. In *Operation Shylock,* for example, the murkiness of the characters reflects the murkiness of the Middle East, as Roth envisions it (Ziad, it appears, may be an Israeli informant playing the role of a Palestinian radical; Roth's double may also be a Mossad operative setting the stage for Roth's hazily disclosed mission in Athens to expose Jewish financial supporters of the PLO). Both of the novels' strengths, I would argue, lie in Roth's extensive depiction of this murkiness. It is just this lack of a satisfyingly clear moral perspective of the Middle East which dogs thoughtful Jewish and non-Jewish intellectuals today. Moreover, Roth deserves credit for entering the fray at all. Toward the end of *Operation Shylock,* the Mossad operative, Smilesburger, admonishes the American Jews' complacency when it comes to matters of the Middle East:

> You are free to indulge your virtue freely. Go to wherever you feel most blissfully unblamable. That is the delightful luxury of the utterly transformed American Jew. Enjoy it. You are that marvelous, unlikely, most magnificent phenomenon, the truly liberated Jew. The

Jew who is not accountable. . . . you are the blessed Jew condemned to nothing, least of all to our historical struggle. (*OS* 352)

Smilesburger, indeed, could easily be referring to Jewish-American writers, who, as a group, have largely ignored Israel in their work until recently. Roth, to his credit, engages the "historical struggle" in both of his Middle East novels by assessing the considerable accomplishments and the more troublesome failings of the Jewish state (and only occasionally lapsing into what current post-colonial critics would call, "colonialist discourse"). Several critics have given Roth his due in this regard. In a review of *Operation Shylock*, John Updike comments, "Relentlessly honest, Roth recruits raw nerves, perhaps, because they make the fiercest soldiers in the battle of truth" (111). Reflecting upon both of Roth's Israel novels, Hillel Halkin notes that the "sheer, almost abstract passion for being Jewish seems to grow stronger in Roth's work all the time" ("How to Read" 48), while Sanford Pinsker commends Roth for "wrenching Jewish-American fictions about Israel from the conventional pieties into which they have too often fallen" ("They Dream" 8–X). Most interestingly, perhaps, Cynthia Ozick—a staunch Zionist who has little use for its current "post" prefix, thank you—could not say enough good things about *Operation Shylock* in a recent interview: "[*Operation Shylock*] is totally amazing, in language, intellect, plotting, thesis, analysis, reach, daring. . . . He's now the boldest American writer alive" ("An Interview" 394). All of which is simply to say that Philip Roth's *The Counterlife* and *Operation Shylock* show just how far Jewish-American fiction on Israel has come since Leon Uris's *Exodus*, and suggest the directions in which we can expect it to go in the not too distant future. I pursue perhaps the most prevalent of these new directions—the Jewish-American feminist approach toward Israel—in the final two chapters below.

Chapter 8

ANNE ROIPHE'S ANGST
A Jewish-American Feminist Looks at Israel

> *If Israel is the redemption of the Jewish peo-*
> *ple, God's sign after the Holocaust, then if one*
> *is connected to the Jewish experience, one*
> *must be connected to Israel—but how and to*
> *what degree and what is asked and what can*
> *be given?*
>
> —Anne Roiphe (GWM 17)

In a short piece which appeared in *The New York Times* in December 1978, Anne Roiphe revealed that her secular Jewish family did not celebrate Chanukah and (worse yet) bought a Christmas tree each year. Her article prompted a hostile response from scores of Jews. Says Roiphe, "Housewives, rabbis, lawyers, doctors, businessmen, all but Indian chiefs phoned or wrote in, furious that the paper had published an article that advocated assimilation, displayed ignorance of Judaism, and seemed to express contempt for the Jewish way of life" ("Taking Down" 58). Roiphe, by her own admission, would not have written the piece had she anticipated the public berating she would subsequently be forced to endure; however, she has reason to be thankful for the unsavory episode. The angry responses to her inflammatory article caused her to reflect upon the importance of Judaism in her life and to recognize that assimilation into the dominant culture had nearly stripped her of this central element of her identity. Roiphe immediately began to study Jewish history and the Talmud. Moreover, she began to explore Jewish issues overtly in her works. In a memoir, *Generation without Memory* (1981), and a more recent novel, *The Pursuit of Happiness* (1991), she examines the questionable viability of assimilation; in the novel *Lovingkindness* (1987) she scrutinizes Israel and its growing ultra-Orthodox population; and she suggests the role that Holocaust remembrance should play in a "living Judaism" in *A Season for Healing; Reflections on the Holocaust* (1988).

One must admire Roiphe's courage. She surely realized that several of those who excoriated her for expressing her alienation from Judaism, as embodied in her purchase of Christmas trees, would be eager to attack her *chutzpahdik* [nervy] exploration of Jewish issues (*chutzpahdik* since Jews who allow Christmas trees past their threshold know enough to expect a special kind of scrutiny from fellow Jews). I offer one recent assault for both its insight and its blindness. In a fairly mean-spirited essay, "The Odyssey of Anne Roiphe: Anatomy of an Alienated Jew," Bernard Zelechow reviews the breadth of Roiphe's writing and, perplexed, concludes that "Anne Roiphe holds Jewish values in low esteem intellectually and morally yet she desires Jewish affirmation for her unreflected attitudes and opinions" (44). He can only wonder "[w]hy is it that a well-educated woman who seeks to identify with Judaism is so paralyzed in her quest?" (44). To Zelechow's credit, he identifies the essential element of Roiphe's relationship with Judaism as it manifests itself in her fiction and non-fiction—ambivalence. That said, he finds this ambivalence inexplicable (or, at least, unworthy of careful inspection). He never attempts to answer the rhetorical question he poses above, even though its answer lies within the question itself. For, indeed, Roiphe's very identity as a well-educated woman accounts, in large part, for her uneasy relationship with Judaism.

This is not to say that traditional Judaism stands foursquare against progressive politics. Interestingly, biblical Judaism—with its emphasis on social justice and *tikkun olam* [the repair of the world]—continues to encourage the vast majority of Jews to embrace progressive liberalism. Although many second-generation American Jews have joined ranks with political conservatives over the past twenty years (a trend exemplified by the ideological shift to the right of Norman Podhoretz and the concomitant shift of his magazine, *Commentary*), polls indicate that an overwhelming majority of American Jews—78 percent in fact—voted Democratic in the Republican landslide that was the November 1994 election.

Still, a fierce tension exists today between traditional Judaism, which inspires such political liberalism, and one contemporary liberal movement, feminism. It is a tension one must appreciate to contextualize

Roiphe's exploration of the Jewish state, Israel, in her fiction. For just as Israel represents "the paramount source of Jewish identity," as Theodore Solotaroff puts it, the state is also the site—thanks to the political and numerical power of the ultra-Orthodox, or *Haredim*—where the patri-archal problems of Judaism manifest themselves most prevalently ("American-Jewish" 33). Thus, when Anne Roiphe looks toward Israel in her writing, she sees the answer to the Holocaust, the most triumphant expression of Jewish self-determination and perseverance, a viable alter-native to assimilation; however, she also sees a state foundering in the strengthening grip of the ultra-Orthodox Jews whose rigid interpreta-tion of the *halakah* perpetuates the subordination of women in Israeli society.

First, let us explore my premise that Jewish-American women have ample reason to feel ambivalent about the "Jewish" component of their hyphenated identity. Letty Cottin Pogrebin's recent book, *Deborah, Golda, and Me: Being Female and Jewish in America* (1991), proves instructive since she explores in some depth this tension between fem-inism and Judaism. In this thick and impressive study, Pogrebin uses the term "double marginality" to describe the experience of being both Jewish and a woman living in America. Neither of a Jewish woman's affinity groups, Pogrebin insists, represents a cultural norm. That is, while a Jewish male lives in the margins of mainstream American life, he "can never be an outsider the way a Jewish woman is an outsider. . . . With other *women* she remains The Jew, and with male *Jews* she remains The Woman" (xvi). What interests me, given the focus of my essay, is the second half of Pogrebin's equation. For, just as women are devalued in mainstream America, they are marginalized and given subordinate status as Jews in Orthodox and most Conservative syna-gogues. Pogrebin calls upon several painful childhood reminiscences to illustrate the inherent sexism of Judaism. Perhaps most poignantly, she remembers her exclusion from the memorial service minyan—a quorum of ten men required for communal prayer—for her mother, despite pleading with her father: "'I know the Hebrew.' I say. 'You can count *me*, Daddy.' I meant, *I want to count*. I meant, don't count me out just because I am a girl. 'You know it's not allowed,' he replies, frowning. . . . He calls the synagogue and asks them to send us a tenth man." (Pogrebin 43). Such reminiscences are essential in Pogrebin's attempt to "illuminate in personal terms one woman's struggle to rec-oncile Judaism and feminism" (xvii).

Pogrebin's upbringing in a fairly mainstream American Jewish household leaves one with the nagging and downright disconcerting sense that the highly personal struggle she illuminates in her book is one that faces several Jewish-American women, that her sense of double-marginality is not at all atypical. Small wonder that in Anne Roiphe's memoir, *Generation without Memory* (1981), she reflects upon her own painful formative years as a Jewish female (see also Kendall, Umansky, Feld, Susan Alter, and Penkower). Consider, for a moment, Roiphe's childhood initiation into Judaism:

> In the basement of the synagogue I learned that the law was for men, women were supposed to take care of the house and the children, and that it wasn't too smart for a girl to be too smart. I discovered that women were excluded from the minyan ... from the daily observances, from the sacred obligations, from the honors of the congregation, from the handling of the Torah itself. All the talk about the woman's importance in the home, the bringing of the Sabbath Queen, I dimly recognized as the sugar candies on the gingerbread house of misogyny. In the basement of the synagogue I began to lose my interest, and my theological passions turned instead to secular matters. (*GWM* 22)

Given the virtual exclusion of women from the 613 Jewish commandments (or *mitzvot*), it should come as little surprise that educated women like Roiphe distanced themselves from Judaism pretty early on in their lives and, instead, devoted their energies toward a secular world considerably more receptive to their spiritual and intellectual gifts. Roiphe's early alienation from Judaism, expressed above, seems perfectly natural.

However, Roiphe and other Jewish feminists discovered that their flat rejection of Judaism left a tremendous spiritual void in their lives. After all, Jewish women, like it or not, are inextricably connected to Jewish history. Once Roiphe began her Jewish re-education as an adult, she realized that the Jewish story was "finally my real story" ("Taking Down" 59). What is more, the American identity, Roiphe argues, "if it is not grafted onto something firm, turns to vapor, a substance that cannot sustain or nourish" ("Taking Down" 59). Judith Plaskow, whose sentiments reflect the prevailing spirit within the Jewish feminist movement, shares Roiphe's commitment to both Judaism and feminism, because she recognizes that "sundering Judaism and feminism would mean sundering my being" (xiii). Hence, the Jewish feminists' need to reconcile Judaism and feminism—two seemingly irreconcilable entities. We are in the midst of this precarious, but necessary, reconcilement today. Thankfully, several men and women in the Jewish community are beginning to address and rectify the problems of Judaism's entrenched sexism. Two intellectual periodicals at the center of Jewish thought, *Judaism* and *Response*, recently devoted issues to an intensive reexamination of Judaism and gender (see *Response*, Fall 1993 and *Judaism*, Fall 1993). Marla Bretschneider's "Feminist Judaism: Providing Models for Continuity through Multiculturalism" embodies the key precept of this feminist movement within Judaism, as she suggests the ways in which "feminist Judaism can guide us towards a coming to terms with the crisis of Jewish life in modernity such that what will emerge will be both authentically Jewish and radically transformed" (18).

This desire to preserve an "authentically Jewish" element of a "radically transformed" Judaism accounts for the surge today in the reinterpretation, rather than the abandonment, of biblical scripture and *halakah*. In the Torah's five daughters of Zelophehad (who lobbied for and won certain hereditary rights for daughters), an exuberant Haim Chertok locates a "structural model for ameliorating the status of [Jewish] women" (66). Judith Hauptman also relies upon traditional Jewish sources to elevate the status of Jewish women. In "Women and Prayer: An Attempt to Dispel Some Fallacies," she criticizes Orthodox men who errantly cite *halakah* to "answer feminists who wish to be counted in the quorum of ten and serve as prayer leaders" (94). To "set the *halakhic* process in motion," she argues that women should be counted in the *minyan* and should even serve as prayer leaders, since *halakah* requires that women pray daily. Michael J. Broyde and Joel B. Wolowelsky dispute Hauptman's *halakhic* interpretation. Broyde, grounding his argument in "classical Jewish law," agrees with Hauptman that Jewish women must pray daily but disputes her contention that this law authorizes women to serve as the *shaliah zibbur*/cantor in communal prayer (387). Wolowelsky also insists that Hauptman "has not yet provided enough material to build a responsum allowing a woman to serve as *shaliah zibbur*" (394). To refute Broyde and Wolowelsky's counter-arguments, Hauptman goes back to the *halakhic* drawing-board. She "writes as one who believes in *halakah*, but also as one who believes that research, including a fresh look at long held views and practices based on careful examinations of the classical texts that underlie those views and practices, is a worthwhile endeavor for the ongoing *halakhic* process" ("Some Thoughts" 406). She, thus, investigates the "textual underpinnings" of the very laws to which Orthodox men allude in their efforts to exclude women from the *minyan*; her scrutiny of these texts goes a long way toward convincing one that *halakah* affirms a woman's participation in the *minyan*, even as a prayer leader.

Additional recent articles like Tamar Ross's "Can the Demand for the Change in the Status of Women be *Halakhically* legitimized?," Simcha Fishbane's "'In Any Case there are no Sinful Thoughts'—The Role and Status of Women in Jewish Law as Expressed in the *Arukh Hashulhan*," and Rachel Adler's "'The Jew who wasn't there': *Halakhah* and the Jewish Woman," suggest that the reinterpretation of scripture to re-envision the woman's role as Jew is currently the rage (for recent book-length studies see Wegner, Weiss, Kaufman, Grossman/Haut). What this trend in the reinterpretation of scripture tells us, I believe, is that an increasing number of Jewish feminists—both male and female—seek to expunge the misogynous precepts from Judaism (hence, the gender equity that now flourishes in Reform and Reconstructionist synagogues, and in a growing number of Conservative synagogues); but these same Jews also recognize their ineffable, spiritual need for authentically Jewish rituals, myths, and symbols. Judith Plaskow's "It's Feminist But is it Jewish?" (which serves as the introduction to her 1990 book, *Standing at Sinai: Judaism from a Feminist Perspective*), illustrates this tension within the Jewish feminist movement.

Which brings us back finally to the most powerful contemporary *Jewish* symbol—Israel—and the distinctive *tsores* [troubles] of the Jewish-American woman. As I have already suggested, any ambivalences that Jewish-American women harbor concerning their Judaism intensify as they fix their gaze upon Israel because the state functions as the spiritual core for Jews everywhere, but, at the same time, perpetuates the gender discrimination mandated by *halakah*. One need not search long or hard to locate Roiphe's Zionism, to see that she does indeed embrace Israel as the spiritual core for Jews everywhere. "All Jewish rivers," Roiphe insists, "run toward Israel" (*GWM* 31). In this terse statement, she cuts to the heart of her commitment to the Jewish state. Simply put, if one chooses—as Roiphe has—to identify with Judaism, one almost necessarily chooses to support Israel. Now, I say this with the conviction that constructive criticism of the state's policies represents, perhaps, the most ardent form of "support." For as a contributing editor to the liberal

Jewish magazine, *Tikkun,* Roiphe has been a clear supporter of Palestinian rights. Along with several other liberal Jews, she signed a full-page
ad placed by the *Tikkum* in *The New York Times* on April 17, 1994 (in
the wake of the September 1993 peace accord between Israel and the
PLO), calling for the dismantling of the Jewish settlements in Hebron,
Kiryat Arba, and in the Gaza Strip, areas located in the Occupied Territories seized by Israel after its victory in the Six-Day War of 1967. The
continued presence of these Jewish settlements in the Occupied Territories, of course, remains the most divisive issue between the Israelis
and the PLO (and even between Israelis themselves). Roiphe's Palestinian sympathies, however, do not detract from her commitment toward
Israel (albeit within the U.N. mandated, pre-1967 borders). Says
Roiphe, "The safety of Israel is of intense mythic and realistic propor-
tions to all American Jews. . . . I too feel that Israel, a political entity,
with brave soldiers and terrible bombs, marks a necessary turning point
in Jewish destiny" (*GWM* 53, 187). Necessary, of course, given Auschwitz, Dachau, Treblinka, Bergen-Belsen, Buchenwald . . . or, in
Roiphe's words, necessary since "Jewishness appears indigestible to
other countries" (*GWM* 32).

In *Generation Without Memory* and *The Pursuit of Happiness* (1991),
Roiphe joins the ranks of several feminists—Jews and non-Jews alike—
who may be critical of Israel's sexism and its militancy against the Palestinians but make no bones about their Zionist convictions. In Grace
Halsell's travel narrative, *Journey to Jerusalem* (1981), she devotes
roughly a third of the book to sympathetic accounts of the Palestinians'
plight (in chapters such as "Abdul and Stories of Torture" and "A Palestinian Refugee Camp: The West Bank"), but accepts Israel's right to
exist as well. Moreover, in *The Issue is Power: Essays on Women, Jews,
Violence and Resistance* (1992), Melanie Kaye/Kantrowitz begins her
chapter in which she admonishes Israel for its treatment of the Palestinians by making it clear that she has "deep attachments to friends and
family [in Israel], to the sounds of Hebrew, the smells and tastes of the
place" (151). It also rankles her when some Palestinians and their supporters "toss the term *Holocaust* around, as if by invoking it against
Israelis they can cancel out the past, even-steven, leaving the Jews
stripped of history, devoid of credentials" (Kaye/Kantrowitz 152). Kaye/
Kantrowitz clearly believes that the Jews' tragic history in this century
gives them ample credentials for their own state. Pogrebin joins Kaye/
Kantrowitz in both criticizing Israel's treatment of the Palestinians and

expressing her spiritual investment in Israel: "when my feet first made contact with the ground, the actual *land* of Israel, tears flooded my eyes" (Pogrebin 168). Likewise, Plaskow laments the "contradictions of a democracy in which 17 percent of all citizens [the Palestinians] are suspected as a third column and subjected to discrimination . . ." but celebrates Israel's potential: "In providing an opportunity to bring renewed life to traditional Jewish values while taking seriously the lessons of the modern world, a Jewish homeland challenges Jews to create a culturally rich and diverse society on the basis of a new understanding of difference" (111, 109).

Roiphe's own conviction that Israel represents a necessary turning point in Jewish history emerges rather straightforwardly in her novel, *The Pursuit of Happiness*. In many respects, the novel represents the author's most ambitious fictional undertaking to date as she chronicles the immigrant assimilation of the Gruenbaum family in America. Roiphe begins her exploration in a small Polish village in 1878, where Moses Gruenbaum struggles as a tailor's assistant to support his family. His wife, Naomi, intoxicated with the stories of economic opportunity in America, prods him until he agrees that they should undertake the journey. Roiphe then explores the lives of five generations of "American" Gruenbaums as the narrative runs to the present. Given the chronology of the work, the Holocaust looms throughout. Roiphe presages the advent of the Holocaust by starting the narrative in the late nineteenth century, just as fierce pogroms against the Jews were beginning to spread throughout Europe. In addition to the actual Holocaust, then, Roiphe's depiction of a hostile European Diaspora which facilitated the atrocity suggests the moral necessity of a Jewish state.

We can, literally, see the Holocaust coming as Roiphe depicts the anti-Semitism that runs rampant in the European Diaspora, sated only by the flow of Jewish blood. For example, the Poles in Moses Gruenbaum's village burn down the Jewish synagogue and nearly kill Moses and his fellow Jews, who must break through a wall of the temple to escape. Roiphe also describes, in some detail, the rape and murder of a rabbi's wife by Cossacks during a pogrom in a Ukrainian village: "Her screams were heard in the cellars where the Jews were hiding, pressed up against the darkened walls, bolts and chains drawn. Men with *payos* [earlocks] wet with sweat prayed and rolled their hands into fists and swung them in the air, as if they could, as if they knew how to, protect the women and children who listened to the rebbe's wife as she called for mercy to the unmerciful who sucked at her breasts and pulled at her hair in their excitement, who bit her shoulders and smashed themselves against her buttocks . . ." (*TPOH* 90). Through these scenes, Roiphe dramatically affirms her contention that Jewry is "indigestible" to other countries and implicitly justifies Israel's existence as a political necessity. To be sure, the existence of a strong Jewish nation with defensible borders seems a welcome alternative to Jewish existence in the European Diaspora where meek Jewish men, like the ones above, can only pray impotently to drown out the screams of Jewish women in the clutches of Cossacks.

The Holocaust itself only cements Roiphe's Zionist argument in *The Pursuit of Happiness*. In one chapter, "Although She Doesn't Know It, the Moment Hedy Became a Zionist: 1944," Roiphe describes Hedy's encounter, as a child, with a Holocaust survivor on a public bus. The woman disturbs the other passengers when she begins singing and speaking loudly to herself, finally shouting "All gone" in heavily accented English. As she catches Hedy's curious eyes, she tells the child, "I had a little girl . . . I had a little girl too. . . . Are you a Jew?" (*TPOH* 315). Roiphe suggests that Hedy's youth keeps her from understanding the significance of the scene that unfolds before her; the message, however, rings clear enough for the reader. The Holocaust left in its wake all too many isolated and psychologically scarred survivors. Where else but in a Jewish state will the government commit itself to the ingathering of these beleaguered survivors (today, in fact, the largest population of Holocaust survivors live in Israel)? Realizing the necessity for a Jewish state, the Gruenbaum men—who prosper financially in America as garment manufacturers—become generous contributors to the Zionist cause, and Hedy's father, Frank, helps smuggle guns to Palestine as the Jewish forces fight the British occupiers and prepare for the War of Independence against the Arabs.

The "safe haven" aspect of Israel, of course, only begins to account for the state's significance to Jews. As Roiphe herself argues, "[Israel] means more than a refuge from catastrophe—although that in itself might be validation enough. The State of Israel signifies redemption, the fulfillment of God's covenant to Abraham. It offers a religious confirmation of the worth and the truth of the long line of struggle from past to present" (*GWM* 55). Roiphe, then, appreciates the spiritual stock Jews place in Israel's existence. This conviction, no doubt, provokes her to envision Israel as more than merely a political refuge in *The Pursuit of Happiness.* Indeed, settling in the Jewish state ultimately allows the youngest Gruenbaums to find fulfillment through living a meaningful Jewish existence.

Roiphe suggests that life in materialistic America precludes such fulfillment because a Jewish existence, in the first place, lies out of reach. As one reviewer of the novel aptly notes, "To do well in American terms is to renounce what it means to be Jewish" (Sellers 7). To be sure, the Gruenbaums retain precious little of Moses Gruenbaum's *Yiddishkeit.* As they amass their considerable fortune, they increasingly congregate at the local country club rather than the synagogue. Unfortunately, though they prosper financially, they do not prosper in any general sense. Their relationships are sterile to say the least. After all, Flora Gruenbaum's husband murders her with a rifle, and the wives of Max and Arthur Gruenbaum abandon them. Moreover, heart disease plagues the Gruenbaum men. One wonders how much symbolic weight Roiphe means to place on the Gruenbaums' infirmity. For it does appear that assimilation has corroded both the physical and spiritual Gruenbaum heart. Emblematic, I believe, of the assimilated American Jews' moral corruption, Hedy asks a favor of God in 1944, but not the favor one might suppose given this cataclysmic time in Jewish history. She vows never to ask God another favor if he breaks the Brooklyn Dodger's hitting slump (*TPOH* 86). In thus documenting the "descent of a spiritual people into materialistic worldliness," Roiphe tells a familiar Jewish-American tale of immigrant disillusionment, joining the eminent ranks of Abraham Cahan, Anzia Yezierska, Michael Gold, and Daniel Fuchs (Lehmann-Haupt C18).

Roiphe, however, in contrast to her literary predecessors earlier in this century (with the exception of Ludwig Lewisohn), envisions an encouraging transition from immigrant disillusionment in America to Jewish redemption in Israel. Three of Moses and Naomi Gruenbaum's great-grandchildren—Caleb Herzberg, Teddy Gruenbaum, and Hedy Sheinfold—make *aliyah* to Israel and discover that settling in the Jewish state imbues their lives with a sense of purpose that eludes them in America. Caleb feels a religious responsibility for Israel in 1948, a fledgling state embroiled in its War of Independence. Israel needs Caleb Herzberg and, well, America simply doesn't. Caleb tells his father, "I must go" (*TPOH* 359). A religious Zionist (not to be confused with the more numerous Zionists of a socialist bent at the time), Caleb feels that he fights for God, for the restoration of the temple. In the following passage, Roiphe most evocatively dramatizes Caleb's spiritual affinity for the land:

> In the morning . . . he would go to the window and look out over the hills and watch the cypress trees take shape out of the mist and clouds. He would run his hands across the sill and, smelling the lemon tree in the courtyard and the winds that blew off the distant lake carrying the smell of pine and cedar, watching the rocks turn ink with the rising sun, he would hit his head against the wall, its loveliness so overcame him. In the evenings he would smell the cooking oils and the leaving of the goats that were kept in a pen down the street. In the night he would watch the stars come up in the sky and the moon hang over the old synagogue where the mosaics showed Romans marching under an arch, and his heart would beat with a joy that he had come to this place where everything began, and he knew he would serve it with his entire soul. (*TPOH* 360–361)

Much ado, one might argue, over goat feces. Still, for what it may be worth, none of the Gruenbaums manage to muster up such sentiments about Brooklyn. Caleb, like several Jews today, believes that Israel is *the* place for Jews to live. "No longer 'Next Year,'" he writes his father, alluding to the Passover toast, "Next year in Jerusalem."

What Teddy Gruenbaum lacks in Caleb-like religiosity, he makes up for in a secular Zionism of his own. While Caleb fights in Israel for God, Teddy fights against the two forces that threaten to wipe out Jewry: the violent European Diaspora and the vacuous American Diaspora. Disillusioned by the anti-Semitism of Choate, the drudgery of the family business (he makes coffee for his Uncle Frank), and the idleness of life as a rich boy in his parent's Park Avenue apartment, Teddy smuggles guns to the Jewish forces in Palestine by swimming them ashore from the Mediterranean Sea under the noses of the British. Says the narrator, "Teddy felt the joy of knowing exactly what he was doing" (*TPOH* 350). He adopts the Hebrew name, Ari, and the narrative voice only half-jokingly comments, "Teddy was catching identity" (*TPOH* 350). Teddy thrives as a soldier in the Israeli Defense Force and rejects the ethically bankrupt, materialistic credo of America which his parents, grandparents and great-grandparents mistakenly embrace: "He didn't want the business. He didn't want a Cadillac car with fins. He didn't want an apartment like his father's with two maid's rooms behind the kitchen. He didn't want to marry a woman who knew how much to tip the doorman at Christmastime" (*TPOH* 399). Teddy/Ari accordingly gives up an emotionally sterile life of servants and Sevilles and gains a viable Jewish identity in Israel.

Teddy/Ari writes his cousin, Hedy, "Someday you will come and visit me and see for yourself how Jews are meant to be" (*TPOH* 369). Hedy does, indeed, visit Israel and, like her two cousins, decides to make *aliyah*. Also like her cousins, she thrives. Hedy marries and, in Israel, her children enjoy feelings of self-worth that eluded her as a child and also eluded her mother, Flora. The childhoods of Hedy and her mother in America are marked by an inculcated sense of inadequacy as they are forced to assimilate to mainstream, upper-class mores. Flora leads a debutante's life, but is overweight and, thus, miserable. At one point, her mother forces her to attend a costume party encased in a box (the symbolism speaks for itself) and she wets herself as the judges ponder the quality of the costume. Flora's lamentable childhood, however, does not keep her from forcing Hedy into boxes, as well. To unkink her daughter's "Jewish" hair, Flora forces Hedy to endure a painful and malodorous conk in a Harlem beauty parlor. In contrast to Flora's and Hedy's unhappy childhoods, Hedy's daughter in Israel "believed that she counted, what she did, what she felt, how she behaved toward others, mattered" (*TPOH* 257). In *The Pursuit of Happiness*, then, Roiphe allows the youngest Gruenbaums to resist the comfortable materialism of America (the "fat gods" as Saul Bellow once quipped). She allows the Gruenbaums, finally, to triumph. That both male and female Gruenbaums do so by making *aliyah* to Israel bespeaks Roiphe's pride in the Jewish state and attests to her conviction that Israel can play a key role in forging a viable Jewish identity.

Would that contemporary Israel merited such unambiguous kudos from Jewish-American women. Alas, such is not the case. In "Political Empowerment of Women in Israel," Colette Avital—the Consul-General of Israel in New York and Israel's highest-ranking woman diplomat—shatters the myth of the Jewish woman's "equality" in Israel. Avital notes that "women's representation in [Israel's] 120-member parliament, the Knesset, has varied from a low of six percent to a high of merely nine percent" (18). In private life women scarcely fare better. Avital argues that "[i]n family life there is still no equality—women and men do not have equal or even similar roles. The educational system from kindergarten to university is replete with and has encouraged stereotypical images, impacting not only our attitudes to politics but also our choices of work and career" (19). Plaskow explores some specific manifestations of this gender inequity. For example, she notes that "of the 50 percent of women who serve at all in this major socializing insti- tution [the Israeli military], the majority do the same kind of office work they perform in the civilian market" (111). Plaskow also under- scores the "sexual division of labor" that, interestingly, persists in most *kibbutzim* (110). Says Plaskow, "while there were women who fought for and won the right to do men's work, no one ever suggested that men ought to be in the kitchen and nursery" (110) (see also Hazleton for her exploration of gender-equality myths). The question arises: How can such institutionalized gender discrimination thrive in a state created as a refuge from institutionalized persecution? As Avital suggests, the political power of the ultra-Orthodox lies at the root of Israel's patriar- chal problem:

> In the Jewish tradition there is mutual respect but separation of the genders. This implies a clear-cut difference in the roles played, or allowed to play; this implies a strong set of rules, and setting a strong borderline between private life—where women have an educational role to play in the home and public life from which they are excluded. The growing power of religion and of religious groups has had a neg- ative impact on the status of women (even in legislation). (20)

Avital refuses to hedge on the issue. As the ultra-Orthodox gain power, women lose power. For this simple reason, Leah Shakdiel—the first woman member of an Israeli religious council—"firmly believe[s] that the monopolistic claim of the ultra-Orthodox to speak for authentic Judaism, in the end, must be challenged" (Qtd. in Chertok 82). Letty Cot- tin Pogrebin wholeheartedly agrees with Avital and Shakdiel that the ultra-Orthodox only exacerbate the problem of women's inequality in Israel. She documents the political power of the ultra-Orthodox by not- ing their control of Israel's marriage, divorce, and child-custody laws. Under these laws, men literally control all facets of matrimony in the state, resulting in the persecution of women. For example, an Israeli man can refuse to grant his wife a divorce; thus, some men blackmail their wives before agreeing to give her the divorce certificate, called a *get*. Pogrebin explains that "[a] woman in such a situation is considered an *agunah*, a chained wife . . ." (170). Furthermore, when a husband dies, the wife— if she is childless—must either marry her husband's brother or get the brother's permission to marry someone else. This law, like the divorce law, facilitates extortion, as a man can withhold permission from his sis-ter-in-law if she refuses to meet his terms. Says Pogrebin, "Israelis have freedom *of* religion; what they want now is freedom *from* religion, that is, from Orthodox interference in the civil affairs of the nation" (201).

The ultra-Orthodox, however, show few signs of backing off. Their success in upholding *halakah* at the Western Wall proves their determi-nation to perpetuate the demeaning gender roles prescribed by these laws. Anat Hoffman, a member of Women at the Wall (WAW), describes the melee that ensued once she and fellow members attempted to lead the Torah service on the women's side of the Wall in 1989: "Shortly after we started praying, *haredi* women started to berate us. One called me a prostitute. Then one of their men tossed a metal chair at us from his side of the *mehitza*. . . . Two of them grabbed me and started to drag me away from the Wall. I clung to another woman, but then we were both hauled across the ground like sacks of potatoes. My knees and elbows were skinned and bleeding. . . . All the while, *haredi* women were cursing and spitting at us" (Qtd. in Chertok 92; see Haut also for a vivid account of her earlier attempt to lead the Torah service at the Western Wall). Indeed, the ultra-Orthodox stand ready to squelch any feminist stir-rings in Israel and represent, probably, the most serious obstacle to gen-der equality in the Jewish state.

It seems appropriate, given the tumultuous milieu described above, that Anne Roiphe engages the tension between feminism and the ultra-Orthodox in her only novel set largely in Israel, *Lovingkindness* (1987). Roiphe's depiction of Israel in this novel contrasts sharply with the Israel she envisions in *The Pursuit of Happiness* (in the latter novel, Roiphe does dramatize the senseless violence inflicted by both Arabs and Jews, but does not broach the state's gender problems). The plot in *Lovingkindness* revolves around Annie Johnson, a nominally Jewish feminist scholar, who must come to terms with her estranged daughter's decision to join an ultra-Orthodox sect in Israel. Although the story may strain credulity for some, given the daughter's feminist upbringing, Thomas Friedman notes the allure of the ultra-Orthodox way of life to several alienated Jews in the Diaspora: "practically the only Jews coming to Israel these days from America and Western Europe are ultra-Ortho-dox or their recruits" (302). Indeed, these are heady times for the ultra-Orthodox; in *Lovingkindness*, Roiphe dramatizes a trend rather than an anomaly, as a significant number of American Jews today—disillu-sioned with the self-centered individualism and liberalism of America—make *aliyah* to join ultra-Orthodox sects in Israel. Hence, after not hearing from her daughter, Andrea, for five months, Annie finally receives a phone call one night: "I am staying at the Yeshiva Rachel, I am different from when you last saw me. . . . Mother . . . don't be upset. I love you, I made my own decision, by myself. I am peaceful. I honor you, of course" (*L* 2). Annie realizes the significance of the Yeshiva Rachel and her daughter's deliberate allusion to one of the ten commandments. Andrea, who once put a "God sucks" sign over her mirror (as Annie reminds her), has embraced ultra-Orthodox Judaism and, perforce, has rejected the feminist precepts of her mother. One of Annie's friends tells her, "They will encourage her to have twelve children" (*L* 3), whereas the reviewer of the novel for *The New York Times Book Review* puts it a bit more bluntly: "Goodbye liberalism, feminism . . . Hello womb" (d'Alpuget 9).

The *Ms. Magazine* reviewer does not overstate matters when she describes the novel as a "feminist nightmare" (34). Annie, like most feminists, one can be fairly sure, sees ultra-Orthodox Jewish life as a retrogression into archaic, stifling gender roles. The fervor with which Andrea (who adopts the Hebrew name, Sarai) embraces the woman's subordinate role provides comic relief to this disconcerting plot. Restricted primarily to the Yeshiva kitchen, as prescribed by *halakah*, Sarai boasts to her mother, "We make this incredible bread. We put the dough in big white bowls on the stove and it rises, I mean really rises" (*L* 35). Now, I would like to tread softly here, as I do not wish to duplicate Hillary Clinton's 1992 campaign gaffe (as you probably remember, she indirectly, but clearly, derided cookie-baking housewifery). However, Roiphe encourages us to question, at least, Sarai's exuberance in her domestic duties. Consider Sarai's ode to the woman's divinely assigned cleaning chores: "When I sponge the table and the crumbs are gone and the board is again honey-colored and the patches of light from the window shine on my part of the floor, the One Above is pleased with me" (*L* 37). Annie, of course, does not share her daughter's euphoria. She named her Andrea, in the first place, because it did not "hint of limit or confinement" like the name Sarai (*L* 8). Annie explains to Sarai,

> I want you to go on learning new things. I don't want you frozen in a time warp that experienced its grandeur in the backwoods of Poland several centuries ago. . . . I don't understand how you are tolerating the discipline of being part of a group that makes so many demands

on your innermost thoughts and requests so much conformity of
behavior. . . . Don't you still want to see and do and belong to as great
a variety of human events as possible? (*L* 45)

In a more comic attempt to poke holes in the credibility of the ultra-
Orthodox, Annie asks her daughter, "Is lobster really an immoral creature of the deep?" (*L* 18). Sarai, however, readily accepts the ultra-Orthodox's strict interpretation of the Jewish law, even their contention that
women do not need to study Talmud because they are "naturally" in
touch with God's wonder. She tells her mother, "We are the sun, the
moon, the stars, the ocean, the forest and the field. We make the learning
possible" (*L* 36). Annie, of course, recognizes this familiar argument as
a convenient justification for women's subordination in ultra-Orthodox
society. She would, no doubt, sympathize with one Jewish feminist's
recent quip, "Terrific! Next you're going to tell us that Jewish tradition
maintains that we women eat, drink, and screw on such a higher plane
than you men that we have no need to engage in serious learning" (Qtd.
in Chertok 62).

Despite her general abhorrence for the insidious misogyny of the
ultra-Orthodox, Annie does her best to appreciate her daughter's religious epiphany. However, when the leader of the Yeshiva Rachel, Rabbi
Joshua Cohen, writes Annie to thank her for the "gift of your daughter,"
she must finally say, enough is enough. She composes a hostile letter
(which she restrains herself from sending) castigating fundamentalism
and the Yeshiva Rachel, specifically. She compares Rabbi Cohen and his
cohorts to "muggers in black coats" and continues, "in ancient language,
with soothing words, with rules and promises, you have bruised my
daughter, brainwashed my daughter, so that she considers giving up what
she had not yet given up, her mind, her independence, her knowledge
of the multiple realities, the multiple choices, her willingness to be
accountable to herself, for herself, under the sky, to be human without
wailing to the clouds . . ." (*L* 67). Push, inevitably, comes to shove when
Sarai informs her mother of the arranged courtship and imminent marriage between herself and another American recruit to a yeshiva affiliated
with the Yeshiva Rachel (he also adopts a Hebrew name, Micah). Annie
cancels her summer teaching load and journeys to Israel to rescue her
daughter.

Roiphe uses Annie's visit to Israel, in large part, to expose and criticize several manifestations of Israel's gender discrimination, some of

which I have already discussed. For example, Annie reflects that she wouldn't visit the segregated women's section of the Western Wall to place a note in its crevices "even if an angel of the Lord were holding out his hand for my message" (*L* 141). She ultimately does visit the Wall for curiosity's sake, and notes that "the women's section was a third the size of the men's and they seemed crowded together" (*L* 147). Roiphe delivers a more pointed attack on Israel's patriarchal legal system during Annie's first visit to the Yeshiva Rachel. While there to see her daughter, she sees, in action, the ultra-Orthodox control of the laws concerning the family. A Jewish woman comes into Rabbi Cohen's office and bursts into tears. Cohen explains to Annie that the rabbinical court has taken away the woman's children. When Annie asks, "Why? What has she done?" the rabbi tersely states, "It is the law" (*L* 151). Cohen's refusal to justify the court's actions on more specific grounds epitomizes, the scene suggests, the obdurate allegiance of the ultra-Orthodox to their traditional interpretation of *halakah,* which all too often smacks of misogyny (one, at any rate, certainly suspects an impropriety in this woman's case). There is simply no room, given the ultra-Orthodox control of the laws concerning the family, to debate the woman's proper role and conduct.

Roiphe further emphasizes the perniciousness inherent in the ultra-Orthodox control of the marriage, divorce, and child custody laws when Annie, exploring possible ways to extricate her daughter, visits a feminist Israeli lawyer, Naomi Shen Lov. Shen Lov has little sympathy for Sarai's predicament since she has her hands full trying to represent "a victim of the law of [Sarai's] adopted religion" (*L* 196). The client explains to Annie that the rabbinical courts have denied her permission to remarry, even though her husband was killed while serving for the Israeli military in Lebanon: "By the law of the religious courts, which is here the law of the land, I cannot remarry without the ceremony of release being performed by my husband's younger brother. He will not do this for me unless my family gives him fifty thousand dollars" (*L* 196). This is the Israeli woman's nightmare, of course, which Pogrebin describes in *Debra, Golda, and Me.* Unsurprisingly, Shen Lov sees little hope of a legal victory; there are no women on the rabbinic court "because no women are allowed to become rabbis" (*L* 196).

Roiphe not only exposes, in the above scene, the sexist laws that remain the order of the day in Israel, but also engages the heated debate concerning the refusal of the ultra-Orthodox to serve in Israel's military.

Shen Lov tells Annie, "These Orthodox are going to turn the Knesset into a shul [synagogue] and all of Israel into a shtetl. We will be armed with prayers when the invaders come" (*L* 197). Her feelings are not uncommon. The like-minded sentiments expressed by Ruth Wisse in her study, *If I am Not for Myself . . . The Liberal Betrayal of the Jews* (1992) epitomize the anti-Orthodox position of several Jews in America and in Israel when it comes to the refusal of the *Haredim* to serve in the military. Says Wisse, ". . . exemption from national service in the name of the Lord, in a country that requires so much self-sacrifice from its citizens, corrupts the moral integrity of both religion and politics" (105). Wisse argues that the untenable moral stance of the ultra-Orthodox—who scorn military service but benefit greatly from military protection—provokes their inflated spiritual claims, their need to, say, "burn bus shelters featuring provocatively sexual ads" (106). "In order to justify their abdication of national responsibility," Wisse continues, "they have to be convinced that they too are really 'soldiers' in a truer struggle . . ." (106). Several secular Israelis (perhaps most secular Israelis) share Wisse's and Shen Lov's antipathy toward the ultra-Orthodox, largely because of their refusal to serve in the Israeli military. Moreover, since a disproportionate number of Americans making *aliyah* today do so to join ultra-Orthodox sects, anti-American sentiments in Israel have escalated. The Israeli newspaper, *Maariv,* recently complained about American parents who "send their lunatic children to Israel" (Qtd. in Haberman, "Massacre" 4). Roiphe's Shen Lov gives voice to these anti-American sentiments when she tells Annie, "We are in need of true Zionists, of people of learning and technology and democratic principles, and what do you send us, your broken, drug-riddled, starry-eyed, wiped out dropouts. And what do they do when they get here? They breed and make more of themselves, exactly what we don't need, thank you very much" (*L* 195).

We can be fairly certain that Roiphe shares most of Annie's and Shen Lov's anti-Orthodox sentiments. Roiphe has made no secret of her antipathy toward fundamentalists of any ilk. In a recent article, she laments the rise of fundamentalism in Israel: "Fundamentalism, the oh-so-sweet certainty that your truth is the truth, that the word has been given and must not be changed, that law and order will follow the revealed truth—this fundamentalism, the tranquilizer of ambivalence, the amputator of doubt, is with us again" ("The Whole" 86). Roiphe takes particular exception to the "fundamentalists who know that women were not meant to hold the Torah, who have likened women who hold the Torah to pigs" ("The Whole" 86). She imagines that these Orthodox Jews still pray each morning and thank God "for not having made them female" (*GWM* 12). Indeed, one would be hard pressed to argue that Roiphe envisions ultra-Orthodox Judaism, in *Lovingkindness* or anywhere else, as an appealing option for American or Israeli women. But having said that, one must also acknowledge that, in the final analysis, the Yeshiva Rachel comes off rather positively in the novel. Roiphe, as Naomi Sokoloff rightly suggests, is "not glibly dismissive of the alleged fanatics" (66). True, Roiphe's critique of the ultra-Orthodox seems unrelenting at times. However, she delivers an equally unrelenting critique of political liberalism in America and, therein, explores some redeeming features of ultra-Orthodox Judaism.

To Roiphe's credit, she gives ultra-Orthodoxy its due through her depiction of Sarai as a lost, alienated child in "liberal" America who seems to thrive only after entering the yeshiva and the world of the spiritual, if patriarchal. As d'Alpuget notes, "[Roiphe] allows Sarai to know what Annie cannot: that despite all the demands of intellectuals and moralists, Judaism is spiritual . . . To ask that it be liberal, rational, non-patriarchal is to miss the point—and the beauty—and to ask that Judaism descend into the service of Caesar, into the world of the outer life, the territory of power, morals and politics" (9). This "outer life" of liberalism in America, one must remember, proves disastrous for Sarai. Feminism, as Annie reflects, tragically backfires in Sarai's case: "brought up to admire her body, to accept her biology, no facts hidden, no disgrace or limitations in girlhood, and she was falling, free falling, hang gliding, dizzy, scared" (*L* 28). Unbridled "liberation" leads to Sarai's loneliness and alienation. As a gloomy adolescent, she experiments with several drugs, undergoes three abortions, starves herself to lose weight, and attempts suicide. Annie reflects, "Some of our children just can't make it [free]. They're not strong enough" (*L* 191–192). At the very least, a life of happy domesticity at the Yeshiva Rachel restores Sarai's physical health. When Annie finally sees her daughter at the yeshiva, she notices Sarai's white teeth and healthy weight. She later notes that her daughter "looked calm, almost like a Cezanne apple, rosy-toned and solid" (*L* 206). As Annie relates to a friend in America, "[Sarai] says she feels peaceful, no drugs, only scrubbing floors" (*L* 98). While Roiphe, then, does not endorse ultra-Orthodox life as a viable option for most women, life at the Yeshiva Rachel does seem a prudent choice in Sarai's case. She asks her mother, "Do you understand that I am happy?" (*L* 40).

Let me stress that Roiphe does not relegate ultra-Orthodox Judaism to merely "lesser-evil" status, either. Annie's inability to repel the specter of Rabbi Nachman of Bratslav, who visits her in a series of hallucinatory dreams, illustrates how even the most secular Jews cannot, and should not, eschew Judaism. As Lewis Fried suggests, these dreams give way to "the human need to encounter the holy" (*L* 178). Annie can insistently reject religion in her wakefulness; that she cannot shut out religion in her sleep reveals that she suppresses very real spiritual yearnings. In Israel, Annie can throw away the panty hose the yeshiva forces her to wear, but she interestingly cannot throw away a bible they give her as a gift. Moreover, while Annie argued in her scholarly book that the spinsters of nineteenth-century New England (utterly free of the stifling gender roles of ultra-Orthodox women) led happier and more fruitful lives than their married counterparts, she remembers crying for them because they "missed the brightest bondage of them all" (*L* 10). Annie, then, recognizes the appeal of the loving relationships fostered in an ultra-Orthodox community.

Annie (and, admirably, Roiphe) is not so blind to the failings of American feminism that she cannot respect Sarai's decision to embrace the close-knit, ultra-Orthodox society in Israel. While Annie feels "like a ghost adrift in the universe" upon her arrival in the Jewish state, a more profound alienation plagues Sarai in America (*L* 144). In thus criticizing the rampant, self-centered individualism that, unfortunately, accompanied the feminist movement of the 1960s, Roiphe joins the ranks of other contemporary American feminists who are beginning to reassess the successes and failures of the movement. Elizabeth Fox-Genovese, for example (who frequently criticizes, in her words, the "do me" feminists) suggests that "the worst of the inner cities are giving us some harbinger of what a world of unbridled ids might look like. And progressives have yet to explain satisfactorily how that sinister world is to be distinguished from individual liberation" (53). She continues to argue that "the campaign to liberate women has increasingly pointed toward a liberation from responsibility for children in particular and the moral work of society in general" (53). Whatever the failings of the Yeshiva Rachel, "responsibility," and responsibility toward the rearing of children, specifically, is not one of them.

Recognizing the virtues of ultra-Orthodox life and the failures of American feminism, Annie lets her daughter go; it is an act of maternal "lovingkindness." The argument of Annie's friend—"Andrea has made an independent decision not to be independent in the same way that you were independent, but on the other hand her independence is independence from you and yours was independence from everyone else, so it seems fair to let her try it her way"—makes good sense, despite its circuitousness (*L* 177). Thus, while the parents of Sarai's fiancé attempt to kidnap their son and offer to help Annie smuggle her daughter out of the country, as well, Annie refuses to do so and even foils their plans. She remains true to her daughter, while also taking comfort in the possibility that her future grandchildren might renounce fundamentalism, that the pendulum might swing back in the feminist direction.

Israel, then, provokes enigmatic thoughts and feelings from Anne Roiphe. She sees the potential of Israel to rescue Jews from a life of sterile, American-style assimilation (downright destructive in Sarai's case); but Roiphe also cannot ignore the special agonies of the Israeli woman, agonies to which Jewish-American women become susceptible upon making *aliyah*. Roiphe suggests, in her fiction and non-fiction, that American Jews need both Judaism and Israel. But what kind of Judaism and what kind of Israel? Certainly not the precise kinds inextricably connected with one another today. That is, she laments both the entrenched sexism of the ultra-Orthodox Jews and the political system in Israel that lends them legislative power, as moderate, secular parties must necessarily form a coalition with the right-wing religious parties to achieve ruling power in the Knesset. Still, Roiphe takes comfort in Judaism's fluidity and vision. "It is in the Jewish tradition," she notes cheerfully in her memoir, "for the Jewish tradition to change" (*GWM* 219). She encourages fellow Jews to seek this change in a November 1994 article, "O. J. Simpson and Us." In the wake of Nicole Simpson's murder, she urges her readers to examine the archaic *halakhic* laws which facilitate parallel abuses of Jewish women. Roiphe, thus, continues to plant the seeds of a truly nonpatriarchal Judaism in her fiction and non-fiction. One only hopes that these seeds will take root in Israel.

Chapter 9

TOVA REICH'S DARING VISION;
OR,
THE FEMINIZATION
OF ISRAEL'S PENITENT

In addition to Anne Roiphe, an unprecedented number of Jewish-American women writers are finally beginning to garner widespread attention. Women represent slightly more than half of the writers in Ted Solotaroff and Nessa Rapoport's recent collection of Jewish-American stories, *Writing Our Way Home* (1992), in contrast to the few women writers included in Irving Howe's 1977 anthology, *Jewish American Stories*. These contemporary women writers, like their more established female colleagues (one thinks of Anzia Yezierska, Cynthia Ozick, Grace Paley, Rhoda Lerman, and Tillie Olsen), contribute to the existing generic concerns of Jewish-American literature, to be sure; but they also give voice to the specific perspective—long overshadowed but never altogether silent—of the Jewish-American woman. Moreover, in taking on relatively new Jewish-American fictional terrain, Israel, they have produced a surge of exciting work indeed.

Tova Reich, perhaps, represents the most promising of these American writers who have chosen Israel as the site at which to explore the issue of Jewish identity. For in her second novel, *Master of the Return* (1988), Israel emerges as more than merely a "background." Under Reich's surreal touch, it transcends the role of physical locale altogether. Rather, Reich's Israel is a spiritual locus at which the lunatic fringes of Jewish, Moslem, and Christian society meet and clash, usually in humorous ways. As Hugh Nissenson argues, "Almost everyone in 'Master of the Return' is a fanatic of one kind or another. Jews, Arabs, Moslems, Christians, even agnostics and atheists, are possessed by their respective beliefs, which emanate from the land itself. For Ms. Reich's

Israel is a state of mind, a kind of collective dream, where linear time doesn't exist" ("High" 10). Reich uses highly charged poetic language and evokes the biblical landscape for all it is worth to carry off this effect, figuring into the plot the most significant and symbolically loaded Jewish sites: the Western Wall, martyr's tombs, Mount Moriah, and Sinai. Amid such magical surroundings, anything can happen and, as Elie Wiesel observes, one accepts it without so much as a flinch (8). The penitent can levitate, emanate light, come back from the dead even; petitions lodged in the crevices of the Western Wall are occasionally answered (through the regular post no less!); and whereas Philip Roth's postmodern touches in his first novel set in Israel smack of trickery (nobody can quite seem to remain safely dead in *The Counterlife*), we suspend our disbelief in *Master of the Return*.

Reich's novel contrasts, however, even more interestingly with Anne Roiphe's *Lovingkindness*. Both novels center around ultra-Orthodox yeshivot in Jerusalem, the Yeshiva Rachel in Roiphe's novel and the Uman House in Reich's novel, where the principal characters have eschewed the secular and downright hedonistic values of mainstream America to embrace the religious restraint of ultra-Orthodox Jewry. Furthermore, both Roiphe and Reich write from an unmistakably feminist orientation. But the similarities, for all intents and purposes, end here. For in *Lovingkindness*, Roiphe manipulates her characters somewhat like chess pieces. Secular Americans, secular Israelis, and ultra-Orthodox Israelis all have distinct and predictable roles to play and, to Roiphe's credit, they carry out these roles competently (Roiphe, thereby, successfully engages the major tensions between feminism and traditional Judaism). However, the match ends at something of a stalemate, as inexorable feminist and ultra-Orthodox voices clash but cancel each other out; Roiphe envisions no inroads between the two camps. One critic notes that, despite the interesting topic, the novel just does not satisfy in the way that "good fiction demands" (Pinsker, "They Dream" 8-x). One senses that Tova Reich succeeds where Roiphe fails because Reich takes joy in her ultra-Orthodox characters in a way that eludes Roiphe. Reich portrays the ultra-Orthodox, in particular, not as rigid stereotypes but as fully rounded human beings, with their own richly detailed pasts and current idiosyncrasies. Faye Kellerman aptly contends that Reich's characters are "touchingly human" (10).

More to the point, unlike Roiphe, Reich readily appreciates the earnest redemptive efforts of her ultra-Orthodox characters. While Roiphe does not mock the ultra-Orthodox perspective (and, indeed, represents their stock, *halakhic* perspective truthfully), we only see the ultra-Orthodox through the narrative perspective of the thoroughly secular and feminist Annie Johnson, whose opinions, we suspect, like her name, closely resemble the author's views. Alternatively, Reich's third-person narration, while especially attentive to the foibles of those seeking redemption, does not disparage the redemptive urge itself. As one reviewer comments, "her manner is astringent, not contemptuous" (DeMott 93). Ultimately, Reich's celebration of the redemptive possibilities in Israel allows her to escape Roiphe's either/or dichotomy (that is, either feminism or ultra-Orthodox Judaism) to envision instead the sprouting of an un-oxymoronic feminist Judaism.

Since I have already alluded to Reich's ebullient approach to her characters, allow me to introduce some of the quirky Uman House residents. There is Bruriah Lurie, formerly Barbara Horowitz of Brooklyn, a champion breeder who spits her babies out soundlessly, "pop, like missiles; the women caught the babies in mid-air" (*MTR* 95). Lurie, a true leader by example, wants to increase the birth rate of the Uman House and thereby retain a numerical advantage against the Arabs, even if this means reinstituting polygamy. After all, she insists, it is just a medieval ban; "it doesn't have the force of law" (*MTR* 110). The wife of Reb Lev Lurie of Uman House, she lets on to one friend that "It's a real trip to be married to a holy man" (*MTR* 139). For his part, Lev Lurie wants to smuggle an IBM computer into the country in a diaper box to help him "demonstrate the perfection of the Torah mathematically, through Gematria" (*MTR* 62). There is also Sora Katz, a convert from Macon, Georgia, whose mother—not wanting to deprive her daughter of life's advantages—"had started Sora in analysis around the age of four, right on the cusp of the Oedipal phase" (*MTR* 181). In Israel, Sora puts her secular skill as a graphic artist to God's use by fashioning instructive signs out of bed sheets: "Rules of modesty for Daughters of Israel: Absolutely no makeup, nail polish, or perfume, God forbid. . . . (*MTR* 140). Let us not ignore the unrelentingly pious Abba Nissim, whose method of curing a boy's burnt foot is to pray to the One Above "to make the child realize he isn't burned" (*MTR* 192). Or, finally, take Tivka Unger, who rejects the secular kibbutz of her mother for the Uman house, but cannot quite escape the idioms carried over from her rebellious, druggie days. During labor, she confides to one nearby friend, "I feel like I'm having a bad trip. I feel so spacy . . . I'm all spaced out" (*MTR* 124). These are but a sampling of Reich's imaginative creations, most of whom harken back to the saintly *schlemiels* of Yiddish writers like I. B. Singer, Sholom Aleichem, and Moishe Kulbak.

Moreover, Tova Reich explores in *Master of the Return* a prevalent thematic concern of the great Yiddish writers: the at once comical, surreal and picaresque quest for "Jewish transcendence over the pomp of the world" (Howe and Greenberg 54). Most of the chapter headings, in fact, allude to the various and often conflicting transcendent strategies of the Uman House residents. The disputes within the house concerning which strategy is "where it's at," as Tivka Unger likes to put it, provide much of the novel's dramatic tension (*MTR* 221). In the first chapter, "Bring Us To Uman," Reich introduces the original redemptive strategy of the Uman House, a physical and spiritual pilgrimage to the grave of Rabbi Nahman of Bratslav, located in the Ukraine town, Uman. The spokesperson for Uman House's founding principle is Samuel Himmelhoch, a penitent who, like most in the Uman House it seems, "had strewn many horrible sins all across the Americas, Europe, Africa, and Asia, not to mention his specialization in Israel" before seeing the light (*MTR* 2). He speaks to us posthumously as the novel begins with Abba Nissim's discovery of Himmelhoch's journal under a jerrycan in Hannah's tomb (shortly after Nissim's discovery, the retired bandit and Himmelhoch's old friend, Shyke Pfeffer, discovers Himmelhoch's corpse).

Himmelhoch's journal initiates the reader into a penitent's frame of mind. For several pages, Reich narrates directly "From the Journal of Samuel Himmelhoch," through which Himmelhoch writes didactically to his son, Akiva (*MTR* 5). The journal, thus, immediately brings to mind *The Autobiography* of Benjamin Franklin, also a didactic narrative written to a son. However, whereas Franklin hopes to provide his son with an instructive model of how one can rise from "Poverty and Obscurity" to a high level of materialistic comfort, Himmelhoch intends to guide his son away from Franklin's secular world of "hideous suffering"; he wants Akiva to become a holy man, "maybe even the harbinger of the Messiah" (*MTR* 6). Put another way, Franklin might instruct his son to relinquish a three-penny loaf to a poor woman provided he has a full stomach and a second loaf under an arm, but Himmelhoch encourages the cessation of all vain appetites. Toward the beginning of the journal, he tells the three-year old Akiva, "I have just risen to remove your hands from your private parts" (*MTR* 6).

In the journal, Himmelhoch documents his own earnest attempts to reject the secular world of vain appetite; for a successful pilgrimage to Rabbi Nahman's grave in Uman promises an end to nocturnal emissions. "[P]riceless in itself," Himmelhoch insists, but also a "mystical metaphor for the more general rewards—a cessation of the cravings for food, money, fame, sleep, desire, the whole corrupt baggage" (*MTR* 10). Hugh Nissenson notes the amusing twist of Jews "trying to get in, not out, of the Soviet Union" and Reich dramatizes each one of Himmelhoch's aborted pilgrimages in other amusing ways as well ("High" 10). Himmelhoch, using a Mexican passport, tries to pass himself off as one Manuel Domingo in his final documented attempt to reach Uman. After all, his sidelocks "could be tolerantly viewed as the logical extension of Domingo's sideburns" (*MTR* 29). While the earlocks might pass muster, their dangling *tzitzit* ultimately give Himmelhoch and his cohorts away in the Soviet Union and they are shipped back home. This is all funny stuff, of course, as Reich intends. However, she deftly uses humor (almost inherent in the implacable piety of former hedons) to expose the serious and problematic misogyny of the ultra-Orthodox.

Humorous details of Himmelhoch's sexism abound. He warns his son not to indulge in too many conversations with women since "[T]en portions of speech were allotted to the world . . . of which nine were appropriated by woman" (*MTR* 8). Reich pokes fun at Himmelhoch's hypocrisy in accosting "immodestly" clad women as he acknowledges an obstacle in this holy duty: "How to pick out these women while averting one's glance?" (*MTR* 23). In a more serious vein, however, Reich dramatizes ultra-Orthodox misogyny through Himmelhoch's monomanic quest to reach Uman, as his desire to achieve redemption supersedes the needs and desires of his wife, Ivriya (a paraplegic who certainly needs the aid of her husband). Himmelhoch, in effect, abandons her for Uman once he impregnates her with Akiva. When she laments, "Oh, Shmuel, what will become of me—pregnant and in a wheelchair," he responds icily, "You are like a pot with a seed in it. . . . Sit out in the sun and in the rain. God will help" (*MTR* 19). Himmelhoch here betrays his unlikely affinity with William Faulkner's Thomas Sutpen, who also treats women as mere vessels for his seed (he impregnates Wash Jones's fifteen-year-old granddaughter and would offer her a decent stall if she were a mare) (Faulkner 357). However, while Sutpen's dehumanization of Milly Jones brings upon his downfall (Wash Jones hacks Sutpen to death after overhearing him liken Milly to a mare), it is perfectly acceptable by Uman House standards for Himmelhoch to, say, instruct Ivriya to use her talents as a floor-scrubber to support Akiva since he must abandon them once again for Uman. Himmelhoch rationalizes to his son in his journal, "You deserved a father who had been brought to Uman" (*MTR* 26).

One does not broach pedantry in recognizing the affinities and contrasts between Faulkner's Sutpen and Reich's Himmelhoch. For echoes of Faulkner reverberate in the novel elsewhere, as well. Once Shyke Pfeffer finds the corpse believed to be Himmelhoch's, several members of the Uman house decide to carry Himmelhoch from Meron, through the Wadi Amud, to Safad for burial. The lengthy episode, of course, evokes Faulkner's *As I Lay Dying* (1930), and while we do not know precisely whether Himmelhoch's decaying corpse smells like a fish, we do know that it smells. Reich, more importantly, emulates Faulkner by narrating the pilgrimage through contrasting perspectives, as various Uman House residents offer eulogies during rest periods along the way to Safad. Reich interestingly reserves the final eulogy for the widow, Ivriya, who effectively revises the preceding male perspectives.

The various male reminiscences of Himmelhoch are rife with humor. Lev Lurie, the first to speak, focuses upon Himmelhoch's transition from a "hard-core bohemian from the major leagues" to a penitent (*MTR* 64). Lurie claims to have recognized Himmelhoch's redemptive potential immediately, "Never mind [Himmelhoch's] trousers that squeezed and accentuated the groin, placing constant pressure on that department and thereby serving to give prominence and priority to the insatiable demands of that department" (*MTR* 64). Lurie gives Himmelhoch the mantra *Gevalt! Gevalt! Gevalt!* to replace the ten thousand dollar Feh, Feh, Feh. Abba Nissim also describes how he guided Himmelhoch beyond his wanton lust for an "astonishing variety of God's creatures on earth, living and dead" (*MTR* 66–67). Through his perspective, Ivriya functions as a "proper, traditional outlet" for Himmelhoch's lascivious passions (*MTR* 69). Marrying a cripple (while horseback riding bare-breasted, Ivryiya fell and injured her spinal cord; God's punishment, of course, for her vanity) should earn Himmelhoch absolution. The eulogies of Shyke Pfeffer, Rami Marom, and Roman Unger—Unger, for one, recalls Himmelhoch's first marriage to a black schizophrenic *shikse* who worked for a German airline—are all variations along Lurie's and Nissim's tack, as they recount Himmelhoch's comically rebellious days and his virtuous about-face.

Feminist issues, of course, permeate the episode. Reich takes care to illustrate, for example, Ivriya's status as an *agunah* (or chained wife) before the discovery of her husband's corpse. According to *halakah* (as I have discussed in the previous chapter), a widow like Ivriya cannot remarry without sufficient proof of her husband's death, although, in Ivriya's case, her husband disappeared more than two years before (one should refer to Letty Cottin Pogrebin's chapter, "Gatekeepers and Gatecrashers: Israel through Feminist Eyes," in *Debra, Golda, and Me: Being Female and Jewish in America* [1991], for a detailed account of the troubling *halakhic* laws which account for many "chained" wives in Israel today). Reich explores the discriminatory tradition of the ultra-Orthodox largely through humor as the Uman House men wrangle over the procedural details that would make it acceptable for a woman, Ivriya, to deliver a eulogy for her dead husband. Abba Nissim, for example, insists that she stand at least four feet from the men with a makeshift barrier set up to separate the men from the women, "or perhaps the women can cross the stream and the widow can speak from the opposite side" (*MTR* 79). When Lev Lurie regrets that Ivriya had not purified herself in the *mikvah* (a ritual bath), Nissim suggests that the men can immerse themselves in one immediately after the burial to "cleanse ourselves not only of the impurities of the dead, but also of the frivolity of female thought and discourse" (*MTR* 80). Haggling ensues, of course, as Pfeffer opines that the widow should sob, not speak, at her husband's funeral (he wonders what Ivriya is saving her tears for), and a group of yeshiva students, who also object to Lurie's leniency, refuse to listen to Ivriya at all.

Ivriya will have her say, however, though the men sit across the stream, most safely out of earshot with plugged ears for good measure. Like the men, Ivriya presents a version of Himmelhoch's bohemian and penitent stages. But while Nissim possesses a relatively utilitarian perspective of the marriage between Himmelhoch and Ivriya, with Ivriya more or less acting as the vehicle through which her husband can achieve redemption, she depicts her relationship with her husband as a reciprocal, spiritual union. She notes that they were "brother and sister, not physically—God forbid—but in the spiritual sense, soulmates" (*MTR* 82). She also insists upon her husband's tenderness toward her and their son, Akiva. Interestingly, Himmelhoch does not betray the companionate nature of their relationship in his journal. Ivriya must insist that "It's not true what Shmuel writes in his journal—that he gave me only minimal assistance with my personal needs"; and she does not understand why "Shmuel refuses to allow the softer side of his nature to be known" (*MTR* 85). Thus, through Ivriya's eulogy, she not only revises Nissim's preceding male perspective of her marriage, but even revises Himmelhoch's own account of their relationship. His refusal to document the reciprocal nature of their union indicates, I believe, his indoctrination into the ultra-Orthodox conception of marriage, from which he might have strayed in reality, but which he refuses to challenge in his journal. Ivriya herself, then, offers this new, feminist vision of marriage and revises the traditional ultra-Orthodox perspective to which Nissim and, ultimately, Himmelhoch adhere.

Let me stress that Reich does not reject ultra-Orthodox Judaism here or anywhere else in *Master of the Return*; rather, she envisions its feminization. The Uman House women, to be sure, do not embrace Israel's version of secularism, as embodied by Ivriya's mother, Dr. Frieda Mendelssohn. Vehemently anti-Orthodox (largely owing to the refusal of the *Haredim* to serve in the military), Mendelssohn weaves defiantly through ultra-Orthodox streets in her scarlet Mercedes, or on foot yelling, "Fanatics, make way!" (*MTR* 230). Upon hearing that Himmelhoch's corpse has turned up, she tells her daughter, "I'll slice him up, Ivriya darling. Believe me, it'll be the biggest thrill of my life—that bastard! He brainwashed you, the no good freak, that's what he did. He seduced you into his medieval cult" (*MTR* 46). In short, Mendelssohn is one of Reich's more memorable characters. Still, the Uman House women reject Mendelssohn's spiritually bereft secular life. All of the Uman House women, Ivriya included, express their longing for a recognizably Jewish redemption. Segregated from the men after Sora's polygamous marriage to Rami Maron, the Uman House women discuss their almost ineffable faith while stoned on hashish (it is, after all, Purim). Take Sora Katz's account of her religious epiphany:

> "Simplicity! Simplicity!" It came to me like that—pure and simple recognition. I wanted to be absorbed. I wanted to be swallowed up. I just wanted to prostrate myself, I wanted to have no choice but to be brought to my knees before the true God. How can you explain it? (*MTR* 156)

Ivriya, like Sora Katz and the other women, believes in the traditional ultra-Orthodox precepts of penitence and redemption. She states fervently, "I believe in penance. I believe in *teshuva*. I believe in the return"

(*MTR* 162). Importantly, Reich does not disparage the faith of the Uman House women, or the faith of the men for that matter. However, in this revelatory scene, Reich does imagine a sororal ultra-Orthodox community of loving kindness as an alternative to the patriarchal community. As Golda massages Sora's feet, she recalls how she escaped her physically abusive Bedouin husband, Munis, and found a physical and spiritual refuge in Ivriya's home. Despite her rotten teeth, her filth, and her bruises, Ivriya takes her in. Ivriya reflects that Himmelhoch would not have extended this welcome to Golda:

> [I]f Shmuel had been home, I'm afraid I could never have earned the *mitzvah* of performing that *hesed* for you, Goldie, of taking you in and nursing you back to health with loving-kindness. As it was, he burned your mattress when he returned, as a precaution against the impurities.... Shmuel, may he rest in peace, was concerned about your spiritual effect on the baby in my womb, and he was very angry at me for letting you in. (*MTR* 160).

Through Ivriya's act of sisterhood, then, Reich offers a feminist model of the ultra-Orthodox community, which tellingly stands in contrast to Himmelhoch's misogynist model. Ivriya's act of loving kindness bolsters the faith of the women and gives Golda faith in God for the first time. Says Golda, "I prayed, 'show me some kindness, bring me some comfort, prove to me that the life of a single individual matters, give me a reason to live, give me a reason to believe in You.' And He heard my prayer, and he acted through you, Ivriya" (*MTR* 161).

Reich continues to dramatize the redemptive urge of the Uman House residents while offering her distinctively feminist vision of how this redemption might come about. Lev Lurie offers an alternative redemptive strategy when he exhorts the Uman House to reclaim the Temple Mount from the Moslems, a lamentably popular initiative today among messianic Zionists. Thomas Friedman describes the most serious, 1984 attempt to "liberate" the Temple Mount in *From Beirut to Jerusalem*: "...the Israeli plotters were convinced that the Messiah would come only once this Muslim 'desecration' was cleared from the very throne of God on earth, the focal point of Jewish national sovereignty.... Fortunately for Israel, and the world, this plot to prod the messiah was never realized" (305). Lurie rationalizes the endeavor this way: "How much could they really care about those Temple Mount mosques anyway? They prostrate themselves five times a day, bowing their heads toward Mecca while pointing their unclean behinds toward Jerusalem. It's only their third-holiest site; for us it's the first, the *first!* 'Finish the job, *Yidden*,' Rav Nahman would have said" (*MTR* 120). For his part, Abba Nissim opposes Lurie and intends to continue striving for the spiritual, if not physical, Uman. He would just as soon forego a battle with the Arabs, occupied as he is with the war against wet dreams. For *shalom bayit* [domestic peace], the two decide to set their respective agendas aside and climb Mount Sinai instead. Through re-enacting the moment of revelation, they hope that God will reveal to them whether to pursue Uman or Moriah.

The Uman House residents embrace the pilgrimage because the re-enactment atop Sinai promises to revitalize their mystical union with God. Moreover, Mount Sinai evokes the possibility of a new beginning, of starting afresh as a Jewish community. That is, because all Jews living and dead are believed to have been at Sinai ("We were at Sinai together," some religious Jews like to say to other Jews), the re-enactment suggests a chance to restructure Jewish society, perhaps along more egalitarian lines. This symbolic element of Mount Sinai does not escape Judith Plaskow, who titled her recent feminist study of Judaism, *Standing Again at Sinai: Judaism from a Feminist Perspective* (1990). Though Ivriya herself does not view Sinai in such overtly feminist terms, she does believe it offers her, as a woman, the greatest chance for spiritual transcendence:

> And in those early days of her penance, how she had been swept away by the possibilities opening up to her: of mystery, of transcendence, of ecstasy, of union with the divine. Abba Nissim had said to her then that such exalted states were indeed possible, even for a woman, and well worth striving for, though in fact the female did not commonly achieve high levels of holiness because she was fettered by nature and by circumstances to practical, mundane affairs. . . . Into his blessed hands she would deliver her crippled body, her gravity-diseased body, and he, Abba Nissim, would bear it, would bear it up to the top of the mountain and launch her soul. (*MTR* 184–185)

Ivriya, then, does not explicitly seek a *feminist* religious transcendence atop Mount Sinai. However, this does not keep Reich from tapping Sinai's symbolic significance to suggest yet another feminist model of Jewish interrelationships. Just as Reich offers a feminist model of the Jewish marriage during the journey to Safad (through Ivriya's eulogy), and a sororal model of community at the Purim/wedding celebration (largely through the recollections of Ivriya's act of loving kindness toward Golda), she offers a revised, feminist model of Jewish parenthood on the journey up Mount Sinai. Concurrently, Abba Nissim, whom Ivriya promises to marry provided that he carry her to the top of the mountain, eagerly takes on the role of Akiva's father on the journey and manifests the qualities of traditional, ultra-Orthodox fatherhood; Abba, in fact, means father in Hebrew.

Reich sets Nissim's stern model of parenthood in sharp contrast to the warm maternal relationship Ivriya enjoys with Akiva. Ivriya and Akiva, like Ivriya and Himmelhoch (as we learn in Ivriya's eulogy), share a spiritual union. They are uncannily in tune to each other's needs and desires. When Akiva burns his foot and it appears that they might have to turn back, Akiva perseveres since he knows instinctively how important the journey is to Ivriya. Says Akiva, "You have your heart set on it. You'd be very sad if we lost our chance. Don't deny it, Ima [mother]" (*MTR* 194). Ivriya, for her part, recognizes Akiva's needs and enjoys seeing even the most basic of those needs fulfilled. She, for example, provides him with a humble meal of bread and cheese "and so tender and indulgent did she feel toward him at that moment that she overlooked the rituals of the blessings and washings and simply sat there reveling in the pleasure of watching her child eat with such appetite" (*MTR* 195). It is significant that Nissim, who embodies traditional fatherhood, interrupts the harmonious scene in an act of paternal authority: "'Eating without a *kippah*, Akiva?' Abba Nissim said severely. . . . 'And it looks as if you haven't even washed,' Nissim went on. 'Sand is raining into your food. I'm afraid to ask if you've said the blessings'" (*MTR* 195). What is more, he temporarily sunders the bond between Akiva and Ivriya when he and the boy mysteriously disappear together. Ivriya, disconsolate, returns to the Uman House and mourns.

Reich, as one would expect, does not conclude the novel with this suppression of Ivriya's feminist model of parenthood. Rather, she celebrates Ivriya's maternal precepts by reuniting Akiva with Ivriya. Importantly, she restores the maternal bond in overtly Jewish terms. Dr. Mendelssohn attempts fruitlessly to restore Akiva to her daughter by pulling out all of the secular stops. She converts Ivriya's apartment into a high-tech headquarters for the search:

> She exploited all her extensive connections with the police, the military, high government officials, and men of power, influence, and

wealth. . . . No possible avenue was allowed to remain unexplored by the energetic Frieda Mendelssohn; she spared no expense whatsoever. . . . The phone in Ivriya's apartment never stopped ringing; using her impressive connections, Dr. Mendelssohn even managed to get several lines installed, which in itself was considered to be a remarkable feat in the State of Israel. (*MTR* 214–215)

Tivka Unger alerts Mendelssohn to the impotence of her secular search. She tells her that Akiva is in the sealed, exclusive world at the center of the religious realm and that her secular efforts are, thus, "futile and hopeless and a pathetic waste of time" (*MTR* 228). To most readers, of course, Mendelssohn's approach smacks of plain old good sense. One sighs with relief that Akiva at least has one sensible person looking for him, especially when one considers the penitents' methods of exploration. Lev Lurie uses his computer (he must settle for a Commodore instead of an IBM) to show that the numerical value of *Shmuel chai* (Shmuel lives) is exactly the same as *yashuv le'imo* (he will return to his mother). Bruriah Lurie reasons to Ivriya, "since Shmuel's mother is no longer on this earth, the Shmuel who lives and will return cannot refer to your husband, who has no mother to return to, and who is, in any case, himself gone to his world, may his memory be a blessing; this 'Shmuel' can only refer to your son, Akiva, for it's not at all uncommon for the father's name to be used cryptically when the son's is intended" (*MTR* 218). I suspect that most kidnapped victims would rather have Mendelssohn than Lurie at the computer terminal; she would at least use it to track leads.

However, one must concede that Mendelssohn's approach fails while the penitent approach which Tivka Unger espouses succeeds. Indeed, only after Ivriya lodges a petition in the Western Wall does Akiva return to her. Part of her supplication reads, "Ivriya bat Frieda is asking for pity: pity her, pity her. Oh, pity me!" (*MTR* 233). Two days later, she receives an answer through the regular post in which the mysterious writer (Nissim? Himmelhoch?) tells her that Akiva will return, and return he does on the back of an unidentified man (probably Himmelhoch, as the novel's title and previous events suggest) who attempts to re-enact the *Akedah,* the binding of Isaac at the Temple Mount. The ending is nebulous and, thus, most critics have hedged on the scene altogether in their discussion of the novel. Kellerman, who, to her credit, does address the scene, only mentions its "abruptly serious tone that dissolves rather than resolves" and calls it "inconsequential" (10).

Despite Kellerman's suggestion that Reich closes the novel incongruously, the final scene dramatically affirms Reich's principal theme throughout the novel—the feminization of traditional Jewish customs and mores. Indeed, through the narrator's reflections, Reich offers a feminist *midrash*—a revelatory commentary of a religious text—of the binding of Isaac. After two Israeli soldiers free Akiva/Isaac from Himmelhoch/Abraham, the narrator ponders why the Biblical account of Sarah's death follows immediately after the account of the *Akedah*:

> [Sarah's] soul did not tarry to hear the end—that the boy had been spared. And, really, had the boy been spared after all? . . . In the flash of vision, she saw that, though the boy might have survived, he surely had not been spared. And, earlier, when a laugh burst out of her at the revelation that she, a woman of ninety, would bear a child, it was not from intellectual arrogance or common skepticism that she had laughed; riding the keen edge of prophecy, she had seen that the child she would bear would not be hers at all; no, as soon as this child was weaned, the moment she released the child, he would be claimed by his father, who, with dazzling alacrity . . . would heed the voice of his God and set out to the land of the Moriah with the boy at his side, to offer him up, his son, his only one, his beloved, in sacrifice. (*MTR* 239)

Since the Talmudic era, of course, writers have been highly critical of Abraham's behavior in the story. To take a more recent example, the Israeli poet Yehuda Amichai questions whether Abraham failed the test atop Moriah by obeying God with such "dazzling alacrity." In the first three lines of his poem, "The Real Hero," the narrator asserts that "The real hero of the Isaac story was the ram,/who didn't know about the conspiracy between the others./As if he had volunteered to die instead of Isaac" (151). But while Amichai sings a song in memory of the ram's suffering, he does not consider in the poem the suffering of Sarah (or of Isaac for that matter), victims also of the "conspiracy" to which the poet refers. Now, I offer this brief explication not to criticize Amichai for a short sighted narrative perspective. One need not be an animal rights activist to sympathize with the ram's perspective, nor a poetry scholar to appreciate the beauty of Amichai's poem. However, the poem does beg the question: who will sing a song in memory of Sarah and Isaac? Through the above *midrash*, Reich does just that by revising in feminist terms our traditional interpretation of the binding of Isaac story (readers interested in additional feminist *midrashim* of biblical stories should see Büchman and Spiegel).

Should we celebrate Abraham's covenant with God and his unconditional faith in God when we read the binding of Isaac story? Reich's narrator undermines this traditional reading of the biblical story by reflecting upon Sarah's often overlooked perspective. The narrator evokes a more fully human Sarah than the matriarch to whom we are accustomed; the narrator's Sarah resents Abraham's hegemony over their son and his utter obsequiousness toward an apparently malicious God. In contrast to Abraham, Sarah realizes that Isaac was not spared atop Moriah, but was permanently scarred from his near-sacrifice at the hands of his father. Reich emphasizes Ivriya's and Akiva's lingering emotional scars after they are reunited to support her feminist *midrash* on the binding of Isaac story: "The child that was returned to Ivriya Himmelhoch was not the same as the one she had lost, nor was she the same woman who had lost the child. That child had been sacrificed, and that woman's soul had burst out of her and surrendered" (*MTR* 239).

As I have already implied, Reich does not conclude the novel by emphasizing the suppression of Ivriya's maternal principles but, rather, celebrates Ivriya's feminist model of parenthood. Reich closes the novel with the image of Ivriya caring for Akiva by feeding him milk and honey, "mother food," whereupon Akiva's breath drips with sweetness (*MTR* 240). Moreover, Reich takes care to emphasize in the final pages that Himmelhoch's journal and the Uman House itself have been bulldozed and left in rubble. The image suggests, I believe, that ultra-Orthodox Jewish life can begin anew in Israel (perhaps only in Israel) and that Reich's feminist model of Jewish interrelationships, dramatized throughout the novel, might take hold—an imaginative and daring vision indeed.

A Postscript on The Jewish War and Other Ugly Fights on the Contemporary Scene

In the Introduction to this study, I suggested that we would see a continuation of the present surge of Jewish-American fiction on Israel. Given this suggestion, it seems only fitting that, as I put the finishing touches on this manuscript for publication, Tova Reich graces us with a new "imagining" of Israel in *The Jewish War*. In the novel, Reich returns to the tension, which she explores briefly in *Master of the Return*, between the Settler Jews and both the secular Jewish state and the ultra-Orthodox, anti-Zionist Jews.

In *Master of the Return*, Reb Lev Lurie, who wishes to seek redemption through wresting the Temple Mount from Moslem control, articulates the perspective of an Israeli Settler Jew. Reich diffuses the tension in *Master of the Return* (and thereby maintains her focus upon the plight of the woman within the ultra-Orthodox Jewish community) as Lev Lurie agrees to pursue a more benign redemptive strategy in a trek up Mount Sinai. By contrast, in *The Jewish War*, Reich creates an implacable Settler Zionist, Yehudi HaGoel, and joins the ranks of Philip Roth as she engages head-on the current "Jewish War" in the Middle East over the heart and soul of a viable Jewish identity—a war which, shortly after the release of Reich's novel, reached a tragic climax in the assassination of Yitzhak Rabin in Tel Aviv.

Of course, the epicenter of this war is not in Tel Aviv but in the city of Hebron in the West Bank: the last bastion of the Settler Jews, the city where both Moslem and Jewish holy places bestir fundamentalists of both ilks into a nationalist frenzy, the city where Arab and Jewish invective most readily escalates into violence. Put simply, Hebron is the city of Baruch Goldstein. Reich's novel begins in the near future as Yehudi HaGoel, formerly Jerry Goldberg of New York, establishes the religious state of Judea and Samaria in the West Bank to preclude the creation of a Palestinian state in the biblical homeland of the Jews. Israeli Defense Force helicopters hover menacingly overhead as HaGoel announces his state's secession from the secular state of Israel. His intentions, as King of Judea and Samaria, are clearly emblazoned in the stitching of his yarmulke: "And ye shall dispossess the inhabitants of the land and dwell therein, for I have given you the land to possess it" (*JW* 10). Through this passage culled from Numbers 33, Reich exposes the biblical imperative that fuels HaGoel's Zionism and informs his myopic perspective concerning the Palestinian problem:

[T]he Arabs [HaGoel later reflects] are nothing more than the modern-day counterparts of the Canaanites whom Joshua and the hosts of Israel subdued and conquered, systematically and methodically, city by city, mostly, except for a few instructive wonders, in a natural, conventional military fashion following the miracles attendant upon the redemption from Egypt. . . . The Arabs are our guests. I have nothing against the Arabs, they can go on living here as long as they remember their place, as long as they keep in mind that they are the guests and that we are the masters of the house. (140–141)

If Reich's depiction of Yehudi HaGoel smacks of caricature, one might recall the Settler Jews' veneration of Baruch Goldstein as a martyr following his massacre of twenty-nine Palestinians and suicide in Hebron, or the blithe way in which these same Jews cited scripture to claim that these twenty-nine Arab lives were not worth even the thumbnail of a Jew. The Israeli authorities, in fact, discovered a book extolling Baruch Goldstein in the room of Yigal Amir, the Jewish law student who murdered Prime Minister Rabin. All of which is simply to say that Yehudi HaGoel and his cohorts in *The Jewish War* are characters only too palpable. Indeed, through Yehudi HaGoel's secessionist Jewish state and in his foreign policy plans (to seize Judea and Samaria from the Palestinians and, eventually one suspects, to purge the land of Arabs altogether), Reich explores through her artistic imagination the direction in which the Settler Jews might logically proceed in the wake of Baruch Goldstein and further Israeli pull-outs from the West Bank. Reich, interestingly, does not dare to "imagine" a Jewish fundamentalist's assassination of Israel's Prime Minister. Nonetheless, she depicts the near future as nightmare.

This is not to say that *The Jewish War* is a humorless novel. For Reich's now trademark comic touches permeate the story. HaGoel's right-hand man, Hoshea HaLevi, recruits the best and brightest young American Jew to devise a method, via Gematria, to "siphon off the oil of Arabia, to coax and lure it by scientific or mathematical or whatever means through invisible networks, like a microscopic nervous or circulatory system, so that it would collect in great pools beneath the surface of Israel . . ." (an Israeli observed wryly to me once that, after forty years of wandering, it could only have been a stroke of bad Jewish luck that Moses settled in the holy land rather than the oil land) (96); Malkie Seltzer, one of HaGoel's three wives, reads religiously the lurid novels of Colette—a writer who "understood her"—and participates in a discussion group with an impostor Colette living in Jerusalem (Reich, once again, documents in vivid detail the sexual antics of her ultra-Orthodox characters); and Reich dramatizes humorously and intriguingly the curious alliance between the Christian Right and the Settler Jews via Chuck Buck, an evangelical Christian who joins HaGoel in a tent to protest recent conciliatory actions by the Israeli government. Buck, of course, wishes to rebuild the Jewish Temple to bring about the *second* coming of the Messiah: "Oh, Brother Jew-dee, a new day is dawning, I feel it coming, the city of Jesus stretched out upon the Temple Mount, a super, mega Christian theme park to penetrate the spirit of even the most hardened of unbelievers . . ." (145). HaGoel welcomes Buck's support, but must tell his newfound ally that Jesus Christ is "not exactly the guy we're expecting, as you may or may not be aware" (145).

Despite these comic elements, *The Jewish War* is a tragic novel, far more bleak than *Master of the Return*. To be sure, the events during the past several months since Israel's peace accord with the PLO have illustrated, in the blood of many, the tragic potential of religious fundamentalism. Reich is far too canny a writer to ignore this lesson in our recent history. Indeed, she depicts the unrepentant violence, inextricably conjoined with religious fundamentalism, more compellingly than any other American writer thus far. HaGoel's unrepentant terrorism emerges most disturbingly when he plants a bomb in the car of a pious, elderly Arab, Abu Salman; the bomb blasts off Salman's right leg. When a Druze demolitions expert examines Salman's garage for additional explosives, another bomb detonates in the Druze's face and blinds him. The Israeli police eventually capture HaGoel and his accomplices, whereupon their followers exalt them as "true lovers of Zion and of Israel. . . . excellent boys" (194). HaGoel himself predictably offers no apologies since "Terror against terror was the only language the Arabs understood" (195). Like Philip Roth in *The Counterlife*, then, Reich challenges the stereotypes of the Arab terrorist and the Jewish victim in the Middle East. She depicts the Jewish Settler as the purveyor of indiscriminate, terrorist violence and portrays the Arab sympathetically as the hapless victim of a car bomb. To Reich's credit, the current Middle East scene corroborates her implicit suggestion that Arabs do not hold a monopoly on terrorist violence, that the facile categories of victimizer and victim to describe either side embroiled in the Middle East crisis do not hold sway.

While Reich, in this regard, ventures onto territory that Roth has previously explored, she plumbs greater depths than Roth in focusing upon the child abuse that naturally accompanies any fundamentalist movement that places little value in our temporal existence. We have taken, of late, to castigating the parents of child athletes who, projecting their own athletic aspirations onto their children, subject them to physical and emotional abuse. In its fervor, of course, HaGoel's monomanic quest for redemption far outstrips the aspirations of a child-athlete's parent; and, as one might suspect, HaGoel's quest takes utter precedence over the physical and emotional well-being of his children and the children of his followers. He, for example, trains his diminutive daughter, At'halta D'Geula, to carry out a dangerous, unauthorized survey of the subterranean passageways and chambers in the Cave of Machpelah. Telling the Israeli social workers, who have their eye on him, that he is giving his daughter "quality time," he tests her skills with a camera and tape measure. When the time comes to lower At'halta into the chamber, she begins to cry and begs for her blanket. HaGoel appears to treat her tenderly as he accommodates his obedient daughter and lowers her into the chamber. However, Reich provides us with a narrative perspective critical of HaGoel's actions in Emunah Halevi. When Carmela, HaGoel's second wife and At'halta's mother, suggests to Emunah that At'halta's descent into the cave represents a rebirth, Emunah replies dolefully, "Maybe . . . but this time I don't hear her singing" (128). Later, Carmela insists that she does hear her daughter singing, "ma, ma, ma" (129); HaGoel posits that she has seen the Messiah and, awestruck, cannot quite form the full Hebrew word, "Mashiach," so naturally mutters "ma, ma, ma." Emunah knows better: "'She's crying,' Emunah screamed frantically, 'that's crying we hear. She wants her mother. Help her! She's frightened out of her wits! She's crying for her *ima!*'" (129). Through this scene, Reich suggests dramatically how fundamentalists like Yehudi HaGoel all too readily turn a deaf ear to the cries of their children when those cries interfere with their redemptive plans.

The novel, as one begins to suspect, inches toward a tragedy from which the children shall not be spared. Reich foreshadows this tragedy in the scene described above and in others worth noting. To revolt against Israel's withdrawal from the northern Sinai after the 1979 Camp David Accords with Egypt, HaGoel and his followers hole themselves up in the northern Sinai town of Yamit; they will not allow Israel to dismantle the Jewish settlement. Though they stop short of committing a mass suicide, they force the Israeli Army—"the enemy"—to remove them by force. As the Israeli Defense Force shuts off the air-conditioning, then turn high-pressure water hoses onto the Settlers, then finally drag them off the roof of their Yamit compound, one wonders how parents could expose their children to such palpable danger. The female soldiers wonder the same thing and scold the Settler women: "How could you bring your children to such a place? How can you place your babies in such danger?" (119).

The standoff ends just short of tragedy as HaGoel and his followers are evacuated, but leave At'halta (a baby at the time) on the rooftop of the building. Fortunately, an Israeli Colonel notices the abandoned baby before they raze the settlement. Colonel Lapidot weeps openly as he reflects, "We nearly finished her off . . . We almost destroyed her with the buildings. We almost had a tragedy" (121). Though he assumes that At'halta was forgotten, one must wonder whether HaGoel intended to sacrifice his daughter for the cause, for the devastating blow that such a tragedy would inflict upon Israel and its policy of dismantling the Jewish settlements in the Sinai. HaGoel, after all, had seriously contemplated mass suicide as a public relations strategy. The sacrifice of only one child would likely seem to him a more moderate option.

The standoff between HaGoel's sect and the Israeli Defense Forces following the Camp David Accords foreshadows the climactic siege in Hebron at the end of the novel. Yamit represents a trial run for HaGoel, who has had some twenty years to strengthen his resolve. Armed to the teeth, HaGoel leads his followers in a trek through their Kingdom of Judea and Samaria—the "so-called West Bank" (217). They are clearly itching for a fight, and the Palestinians at the refugee camp of Dehaishe are only too happy to accommodate them. They assail the Settlers with stones and intermittent gunfire at which point HaGoel and his men shoot with their Uzis and pistols at the "rising and vanishing shadows of young boys masked in checked kaffiyehs" (221). Predictably, the episode ends in disaster as a bullet hits and kills HaGoel's daughter, Golana:

> Golana's hands slid slowly, slowly down along the pole. With a soft moan, she drew herself in. With a rustle, she let herself go, and she folded up like an offering at her father's feet. (221)

Reich deliberately and tellingly depicts the death as a sacrifice. For though HaGoel interprets her death as another murder in the long line of Arab murderings of Jews, HaGoel, Reich implies, sacrifices his daughter (successfully this time) and bears culpability. Moreover, one can be fairly certain that HaGoel and his men, firing Uzis and pistols, succeed in killing a far greater number of Palestinian children, those "young boys" in kaffiyehs.

HaGoel and his followers fortify themselves with weapons and supplies, and prepare for an extended siege in the Forefather's Compound of Machpelah in Hebron. During these final moments of the novel, Reich takes care to evoke HaGoel's distinct brand of fanaticism. For example, his sect establishes the first annual "great Holocaust Contest of the Kingdom of Judea and Samaria" (254). Despite such concrete details that earmark HaGoel's sect as a Jewish Settler group, one cannot avoid reading this final section as a commentary upon cults in general. Reich alludes explicitly to Jonestown (and belabors the parallel as HaGoel's followers meet a fate similar to the fate of Jim Jones's followers), but the tragic events at the Branch Davidian compound in Waco, Texas, resonate even more profoundly. As in Waco, the world media converge upon the scene in droves; Israeli troops encircle the compund and cut off supply lines; Israeli soldiers, like the ATF agents in Waco, are shot down during an ill-advised raid of the compound; HaGoel and his men dig out a subterranean network of passageways and chambers; HaGoel, like David Koresh, is rumored to be at work on a definitive redemptive plan; the siege captures the attention of various "experts" and opportunists in a way that would seem incredulous if it were not for the events at Waco:

> [T]he whole world waited for something to hatch, to crack, to snap, someone to spring, for news; as mental health experts outdid one another with fanciful theories and explanations that all seemed so true, and rabbis' voices trembled and vibrated in prayer and sermons, and millennial prophets and madmen staggered out of the wilderness crying the world's end, and scholars added more and more wonderful footnotes to their cultural and sociological and historical analogies, and doctors and lawyers stood armed and ready with the tools of their trade for any eventuality, and hucksters peddled Kingdom of Judea and Samaria T-shirts and baseball caps and buttons and bumper stickers, and mobs gathered in a holiday mood to watch in fascination as at any grave accident or conflagration or public execution . . . and media people ran around importantly photographing and filming and interviewing the animate and the inanimate . . . (254–255).

Just a scant couple of years ago, one might have attributed the above scene to Reich's flair for the outlandish. But read in light of the events at Waco, Reich's powers as a social satirist emerge more profoundly. Through the above scene, Reich forces the reader to confront the madness that, disturbingly, characterizes our present reality.

That HaGoel, like David Koresh, once again uses the children of his sect as pawns and refuses to spare them from their mass suicide represents the most disconcerting element of the novel's conclusion. When the Israeli General, Uri Lapidot, warns HaGoel that he intends to launch an air attack on the compound, HaGoel sends his "elite" fighting force onto the roof: ". . . there they were revealed, upon the rooftops and the walls of the Compound, the elite force, the crack fighting unit—more than one hundred children, boys under the age of thirteen, girls not yet twelve, many as young as five or six, all of them with their arms raised, some with rocks clenched in both fists, some with slingshots pulled taut, poised for release, each one tensely awaiting the order to fire" (243). The order, of course, never comes, as Lapidot, not wanting to harm the children, orders his troops to retreat. Lamentably, the Israeli Army cannot, ultimately, save the children, who all perish when their elders—intoxicated by HaGoel's allusions to Masada—decide upon suicide.

Reich depicts convincingly in these final scenes the power that someone like Yehudi HaGoel can wield over devout followers—how egoism, messianic fervor, and sheer charisma can mingle in an individual to lead to disastrous consequences. How could someone like David Koresh, several people wondered, lead so many to such a tragic fate? Through the impassioned exhortations of HaGoel, Reich attempts to answer that question. "[T]he spirit," HaGoel begins to assure his followers, "takes comfort in the ending, rest is good, to be gathered back unto one's fathers and mothers is the most generous gift of all, gathered back even to this place, to pass lightly as spirits through these massive stones that are now an impassable barrier, to pass as unencumbered souls easily through these stones into the innermost inner sanctum of these sacred caves where our forebears lie" (267). HaGoel knows just the right buttons to push. His followers poison themselves and die while attempting to scratch their way through the rock separating them from the burial niches of their forebears.

In *The Jewish War*, then, Reich engages the distinct quandaries facing the Israeli Jew today. There is, indeed, a "Jewish War" today between the secular, ultra-Orthodox, and Settler Jews. That said, Israel also serves as Reich's objective correlative. She uses the Middle East as a prism through which to shine light on our worldwide epidemic: cults and child-abuse. In one short passage, Reich suggests why Israel serves the Jewish-American writer today as such a fruitful locus through which to engage these broader crises: "After all, this was Israel, and everything in Israel was pitched at a higher level of drama, intensity, and what might, to citizens of other lands, appear to be craziness, but that was the power and the wonder of the place, there was no mistaking that you were alive" (123).

Chapter 10

CONCLUSION

In my introduction to this study, I suggested that our present outcropping of Jewish-American novels on Israel marks the beginning of a renaissance in Jewish-American fiction. This contention, I am sure, seems rife with hyperbole to several readers, or at least seems premature. To bring this study to a satisfactory conclusion, then, I would like to elaborate upon my initial, optimistic reflections. It strikes me that two essential questions beg to be asked: (1) what happened to Jewish-American literature in the first place, that it should need a renaissance? and (2) what leads one to believe that the recent Jewish-American literature on Israel heralds in this renaissance?

The answer to this first question, I believe, lies in what we might call the cunning of history. For, curiously, the Jewish-American novel moved from the center of the American literary scene toward its periphery at precisely the same time that American Jews eschewed their peripheral, or marginalized, status in America to join the mainstream. Indeed, it was just that nagging sense of alienation in America that provided the essential grist for the fictional mills of those dazzling post-immigrant writers—Henry Roth, Grace Paley, Saul Bellow, Bernard Malamud, and others. These writers were driven by what Irving Howe called an "inescapable subject": "the judgment, affection and hatred they bring to bear upon the remembered world of their youth, and the costs extracted by their struggle to tear themselves away" ("Introduction" 3). Consider, for example, Saul Bellow's memorable protagonist, Moses Herzog. We first meet him long after he has extricated himself from this "remembered world." He is a History professor with solid academic and financial credentials. That said, his alienation from mainstream America prompts him to reflect upon the virtues of his materially impoverished but emotionally rich upbringing on Napoleon Street: "Here was a wider range of human feelings than he had ever again been able to find. . . . What was wrong with Napoleon Street? thought Herzog. All he ever wanted was there" (Bellow, *Herzog* 140).

True, Bellow's *Herzog* (1964) distinguishes itself from other Jewish-American novels in the same stylistic and even thematic ways that separate Bellow's work from, well, any work that one of his contemporaries has produced. However, through Moses Herzog, Bellow engages the tension that earmarks so much of the post-immigrant Jewish-American fiction written primarily between the 1930s and 1960s. These writers almost invariably depicted characters who were both beleaguered by their hyphenated identity as Americans and ambivalent about the degrees to which they should embrace the Jewish and American side of that hyphen. The Jewish-American novel enjoyed its heyday during this prolific period, as the specific cultural burdens of the alienated Jew resonated for mainstream readers. That is to say, while a Moses Herzog (or a David Schearl, an Asa Leventhal, a Morris Bober, a Neil Klugman . . .) suffered from his own distinct brand of alienation, his culturally specific *tsores* seemed to many to cast the human condition at large in sharp, dramatic focus.

This golden age in Jewish-American literature could only last so long. As mainstream America became more and more hospitable toward American Jews and the post-immigrant consciousness of marginality and alienation dimmed, Jewish-American writers had no choice but to search for new "inescapable subjects." As Alvin Rosenfeld observed more than twenty years ago,

> The many legitimate themes created for literature by the immigrant trauma—themes of cultural displacement and discontinuity, of the trials of readjustment in a new land, the embarrassments and excitements of discovery, the early years of sweatshop toil and the middle years of business accomplishment or intellectual pre-eminence, the spiritual failures that can come with worldly success—these and many more constituted a literature of authentic interest at one time among Jewish writers and readers, but it is an interest that has largely since lapsed or been taken over by the other minority-group writers, who are now searching to find their own expression for it. ("The Progress" 119)

Rosenfeld and others, like Ruth Wisse (see "American Jewish Writing, Act II"), anticipated that the next wave of Jewish-American literature would look decidedly more "Jewish"—that having explored the outside world of mainstream America, Jewish-American writers would increasingly look inward. "The next frontier for American Jewry," Alfred Marcus asserts in 1973, "will be an internal one. ... We have surely seen enough of the individual Jew as everyman, the Jew lost in an alien world; we require, at this point, a sense of community, of the people" (4–5). The theologically oriented Jewish-American literature that cropped up in the 1970s and 1980s bore out the predictions of Marcus, Rosenfeld, and Wisse. Several writers like Steve Stern, Curt Leviant, Allegra Goodman, Melvin Jules Bukiet, Nessa Rapoport, and Rebecca Goldstein followed Cynthia Ozick's lead to explore Jewish liturgy, values, and traditions in their fiction.

Jewish-American literature, then, certainly survived the success of American Jews. What is more, amid our zeitgeist which extols cultural particularism, most scholars of Jewish-American literature have welcomed the new "Jewish" Jewish-American literature. Any scholar in the field not itching for a fight these days knows well enough to deride the mere "ethnic" Jewish-American literature of the post-immigrant ilk. But whatever positive things one may have to say about Jewish-American fiction's second wave, one must also reckon with the decline of widespread interest in the Jewish-American novel that accompanied this second wave. Marcus, for one, read the writing on the wall when he anticipated in 1973 that the next internal frontier of Jewish-American literature "may, let us face it, have only a limited audience, and ... will probably not reach the best-seller lists" (4).

Now, Marcus fretted little over the likely prospect that the new work of Jewish-American writers would appeal to a more narrow, mostly Jewish, audience, and I share his disinclination to gauge the quality of literature solely by its general popularity. One need only glance down the *New York Times* best-seller list to remind oneself that literary merit and popular appeal rarely go hand in hand. That the second wave of Jewish-American writers heeded Ozick's call for a literature "centrally Jewish in its concerns" and, in the bargain, enriched the canon of Jewish-American literature is true enough ("Toward" 174). It is also true, however, that as these contemporary writers turned inward to explore the fictional possibilities of the theological imagination, they simultaneously turned their attention away from mainstream America and the secular Jewish experience in mainstream America. This public realm was a central concern of Jewish-American writers during the boom period of the Jewish-American novel in the 1940s, 50s, and 60s.

Philip Roth, writing in 1961, brooded over his responsibility to depict the "American reality":

> [T]he American writer in the middle of the twentieth century has his hands full in trying to understand, describe, and then make *credible* much of American reality. . . . The actuality is continually outdoing our talents, and the culture tosses up figures almost daily that are the envy of any novelist. Who, for example, could have invented Charles Van Doren? Roy Cohn and David Schine? Sherman Adams and Bernard Goldfine? Dwight David Eisenhower? ("Writing American Fiction" 177)

One can scarcely picture one of our young contemporary Jewish-American writers expressing such anxious sentiments. As I have already suggested, their culturally specific agenda has all but precluded their engaging mainstream American figures and issues. Ted Solotaroff underscored this general trend recently while introducing the stories he and Nessa Rapoport decided to include in *Writing Our Way Home: Contemporary Stories by American Jewish Writers.* He notes, "There is a relatively vacant area in which we found very few stories to consider and none that met the standards of our individual tastes. This is the recent public realm" ("The Open Community" xxv). Solotaroff, unlike Marcus before him, regrets the contemporary Jewish-American writers' neglect of the public realm and attributes the neglect partly to the "general withdrawal of interest from political, economic, social, and intellectual concerns in recent American writing . . ." (xxvi).

Scholars might haggle over the degree to which Jewish-American writers partake in a general American literary trend as they neglect the public realm. But of one thing we can be certain. The trend does not bespeak a concomitant American Jewish apathy toward the public realm. To be sure, American Jews continue to grapple on their own distinct terms with a host of mainstream issues. I am thinking, specifically, of the heightened tensions between Jewish and African Americans, the influx of Russian Jews into Jewish-American neighborhoods, the ethnic cleansing in the former Yugoslavia, the curious alliance between Jewish neoconservatives and the Christian right, and, of course, the turmoil in the Middle East.

The intuitive reader may have just inferred why I see a renaissance afoot for Jewish-American literature. For thankfully, the recent Jewish-American fiction on Israel suggests that "political, economic, social, and intellectual concerns" have once again begun to spark the Jewish-American imagination. The Middle East, that is, represents the most promising site at which Jewish-American writers presently engage the public realm. It comes as little surprise that Israel should serve this function. After all, some of the most pressing dramas that define our culture play themselves out in the Middle East. To wit, if one were to update Roth's list of personages above, one might very well include several names enmeshed in the Middle East crisis and etched into our nation's collective psyche: Yasir Arafat, Jonathan Pollard, Baruch Goldstein, Yigal Amir, John Demjanjuk, Hanan Ashrawi, Edward Said, Yitzhak Rabin, and Shimon Peres. Forget Charles Van Doren! Who, indeed, could have invented *these* public figures? Perhaps no one. But Roth, Roiphe, and Reich, to their credit, have already begun to imagine these figures, or compelling composites, in their fiction.

I suspect that additional Jewish-American writers will follow their lead to engage the Middle East and the other public issues listed above which daily inform Jewish life in America. Jews, after all, continue to take on public issues with an intellectual intensity and moral rigor that far outweighs Jewish numbers. Jewish-American writers must take on these issues, as well. Until they do, the mosaic of Jewish-American literature, brilliant though it may be, will remain incomplete.

WORKS CITED

"A Zionist Colony." Rev. of *Yehuda*, by Meyer Levin. *The New York Times Book Review* Mar. 1931: 21.

Abel, Lionel. "American Jews and Israel: A Symposium." *Commentary* Feb. 1988: 21–75.

Adam, Yehudi. "Zionism and Judaism." *Judaism* 29 (1980): 279–285.

Adler, Rachel. "'The Jew who wasn't there': *Halakhah* and the Jewish Woman." *On Being a Jewish Feminist*. Ed. Susannah Heschel. New York: Shocken Books, 1983. 12–18.

Alexander, Edward. "American Jews and Israel: A Symposium." *Commentary* Feb. 1988: 21–75.

———. "Imagining the Holocaust: *Mr. Sammler's Planet* and Others." *Judaism* 22.3 (1973): 288–300.

———. *With Friends Like These: The Jewish Critics of Israel*. New York: Shapolsky Publishers, Inc., 1993.

Allen, Woody. "Am I Reading the Papers Correctly." *The New York Times* 28 Jan. 1988: A27.

d'Alpuget, Blanche. "A Daughter Lost to Faith." Rev. of *Lovingkindness*, by Anne Roiphe. *The New York Times Book Review* 30 Aug. 1987: 9.

Alter, Robert. "Defenders of the Faith." *Commentary* July 1987: 52–55.

———. "Enemies, a Love Story: What the Jews, Even Under Siege, Owe Liberalism." *The New Republic* 30 Nov. 1992: 28–33.

———. "Sentimentalizing the Jews." *Commentary* Sept. 1965: 71–75.

Alter, Susan D. "The *Sefer Torah* Comes Home." *Daughters of the King: Women and the Synagogue*. Eds. Susan Grossman and Rivka Haut. Philadelphia: The Jewish Publication Society, 1992. 279–282.

Amichai, Yehuda. *Selected Poetry of Yehuda Amichai*. Trans. and Eds. Chana Bloch and Stephen Mitchell. New York: Harper & Row, 1986.

Angoff, Charles, and Meyer Levin. Introduction. *The Rise of American Jewish Literature: An Anthology of Selections from the Major Novels.* Eds. Charles Angoff and Meyer Levin. New York: Simon and Schuster, 1970. 7–17.

Avital, Colette. "Political Empowerment of Women in Israel." *Midstream* April 1994: 18–20.

Bell, Pearl K. "Meyer Levin's Obsessions." *Commentary* June 1978: 66–68.

Bellow, Saul. "Common Needs, Common Preoccupations: An Interview with Saul Bellow." With Jo Brans. *Southwest Review* 62 (1977): 1–19.

———. "Deep Readers of the World Beware!" *The New York Times Book Review* 15 Feb. 1959: 1, 34.

———. *Great Jewish Short Stories.* New York: Dell, 1963.

———. *Herzog.* 1964. New York: Viking Penguin, Inc., 1988.

———. "Literature and Culture: An Interview with Saul Bellow." With Robert T. Boyers. *Salmagundi* 30 (1975): 6–23.

———. *Mr. Sammler's Planet.* 1970. New York: Viking Penguin, Inc., 1988.

———. "Summations." *Saul Bellow: A Mosaic.* Eds. L. H. Goldman, Gloria L. Cronin, and Ada Aharoni. New York: Peter Lang, 1992. 185–199.

———. "The Nobel Lecture." *The American Scholar* 46 (Summer 1977): 16–25.

———. *To Jerusalem and Back: A Personal Account.* New York: Viking Press, 1976.

Berger, Alan L. "Judaism as a Religious Value System." *Crisis and Covenant: The Holocaust in American Jewish Fiction.* Ed. Sarah Blacher Cohen. SUNY Series in Modern Jewish Literature and Culture. Albany: New York State UP, 1985. 59–65.

Berkove, Lawrence I. "American *Midrashim*: Hugh Nissenson's Stories." *Critique* 20.1 (1978): 75–82.

"Bestseller Revisited." Rev. of *Exodus. Time* 8 Dec. 1958: 110.

Blau, Joseph L. *Modern Varieties of Judaism.* New York: Columbia University Press, 1966. 64–79.

Blocker, Joel. "Fantasy of Israel." Rev. of *Exodus. Commentary* June 1959: 539–541.

Breines, Paul. *Tough Jews.* New York: HarperCollins, 1990.

Brettschneider, Marla. "Feminist Judaism: Providing Models for Continuity through Multiculturalism." *Response* Fall 1993: 18–21.

Brown, Paul. "'This thing of darkness I acknowledge mine': *The Tempest* and the Discourse of Colonialism." *Political Shakespeare: New Essays in Cultural Materialism.* Ithica and London: Cornell University Press, 1985. 48–71.

Broyde, Michael J. "Communal Prayer and Women." *Judaism* 42.4 (1993): 387–394.

Buber, Martin. "An Experiment That Did Not Fail." *Israel, the Arabs and the Middle East.* Eds. Irving Howe and Carl Gershman. New York: Bantam, 1972. 5–15.

Büchman, Christina, and Celina Spiegel, eds. *Out of the Garden: Women Writing on the Bible.* New York: Ballantine, 1994.

Bullock, Florence Haxton. "Some of the New Novels." Rev. of *My Father's House,* by Meyer Levin. *New York Herald Tribune Weekly Book Review* 7 Sept. 1947: 8, 10.

Chertok, Haim. *Israeli Preoccupations.* New York: Fordham Univ. Press, 1994.

Chomsky, Noam. "Bellow, *To Jerusalem and Back.*" *Towards a New Cold War: Essays on the Current Crisis and How We Got There.* Noam Chomsky. New York: Pantheon, 1982. 299–307.

Clayton, John Jacob. *Saul Bellow: In Defense of Man.* Bloomington: Indiana University Press, 1979.

Cohen, Sarah Blacher. "Saul Bellow's Jerusalem." *Studies in American Jewish Literature* 5.2 (1979): 16–23.

Cook, Bruce. "Allegorical Tale Painfully Told, But Impressive." Rev. of *The Chosen. National Observer* 8 May 1967: 23.

Cronin, Gloria. "Faith and Futurity: The Case for Survival in *Mr. Sammler's Planet.*" *Literature and Belief* 3 (1983): 97–108.

———. "Searching the Narrative Gap: Authorial Self-Irony and the Problematic Discussion of Western Misogyny in *Mr. Sammler's Planet.* " *Saul Bellow: A Mosaic.* Eds. L. H. Goldman, Gloria L. Cronin, and Ada Aharoni. New York: Peter Lang, 1992. 97–122.

Crossman, Richard. "Framework for the Jewish State: The New Boundaries of Zionist Aspiration." *Commentary* Nov. 1947: 401–407.

Daiker, Donald A. "Reviews." Rev. of *In the Reign of Peace. Studies in Short Fiction* 10.3 (1973): 291–292.

Darby, William. "The On-going Thing That She Had Started . . . Was Now More Powerful Than She." *Necessary American Fictions: Popular Literature of the 1950s.* William Darby. Bowling Green: Bowling Green State University Popular Press, 1987. 93–100.

Decter, Midge. "American Jews and Israel: A Symposium." *Commentary* Feb. 1988: 21–75.

———. "Popular Jews." Rev. of *Mila 18. Commentary* Oct. 1961: 358, 360; Rpt. in *The Liberated Woman and Other Americans.* Ed. Midge Decter. New York: Coward, 1971. 177–20.

DeMott, Benjamin. "The Frightful and the Sublime." Rev. of *Master of the Return,* by Tova Reich. *Atlantic Monthly* May 1988: 92–93.

Dershowitz, Alan M. *Chutzpah.* Boston: Little, Brown and Co., 1991.

Dickstein, Morris. "Philip Roth's Diasporism: A Symposium." *Tikkun* May/ June 1993: 41–45, 73.

Ehrenkrantz, Louis. "Bellow in Jerusalem." *Midstream* Nov. 1977: 87–90.

Ehrlich, Leonard. "The Nation of Israel." Rev. of *Yehuda,* by Meyer Levin. *Saturday Review of Literature* June 1931: 880.

Ellenberg, Al. "Saul Bellow Picks Another Fight." *Rolling Stone* 4 Mar. 1982: 14–16, 64.

Eisenberg, Judah M. "American Jews and Israel: Two Views, II." *Midstream* Feb. 1972: 62–67.

Emerson, Ralph Waldo. "Art." *Selected Writings of Emerson.* Ed. Donald McQuade. New York: The Modern Library, 1981. 289–299.

Faulkner, William. *Absalom, Absalom!* 1936. New York: Random House, 1987.

Feingold, Henry L. "American Zionism *In Extremis?*" *Midstream* June/July 1994: 22–25.

Feld, Merle. "Egalitarianism and the *Havurah* Movement." *Daughters of the King: Women and the Synagogue.* Eds. Susan Grossman and Rivka Haut. Philadelphia: The Jewish Publication Society, 1992. 245–250.

Fiedler, Leslie. *Fiedler on the Roof: Essays on Literature and Jewish Identity.* Boston: David R. Godine, 1991.

Field, Leslie. "Israel Revisited in American Jewish Literature." *Midstream* Nov. 1982: 50–54.

———. "Saul Bellow: From Montreal to Jerusalem." *Studies in American Jewish Literature* 4.2 (1978): 51–59.

Fisch, Harold. "High Adventure and Spiritual Quest." Rev. of *In the Reign of Peace. Midstream* Jan. 1973: 71–72.

Fishbane, Simcha. "'In Any Case there are no Sinful Thoughts'—The Role and Status of Women in Jewish Law as Expressed in the *Arukh Hashulhan." Judaism* 42.4 (1993): 492–503.

Fox-Genovese, Elizabeth. "The State of Contemporary Politics and Culture." *Tikkun* March/April 1994: 50–53.

Fried, Lewis. "Living the Riddle: The Sacred and Profane in Anne Roiphe's *Lovingkindness." Studies in American Jewish Literature* 11.2 (1992): 174–181.

Friedler, Egon. "Secular Judaism: New Answers for Old Questions." *Midstream* Oct. 1992: 15–18.

Friedman, Thomas L. *From Beirut to Jerusalem.* 1989. New York: Doubleday, 1990.

Gendel, Evelyn. "The Successful Novelist and the Committed Jew." *Jewish Digest* July 1966: 77–80.

Gilman, Sander. *Difference and Pathology: Stereotypes of Sexuality, Race and Madness.* Ithaca: Cornell University Press, 1985.

Gilroy, Harry. "The Founding of the New Israel." Rev. of *Exodus. The New York Times Book Review* 12 Oct. 1958: 32.

Gittelsohn, Roland B. "American Jews and Israel: Two Views, I." *Midstream* Feb. 1972: 58–61.

Golan, Matti. *With Friends Like You.* New York: Free Press, 1993.

Goldman, Leila H. "Hugh Nissenson." *Twentieth-Century American-Jewish Fiction Writers.* Ed. Daniel Walden. Detroit: Gale, 1984. Vol. 28 of *Dictionary of Literary Biography.* 94 vols. to date. 1978–. 189–195.

Goldman, Solomon. "Zionist Education: The Essential Conflict." *Midstream* May 1993: 25–28.

Goodheart, Eugene. "Writing and Unmaking the Self." *Contemporary Literature* 29 (1988): 438–453.

Gorenberg, Gershom. "Gone Shopping." *The New Republic* 17 Oct. 1994: 18, 20, 22, 24.

Graff, Gerald. "What Has Literary Theory Wrought?" *The Chronicle of Higher Education* 12 Feb. 1992: A48.

Graver, Lawrence. *An Obsession with Anne Frank: Meyer Levin and the Diary.* Berkeley: University of California Press, 1995.

Grebstein, Sheldon. "The Phenomenon of the Really Jewish Best-Seller: Potok's *The Chosen.*" *Studies in American Jewish Literature* 1.1 (1975): 23–31.

Greenberg, Joel. "Israel Rethinks Interrogation of Arabs." *The New York Times* 14 Aug. 1993: A3.

Grossman, Edward. "The Bitterness of Saul Bellow." *Midstream* Aug./Sept. 1970: 3–15.

———. "Unsentimental Journey." *Commentary* Nov. 1976: 80, 82–84.

Grossman, Susan, and Rivka Haut, eds. *Daughters of the King: Women and the Synagogue.* Ed. Susan Grossman and Rivka Haut. Philadelphia: The Jewish Publication Society, 1992.

Guttmann, Allen. *The Jewish Writer in America: Assimilation and the Crisis of Identity.* New York: Oxford University Press, 1971.

Haberman, Clyde. "Doctor, an Old Ally, Confronts Arafat." *The New York Times International* 23 Jan. 1994: A12.

———. "Massacre at Hebron Exposes Anti-American Mood in Israel." *The New York Times* 20 March 1994: A1, A4.

———. "Meet a New (and Younger) Breed of Israelis." *The New York Times* 12 Jan. 1995: A1, A7.

Halkin, Hillel. "How to Read Philip Roth." *Commentary* Feb. 1994: 43–48.

———. "Israel Against Itself." *Commentary* Nov. 1994: 33–39.

———. *Letters to an American Jewish Friend.* Philadelphia: Jewish Publication Society, 1977.

Halpern, Ben. "The Problems Of Israeli Socialism." *Israel, the Arabs & the Middle East.* Eds. Irving Howe and Carl Gershman. New York: Bantam, 1972. 45–68.

Halsell, Grace. *Journey to Jerusalem.* New York: Macmillan, 1981.

Hauptman, Judith. "Some Thoughts on the Nature of *Halakhic* Adjudication: Women and *Minyan.*" *Judaism* 42.4 (1993): 396–413.

———. "Women and Prayer: An Attempt to Dispel Some Fallacies." *Judaism* 42.1 (1992): 94–103.

Haut, Rivka. "The Presence of Women." *Daughters of the King: Women and the Synagogue.* Ed. Susan Grossman and Rivka Haut. Philadelphia: The Jewish Publication Society, 1992. 274–278.

Hazleton, Lesley. "Israeli Women: Three Myths." *On Being a Jewish Feminist.* Ed. Susannah Heschel. New York: Shocken Books, 1983. 65–87.

Hedges, Chris. "Dozens of Islamic Rebel Suspects Slain by Algerian Death Squads." *The New York Times* 24 Jan. 1994: A6.

Hendrickson, Paul. "*Exodus* to *Trinity*: The Impact of Leon Uris' Runaway Epics." *The Washington Post* (2 May 1978): B1, B3.

Hertzberg, Arthur. *Jewish Polemics.* New York: Columbia University Press, 1992.

———. *The Jews in America.* New York: Simon & Schuster, 1989.

———. *The Zionist Idea: A Historical Analysis and Reader.* New York: Doubleday, 1960.

———. "Turmoil at Home, Glory in Israel." *The Jews in America.* New York: Simon & Schuster, 1989. 350–376.

Himmelfarb, Milton. "American Jews and Israel: A Symposium." *Commentary* Feb 1988: 21–75.

Hochman, Baruch. "The Jewish Vogue." Rev. of *The Chosen. Commentary* Sept. 1967: 107–108.

Holtz, Barry W., ed. *The Schocken Guide to Jewish Books: Where to Start Reading about Jewish History, Literature, Culture, and Religion.* New York: Schocken Books, 1992.

Horowitz, David. "Founding the New State." *Commentary* Feb. 1948: 97–103.

Horowitz, Irving Louis, and Maurice Zeitlin. "Israeli Imperatives and Jewish Agonies." *Israel and Zion in American Judaism: the Zionist Fulfillment.* Ed. Jacob Neusner. New York: Garland, 1993. 61–84.

Howe, Irving. "American Jews and Israel." *Tikkun* May/June 1989: 71–74.

———. Introduction. *Jewish American Stories.* Ed. Irving Howe. New York: NAL Penguin Inc., 1977: 1–17.

———. "People on the Edge of History—Saul Bellow's Vivid Report on Israel." *The New York Times Book Review* 17 Oct. 1976: 1–2.

———. "Philip Roth Reconsidered." *Commentary* Dec. 1972: 69–77.

———. *Politics and the Novel.* New York: Horizon Press, 1957.

———. *World of Our Fathers: The Journey of the East European Jews to America and the Life They Found and Made.* 1976. New York: Simon & Schuster, 1983.

Howe, Irving, and Eliezer Greenberg. Introduction. *A Treasury of Yiddish Stories*. Eds. Irving Howe and Eliezer Greenberg. 1954. New York: Penguin, 1990.

Husseini, Faisal. "Faisal Husseini: A Conversation."*Tikkun Anthology*. Ed. Michael Lerner. Oakland, Calif.: Tikkun Books, 1992. 358–364.

Jacobson, Kenneth. "Now is Not the Time to Speak Out." *Tikkun Anthology*. Ed. Michael Lerner. Oakland, Calif.: Tikkun Books, 1992. 346–348.

Johnson, Alvin. "Palestine: A Possible Solution: The Case for a Non-Territorial Federal State." *Commentary* Jan. 1947: 33–39.

Kakutani, Michiko. "A Talk with Saul Bellow: On His Work and Himself." *The New York Times Book Review* 13 Dec. 1981: 1, 28–31.

Kaufman, Michael. *The Woman in Jewish Law and Tradition*. Northvale, N.J.: Jason Aronson Inc., 1993.

Kauvar, Elaine M. "Introduction: Some Reflections on Contemporary American Jewish Culture." *Contemporary Literature* 34.3 (Fall 1993): 337–357.

Kaye/Kantrowitz, Melanie. *The Issue is Power: Essays on Women, Jews, Violence and Resistance*. San Francisco: Aunt Lute Foundation Books, 1992.

Keinon, Herb. "Peace Without Guarantees." *The Jerusalem Post International Edition Magazine* 13 Nov. 1993: 9

Kellerman, Faye. "Jewish Pilgrims, Comic Progress." Rev. of *Master of the Return*, by Tova Reich. *The Los Angeles Times Book Review* 19 June 1988: 10.

Kelly, Michael. "In Gaza, Peace Meets Pathology." *The New York Times Magazine* 27 Nov. 1994: 56–63, 72, 74, 76, 78–79, 96–97.

Kendall, Thena. "Memories of an Orthodox Youth." *On Being a Jewish Feminist*. Ed. Susannah Heschel. New York: Shocken Books, 1983. 96–104.

Kolsky, Thomas A. "The American Council for Judaism's Opposition to Zionism, 1942–1948: An Assessment." *Eretz Israel, Israel and the Jewish Diaspora Mutual Relations*. Ed. Menachem Mor. New York: University Press of America, 1991. 129–150.

Koningsberger, Hans. "Seven People of the Book." Rev. of *A Pile of Stones. The New York Times Book Review* 11 July 1965: 38.

Kremer, S. Lillian. "Chaim Potok." *Dictionary of Literary Biography: Twentieth-Century American-Jewish Fiction Writers*. Ed. Daniel Walden. Detroit: Gale, 1984. 232–243.

———. "The Holocaust in *Mr. Sammler's Planet.*" *Saul Bellow Journal* 4.1 (1985): 19–32.

———. "Post-alienation: Recent Directions in Jewish-American Literature." *Contemporary Literature* 34.3 (Fall 1993): 571–591.

Kupferberg, Herbert. "A Novel of Israel's Birth." Rev. of *Exodus. New York Herald Tribune Books* 28 Sept. 1958: 5.

Kurzweil, Arthur. "An Atheist and His Demonic God: An Interview with Hugh Nissenson." *Response* 11 (Winter 1978–79): 17–23.

Laqueur, Walter. *A History of Zionism.* New York: Holt, Rinehart & Winston, 1972. 385–437.

Lavine, Steven David. "In Defiance of Reason: Saul Bellow's *To Jerusalem and Back.*" *Studies in American Jewish Literature* 4.2 (1978): 72–83.

———. "On the Road to Jerusalem: Bellow Now." *Studies in American Jewish Literature* 3.1 (1977): 1–7.

Lazare, Daniel. "Philip Roth's Diasporism: A Symposium." *Tikkun* May/June 1993: 41–45, 73.

Lechlitner, Ruth R. "Fiction." Rev. of *Yehuda,* by Meyer Levin. *Bookman* Apr. 1931: 196–197.

Lederhendler, Eli. "Interpreting Messianic Rhetoric in the Russian Haskalah and Early Zionism." *Jews and Messianism in the Modern Era: Studies in Contemporary Jewry VII.* Ed. Jonathan Frankel. New York: Oxford University Press, 1991. 14–33.

Lehmann-Haupt, Christopher. "Descent of a People from Spiritual to Worldly." Rev. of *The Pursuit of Happiness,* by Anne Roiphe. *The New York Times* 10 June 1991: C18.

Lerner, Michael. "The Editor: A Personal Note." *Tikkun: An Anthology.* Ed. Michael Lerner. Oakland, Calif.: Tikkun Books, 1992. xxiii–xxix.

———. "Post-Zionism." *Jewish Renewal: A Path to Healing and Transformation.* New York: G. P. Putnam's Sons, 1994. 219–264.

Leviant, Curt. "The Hasid as American Hero." Rev. of *The Chosen. Midstream* Nov. 1967: 76–78, 80.

Levin, Meyer. "After All I Did For Israel." *Commentary* July 1951: 57–62.

———. "A Conversation with Meyer Levin." With Harold U. Ribalow. *Midstream* Jan. 1978: 39–43.

———. "Maurie Finds His Medium." *Menorah Journal* Aug. 1928: 175–181.

————. *My Father's House.* New York: Viking Press, 1947.

————. "The Writer and the Jewish Community." *Commentary* June 1947: 526–530.

————. *Yehuda.* New York: Cape and Smith, 1931.

Liptzin, Sol. "Impact of Israel." *The Jew in American Literature.* New York: Bloch, 1966.

Malin, Irving. Rev of *A Pile of Stones. Chicago Jewish Forum* 113 (Fall 1965): 57–58.

Marcus, Alfred. "The Making of a New Jewish Literature." *Response* 7.1 (1973): 3–5.

Marcus, Amy Dockser. "American Jews Grapple With an Identity Crisis as Peril to Israel Ebbs." *The Wall Street Journal* 14 Sept. 1994: A1, A4.

Marovitz, Sanford E. "Freedom, Faith, and Fanaticism: Cultural Conflict in the Novels of Chaim Potok." *Studies in American Jewish Literature* [Albany] 5 (1986): 129–140.

McDowell, Edwin. "'Exodus' in Samizdat Still Popular and Subversive." *The New York Times Book Review* 26 April 1987: 13.

Melman, Yossi. *The New Israelis: An Intimate View of a Changing People.* New York: Birch Lane Press, 1992.

Merkin, Daphne. "Philip Roth's Diasporism: A Symposium." *Tikkun* May/June 1993: 41–45, 73.

————. "Why Potok is Popular." *Commentary* Feb. 1976: 73–75.

Mintz, Alan. "Hebrew in America." *Commentary* July 1993: 42–46.

Morton, Frederic. "Meyer Levin: A Novel and a Talk." *The New York Times Book Review* 19 Feb. 1978: 14, 32–33.

Myers, Jody Elizabeth. "The Messianic Idea and Zionist Ideologies." *Jews and Messianism in the Modern Era: Studies in Contemporary Jewry VII.* Ed. Jonathan Frankel. New York: Oxford University Press, 1991. 3–13.

Neusner, Jacob. "A Stranger at Home: An American Jew Visits In Israel." *Israel and Zion in American Judaism: The Zionist Fulfillment.* Ed. Jacob Neusner. New York: Garland, 1993. 107–111.

————. "Judaism and the Zionist Problem." *Judaism* 19 (1970): 311–323.

————. "Zionism and 'The Jewish Problem.'" *Midstream* 15 (1969): 34–45.

Nissenson, Hugh. "A Conversation with Hugh Nissenson." With Diane Cole. *The National Jewish Monthly* Sept. 1977: 8–16.

———. "A Conversation with Hugh Nissenson." With Harold U. Ribalow. *The Tie That Binds: Conversations with Jewish Writers.* ed. Harold U. Ribalow. San Diego: Barnes, 1980: 139–163.

———. "High on the One Above." Rev. of *Master of the Return,* by Tova Reich. *The New York Times Book Review* 29 May 1988: 10.

———. *In the Reign of Peace.* New York: Farrar, 1972.

———. *Notes from the Frontier.* New York: The Dial Press, Inc., 1968.

———. *A Pile of Stones, Short Stories.* New York: Scribner, 1965.

Oz, Amos. "Mr. Sammler and Hannah Arendt's Banality." *Saul Bellow: A Mosaic.* Eds. L. H. Goldman, Gloria L. Cronin, and Ada Aharoni. New York: Peter Lang, 1992. 21–26.

Ozick, Cynthia. "An Interview with Cynthia Ozick." With Elaine M. Kauvar. *Contemporary Literature* 34.3 (Fall 1993): 359–394.

———. "Christians Call it Grace, Zen Buddhists Satori, Jews Kavanna." Rev. of *In the Reign of Peace. The New York Times Book Review* 19 Mar. 1972: 4, 22.

———. "Toward a New Yiddish." *Art & Ardor.* New York: Knopf, 1983. 154–77.

Penkower, Yael, Talya Penkower, and Yonina Penkower. "Bat Mitzvah: Coming of Age in Brooklyn." *Daughters of the King: Women and the Synagogue.* Ed. Susan Grossman and Rivka Haut. Philadelphia: The Jewish Publication Society, 1992. 265–270.

Peretz, Martin. "Diaspora But Not Exile: American Jewry and the Triumph of Zionism." Text of an Address in the Annual "State of World Jewry" Series at the 92nd Street "Y." New York, 20 Jan. 1994: 1–15.

Phillips, William. "American Jews and Israel: A Symposium." *Commentary* Feb 1988: 21–75.

Pifer, Ellen. *Saul Bellow Against the Grain.* Philadelphia: University of Pennsylvania Press, 1990.

Pinsker, Sanford. "Jerusalem Without Fictions." *Jewish Spectator* 42.1 (1977): 36–37.

———. *Jewish-American Fiction: 1917–1987.* New York: Twayne, 1992.

———. *The Comedy that 'Hoits': An Essay on the Fiction of Philip Roth.* Columbia: University of Missouri Press, 1975.

———. "The Lives and Deaths of Nathan Zuckerman." Rev. of *The Counterlife,* by Philip Roth. *Midstream* June/July 1987: 52–54.

———. "They Dream of Zion: Jewish-American Novelists Re-create Israel." *Philadelphia Jewish Exponent* 4 June 1993: 1X, 7X–8X.

———. "William Faulkner and My Middle East Problem." *Virginia Quarterly Review* 67 (1991): 397–415.

Plaskow, Judith. *Standing Again at Sinai: Judaism from a Feminist Perspective.* 1990. New York: HarperCollins, 1991.

Podhoretz, Norman. "A Statement on the Peace Process." *Commentary* April 1993: 19–23.

Pogrebin, Letty Cottin. *Deborah, Golda, and Me: Being Female and Jewish in America.* New York: Crown Publishers, 1991.

Polish, David. "Zionist Ideology in America." *Handbook of American-Jewish Literature: An Analytical Guide to Topics, Themes, and Sources.* Ed. Lewis Fried. New York: Greenwood Press, 1988. 261–286.

Porter, M. Gilbert. *Whence the Power? The Artistry and Humanity of Saul Bellow.* Columbia: University of Missouri Press, 1974.

Potok, Chaim. *The Chosen.* 1967. New York: Fawcett Crest-Ballantine, 1987.

———. "A Conversation with Chaim Potok." With Harold U. Ribalow. *The Tie that Binds: Conversations with Jewish Writers.* Harold U. Ribalow. San Diego: Barnes, 1980. 111–137.

———. "A Conversation with Chaim Potok." With S. Lillian Kremer. *Dictionary of Literary Biography Yearbook: 1984.* Ed. Jean W. Ross. Detroit: Gale, 1985. 83–87.

———. "The Invisible Map of Meaning: A Writer's Confrontations." *Tri-Quarterly* 84 Spring/Summer 1992: 17–45.

———. "Judaism Under the Secular Umbrella: An Interview with Chaim Potok." With Cheryl Forbes. *Christianity Today* 8 Sept. 1978: 14–17, 20–21.

Prager, Dennis. "American Jews and Israel: A Symposium." *Commentary* Feb 1988: 21–75.

Rapoport, Nessa. "Summoned to the Feast." Introduction. *Writing Our Way Home: Contemporary Stories By American Jewish Writers.* Eds. Ted Solotaroff and Nessa Rapoport. New York: Schocken Books, 1992. xxvii–xxx.

Reich, Tova. *Master of the Return.* New York: Harcourt Brace Jovanovich, 1988.

Rev. of *Lovingkindness,* by Anne Roiphe. *Ms.* Sept. 1987: 34.

Ribalow, Harold U. "A Look at the 'Israel Novel.'" Rev. of *Exodus. Congress Bi-Weekly* 25 Dec. 1961: 19.

———. "Zion in Contemporary Fiction." *Mid-Century.* Ed. Harold U. Ribalow. New York: The Beechhurst Press, 1955. 570–591.

Roiphe, Anne. *Generation Without Memory: A Jewish Journey in Christian America.* New York: Simon & Schuster, 1981.

———. *Lovingkindness.* 1987. New York: Warner Books, 1989.

———. "O. J. Simpson and Us." *The Jerusalem Report* 3 Nov. 1994: 46.

———. *The Pursuit of Happiness.* New York: Summit Books, 1991.

———. *A Season for Healing: Reflections on the Holocaust.* New York: Summit Books, 1988.

———. "Taking Down the Christmas Tree." *Tikkun* Nov./Dec. 1989: 58–60.

———. "The Whole Truth." *Tikkun* July/Aug. 1989: 86–88.

Rosenbaum, Eli M. *Betrayal: The Untold Story of the Kurt Waldheim Investigation and Cover-Up.* New York: St. Martin's Press, 1993.

Rosenfeld, Alvin H. "Israel and the Idea of Redemption in the Fiction of Hugh Nissenson." *Midstream* Apr. 1980: 54–56.

———. "The Progress of the American Jewish Novel." *Response* 7.1 (1973): 115–130.

Ross, Tamar. "Can the Demand for Change in the Status of Women Be *Halakhically* Legitimized?" *Judaism* 42.4 (1993): 478–491.

Rotenstreich, Nathan. "Can There be a Revival of Zionist Ideology?" *Midstream* 36 (1990): 7–10.

Roth, Philip. "A Bit of Jewish Mischief." *The New York Times Book Review* 7 March 1993: 1, 20.

———. *The Counterlife.* 1987. New York: Viking Penguin, Inc., 1988.

———. "Interview with *The London Sunday Times.*" *Reading Myself and Others.* 1975. New York: Penguin, 1985. 129–137.

———. *Operation Shylock: A Confession.* New York: Simon & Schuster, 1993.

———. *Sabbath's Theater.* New York: Houghton Mifflin, 1995.

———. "Some New Jewish Stereotypes." *Reading Myself and Others.* 1975. New York: Penguin Books, 1985. 193–203.

———. "Writing American Fiction." *Reading Myself and Others.* 1975. New York: Penguin Books, 1985. 173–191.

Rubin, Steven J. *Meyer Levin.* Boston: Twayne Publishers, 1982.

Said, Edward. *Culture and Imperialism.* New York: Alfred A. Knopf, 1993.

———. "Hebron was Inevitable." *The Progressive* May 1994: 25–27.

———. *Orientalism.* New York: Random House, 1978.

———. "Reflections on Twenty Years of Palestinian History." *Journal of Palestine Studies* 20 (1991): 5–22.

Salt, Jeremy. "Fact and Fiction in the Middle Eastern Novels of Leon Uris." *Journal of Palestine Studies* 14.3 (1985): 54–63.

Schemo, Diana Jean. "America's Scholarly Palestinian Raises Volume Against Arafat." *The New York Times* 4 Mar. 1994: A10.

Sellers, Frances Stead. "Souls Lost in the New World." Rev. of *The Pursuit of Happiness,* by Anne Roiphe. *The Los Angeles Times Book Review* 11 Aug. 1991: 7.

Shammas, Anton. "The Art of Forgetting." *The New York Times Magazine* 26 Dec. 1993: 32–33.

Shapiro, Allan E. "Baggage full of racism." *The Jerusalem Post International Edition* 19 Mar. 1994: 6.

Shechner, Mark. "Zuckerman's Travels." *American Literary History* 1 (1989): 219–230.

Shostak, Debra. "'This Obsessive Reinvention of the Real': Speculative Narrative in Philip Roth's *The Counterlife.*" *Modern Fiction Studies* 37 (1991): 197–215.

Siegel, Seymour. "American Jews and Israel: A Symposium." *Commentary* Feb. 1988: 67–68.

Silverman, Hilda. "Palestinian Holocaust Memorial?" *Palestinian Perspectives* Sept./Oct. 1988: 4.

Sokoloff, Naomi. "Imagining Israel in American Jewish Fiction: Anne Roiphe's *Lovingkindness* and Philip Roth's *The Counterlife.*" *Studies in American Jewish Literature* 10 (1991): 65–80.

Solotaroff, Ted. "American-Jewish Writers: On Edge Once More." *The New York Times Book Review.* 18 Dec. 1988: 1, 31, 33.

———. "The Open Community." Introduction. *Writing Our Way Home: Contemporary Stories by American Jewish Writers.* Eds. Theodore

Solotaroff and Nessa Rapoport. New York: Schocken Books, 1992: xiii-xxvi.

Spiegel, Steven L. "American Jews and Israel: A Symposium." *Commentary* Feb 1988: 21–75.

Stampfer, Judah. "The Tension of Piety." Rev. of *The Chosen. Judaism* 16.4 (1967): 494–498.

Stock, Irvin. "Man in Culture." *Commentary* May 1970: 89–94.

Syrkin, Marie. "American Jews and Israel: A Symposium." *Commentary* Feb 1988: 21–75.

———. "'Phony Israel': An Exercise in Nastiness." *With Friends Like These: The Jewish Critics of Israel.* Ed. Edward Alexander. New York: Shapolsky, 1993. 263–272.

Telushkin, Joseph. *Jewish Humor: What the Best Jewish Jokes Say About the Jews.* New York: William Morrow and Company, Inc., 1992.

Todorov, Tzvetan. *The Conquest of America: The Question of the Other.* 1982. New York: Harper, 1987.

Trilling, Lionel. "Modern Palestine in Fiction." Rev. of *Yehuda*, by Meyer Levin. *Nation* 24 June 1931: 684.

Umansky, Ellen M. "Reclaiming the Covenant: A Jewish Feminist's Search for Meaning." *Four Centuries of Jewish Women's Spirituality.* Ed. Ellen M. Umansky and Dianne Ashton. Boston: Beacon Press, 1992. 230–235.

Updike, John. "Recruiting Raw Nerves." Rev. of *Operation Shylock: A Confession*, by Philip Roth. *The New Yorker* 15 Mar. 1993: 109–112.

Uris, Leon. "About *Exodus.*" *The Quest For Truth.* M. T. Boaz. New York: Scarecrow, 1961. 123–130.

———. *Exodus.* 1958. New York: Bantam, 1959.

Varon, Benno Weiser. "The Haunting of Meyer Levin." *Midstream* Aug.–Sept. 1976: 7–23.

Vidal, Gore. "The Empire Lovers Strike Back." *The Nation* 22 Mar. 1986: 350, 353.

Vorspan, Albert. *Start Worrying: Details to Follow: An Insider's Irreverent (But Loving) View of American-Jewish Life.* New York: UAHC Press, 1991.

Walden, Daniel. "Chaim Potok, A Zwischenmensch ('between-person') Adrift in the Cultures." *Studies in American Jewish Literature: The World of*

Chaim Potok. Ed. Daniel Walden. Albany: State University of New York Press, 1985. 19–25.

———. Introduction. *On Being Jewish: American Jewish Writers from Cahan to Bellow*. Ed. Daniel Walden. Greewich, Conn.: Fawcett, 1974. 11–29.

Walzer, Michael. "What Kind of State is a Jewish State." *Tikkun Anthology*. Ed. Michael Lerner. Oakland, Calif.: Tikkun Books, 1992. 303–311.

Wegner, Judith Romney. *Chattel or Person? the Status of Women in the* Mishnah. New York and Oxford: Oxford Univ. Press, 1988.

Weiss, Avraham. *Women at Prayer: A* Halakhic *Analysis of Women's Prayer Groups.* Hoboken, N.J.: KTAV, 1990.

Wiesel, Elie. "In Search of Redemption." Rev. of *Master of the Return*, by Tova Reich. *New Leader* 16 May 1988: 7–8.

Wirth-Nesher, Hana, and Andrea Cohen Malamut. "Jewish and Human Survival on Bellow's Planet." *Modern Fiction Studies* 25.1 (1979): 59–74.

Wisse, Ruth R. "American Jewish Writing, Act II." *Commentary* June 1976: 40–45.

———. "American Jews and Israel: A Symposium." *Commentary* Feb. 1988: 21–75.

———. *If I Am Not For Myself . . . : The Liberal Betrayal of the Jews.* New York: Macmillan, 1992.

———. "Peace Not." *The New Republic* 4 Oct. 1993: 15–16.

Wolowelsky, Joel B. "Joel B. Wolowelsky Reacts to Judith Hauptman." *Judaism* 42.4 (1993): 394–395.

Zelechow, Bernard. "The Odyssey of Anne Roiphe: Anatomy of an Alienated Jew." *Midstream* Aug./Sept. 1989: 43–47.

INDEX